TECHNICALLY SPEAKING:

Oral Communication for Engineers,
Scientists, and Technical Personnel

This book is for scientists, engineers, and technicians.
It contains theoretical material and information, a series of cases
in point, and a number of exercises designed to teach the
principles and methods of good oral communication.

McGRAW-HILL BOOK COMPANY, INC.

New York   San Francisco   London   Toronto

TECHNICALLY SPEAKING:

*Oral Communication for Engineers,
Scientists, and Technical Personnel*

Harold Weiss *and* **J. B. McGrath, Jr.**

Southern Methodist University

TECHNICALLY SPEAKING

Library of Congress Catalog Card Number 62-21906

15 16 17 18 19 20 – MAMM – 7 6

ISBN 07-069085-5

TO WINNIE AND SARAH

PREFACE

"The major reason for the increased emphasis on the need for training in oral communication is the combination of current management philosophies, policies, and practices which add up to greater interaction among people in an organization."[1]

It is a truism in this latter half of the twentieth century that scientists and technically trained individuals have great difficulty conveying their newfound knowledge to the general public and convincing laymen to adopt new ways of existence in this rapidly changing world. It is to answer the compelling need for better oral communication in industry that this text is written. Our aim is to provide speech instructors in engineering schools and training officers in industry with a practical text designed to meet the communication problems of technical men.

This book grew out of the authors' experience in helping to solve communication problems with management and training officers in many technical industries. Our work has been varied and interesting. We have helped many employees make effective goodwill speeches. We have given advice concerning improvement of intracompany reports and conferences. We have assisted scientifically trained individuals to make sales presentations of highly technical equipment. We have taught supervisors how to make effective safety talks. We have assisted departmental managers in organizing and delivering experimentation reports to the executive staff and members of the board. We have helped solve communicative problems in hospitals and medical clinics. We have taught in the oral-communication classes required at schools of engineering, dentistry, and agriculture. We have seen a growing concern on

---

[1] Harold P. Zelko, "Trends in Oral Communication Training in Business and Industry," *The Journal of Communication*, vol. XII, no. 2, June, 1962.

the part of industrial management about the seriousness and complexity of their communication problems.

During our discussions with management in industry, we have heard reports of frequent, costly communication breakdowns in four groups: (1) between company personnel and those outside the company (customers, consultants, government representatives, and the public); (2) between top management and middle management; (3) between middle management and the foreman group; (4) between the foreman group and skilled labor.

An examination of the first three groups reveals that these levels are liberally staffed with engineers, scientists, and other technically trained professional people. These capable people, well prepared in their own specializations, have difficulty in passing on the fruits of their education because they lack knowledge of the processes of oral communication.

This book is designed (1) for use in schools and colleges where scientists, engineers, or other technical personnel are educated; (2) for industrial-training groups; and (3) for individuals who wish to improve their skills in oral communication. Sound principles and practical exercises are furnished to prepare a student for any speaking situation which may arise in his work or during his leisure hours. We have presented practical hints based on intimate knowledge of the oral communication problems that arise in the life of a person engaged in technical matters, from the informal conversation, through the various group situations, to the formal speech. This book will also serve as a continuing guide and reference source for the technical man who seeks greater mastery of oral skills as he advances in his profession.

Each chapter begins with a "case in point." These exemplify the situations in which scientists and engineers frequently find themselves. Although these cases have been culled from real-life situations, some liberties have been taken, and, on occasion, such "cases" have been dramatized by condensing two or three events into one.

The authors are indebted to the various industrial groups with whom they have worked for practical suggestions and encouragement. We are especially grateful to the late Tom Sewell of the Texas Power and Light Company, Tom Hughston of the same company, Doyle T. Brooks, Jr., of the Chance Vought Corporation, W. D. Moore of the Dallas Power and Light Company, members of the Speakers' Club at Texas Instruments, Inc., and Dr. Jacque Yost, research director of the Marathon Oil Company, for assistance in suggesting "Cases in Point;" to Sam G. Whitten, science librarian of Southern Methodist University, who worked diligently with the research material; to Joan Poplinger for invaluable assistance in obtaining permissions; to Winifred T. Weiss for her careful attention to the original draft. We also wish to thank the students in the engineering school at Southern Methodist University who gave helpful reactions to mimeographed copies of an earlier draft of this book.

Harold Weiss
J. B. McGrath, Jr.

CONTENTS

1 HIGH FIDELITY NEEDS A GOOD LOUDSPEAKER

The need for better oral communication

Scientists, engineers, and technicians have all contributed to the flowering of Western civilization. Their specialized knowledge has developed new products, and industry has mass-produced these adjuncts to modern living. But the work of the scientist and technician is not translated from potential (blueprints, equations, etc.) to actuality (superhighways, sun-powered generators, new antidotes for disease, etc.) until, and unless, the scientist can communicate to other scientists and to the general public.

Knowledge is fruitless without the power of communication

A technical man cannot work alone. He must constantly communicate with others. He must obtain advice or skilled assistance, recommend additions to a budget, transmit procedures and plans to others. These are situations which require skill in communication, especially in speech. Professor Francis Horn says: ". . . the increasingly complex political, economic, and technical world which scientific progress had helped create in the twentieth century made oral communication ever more important in the conduct of man's daily life."[1] Letters, memos, telegrams, and written reports play their part in the world of industry but, to quote a publication of the National Association of Manufacturers: "In industry, the important communications take place in face-to-face relationships. The best way to get information across has always been to talk

[1] Francis Horn, "Oral Communication in a Technological World," *The Speech Teacher*, vol. 8, no. 3, p. 197, September, 1959.

directly with those who are to receive it—or at least to those who can pass it along. As a medium for getting ourselves understood and for grasping the thoughts of others, there is no substitute for the spoken word."[2]

The act of communication is difficult

"The cost of effective communication between people is much higher than is commonly supposed. It is expensive in time, in understanding, and in emotional control. The reasons for this are that the process of communication is much less simple than we ordinarily realize."[3]

Few people realize that communication is such a difficult and complex process. Because of our long experience in trying to communicate, we tend to regard speaking as an automatic, almost involuntary act. We speak without regard for accuracy, efficiency, and precision because familiarity with facial expressions, bodily action, and voice has bred neglect of these specialized skills. Some people are amazed that study of speech is necessary. Yet every day we are faced with misunderstandings about instructions, orders, and assignments. Mistakes in scheduling, specifications, and job responsibilities occur because of sloppy, inaccurate, fuzzy speaking. Vague, ineffective use of words causes waste of time, vital materials, and labor.

One practicing engineer puts it this way: "The inability of the average engineering graduate to convey his ideas or plans to others is not only a handicap to him personally, it is one reason that the profession is not recognized as one of the learned professions today. Many engineers devote all of their time to professional study and advancement, but they fail to realize that their ideas are of little value until they can be transmitted to others in a lucid and forceful manner."[4]

[2] *Case Book of Employee Communications in Action,* Industrial Relations Division, National Association of Manufacturers, New York, 1950, p. iv.

[3] Paul Pigors, *Effective Communication in Industry,* National Association of Manufacturers, New York, 1949, p. 1.

[4] C. Bennett Harrington, "A Survey and Analysis of the Speech Courses Taught in Colleges and Departments of Engineering in the United States of America," unpublished thesis, Southern Methodist University, Dallas, Tex., 1950, p. 7.

A case in point **Don't be a "fuzzy-wuzzy"!**

At X Corporation, a foreman of inspection noticed a mistake in the assembling of transmitter cases. The foreman, a shy man when speaking to his immediate superiors, mentioned this matter to the senior supervisor in a weak, ineffectual manner.

The senior supervisor nodded his head and continued to work on a report that he was writing. Later on, a production slow-down occurred, and it was discovered that this flaw in the transmitter was the cause. The chief of production engineering, upset because this error had passed inspection unnoticed, reproved the senior supervisor in a brusque manner.

The senior supervisor called in the foreman of inspection and asked why this error had not been brought to his attention. The foreman said, "I told you the other day they were missing some of the punch-outs in those transmitter cases." The senior supervisor said, *"Yes, but you didn't pound the desk when you told me!"*

Speaking occasions are frequent and crucial

A questionnaire sent to practicing engineers in the Dallas, Texas, area elicited the following:

Question: Do you make talks to groups of eight or more people?
85 per cent answered: "Yes"
Question: Do you think that speech for the engineering student should be part of the engineering school curriculum?
90 per cent answered: "Yes"

It is during oral expression—face-to-face, man-to-man, at the luncheon table, beside the lathe, atop the drilling rig, inside the fuselage, under the main bridge support, over the conference table, at the convention rostrum—that most communication occurs. Whether the technical man is presenting a paper at a professional society meeting, attempting to sell a new engineering process to a group of his prospective customers, or relaying plans at a building site, the speech situation is always crucial. His job and his company's reputation depend upon his ability to speak forcefully, efficiently, and persuasively.

Yet how much time does the average professional man spend in learning to speak? Compare the time consumed in mastering one aspect of a specialized area, such as electrical engineering, with the time spent in learning to speak clearly and effectively. Do you need to devote some study and practice toward improving your ability to communicate orally? Ask yourself these questions:

Is my vocabulary large enough so that I can turn thoughts into precise language?

Can I talk to others to establish proper attitudes and high morale?

Would I be able to make an effective informal address to employees under my supervision about standard operating procedures, insurance benefits, salaries, and promotions?

Do I know how to find and compile research data?

Do I know how to give instructions, orders, and assignments so that they will be understood?

Will I be able to represent my company or a governmental agency by accepting speaking engagements at luncheon clubs, civic interest groups, and professional societies?

Do I know how to make an oral report to an important lay group, to translate technical terms into the other fellow's language?

Do I know how to prepare and deliver a concise, cogent summary report on the progress of an important project for which I am responsible?

As coordinator, would I be able to arbitrate a disagreement among the members of my team so that the work could continue?

Do I know how to ask answerable questions so that I can understand requests and assignments that come down to me from higher echelons?

Do I know how to get my ideas across in a persuasive, forceful manner so that my plans (perhaps for an increased budget or a better operating procedure) will be accepted by top management?

When the time comes for promotion to managerial rank, will I be able to speak in an acceptable manner with top management of other companies, government inspection teams, and important customers?

If you face the problem squarely, you know that some of the above-mentioned speech situations will probably arise. *Will you be able to meet them?*

Technical men communicate with each other on the job

Student engineers report many problems in communication when they leave the classroom for assignments as on-the-job trainees in engineering work. These trainees in the field are often perplexed and confused by supervisory personnel who do not explain orders, processes, and procedures clearly.

Instructions about the design and construction of simple assemblies or the operation of basic machinery often are misunderstood because of ill-defined shoptalk and vague explanatory language. Students report that tools go under many aliases even in one shop. The adjustable pliers might be called the "channel-locks," "pliers," or "dikes." One workman might call a certain tool a "thingamajig" while another might call the same tool a "doodler" or a "stinger."

A case in point **"Say what you mean!"**

My co-op training job was to design small electrical assemblies and to make provisions for other electrical equipment. The following incident concerns a job of designing and installing a bracket for instrumentation probes.

8:00 A.M. Robinson comes to my drawing table with three sets of blueprints. He says, "Here are some blueprints you'll need. Go check out the top drawings and call the EMD vault and have them send up the master." Now that Robinson has me confused with his terms of the trade, he proceeds to open the blueprints and begins to recite dimensions and specifications.

After five minutes of trying to listen to him talk, I interrupt him and ask, "What am I supposed to be designing?" He looks at me with a disgusted expression and says, "A bracket." About this time he is called away to the telephone. While he is away I ask some of the nearby people what "top drawings" are and what is the "EMD vault." After finding out, I carry out his first instructions.

9:30 A.M. Robinson finally remembers me and comes back to see how I'm doing. When he finds out that I've done very little, he wants to know what the trouble is. I try to explain to him politely that I'm not sure what type of bracket he wants and where he wants it. He painfully draws me a sketch and leaves.

11:00 A.M. After fumbling through the specification books and design manuals, I finally draw a bracket that will work. I take the drawing to Robinson. He looks surprised and says, "This was supposed to be made of stainless steel, not aluminum. Aluminum can't stand the high temperatures in this location."

Now that I finally have all the necessary information, I return to my drawing board and complete the design.

The technical man communicates as a supervisor

As the technical man proves himself with his company, he begins to move up the ladder and to meet more challenging responsibilities. Generally these responsibilities take the form of supervising the work of others. Skill in speech is essential to the supervisor, for he must be able to make instructions easy to understand and be able to explain work processes with clarity.

Peter F. Drucker, noted management consultant, says: "As soon as you move one step up from the bottom, your effectiveness depends on your ability to reach others through the spoken and written word. And the farther away your job is from manual work, the larger the organization of which you are an employee, the more important it will be that you know how to convey your thoughts in writing or speaking. In the very large organizations, whether it is the government, the larger business corporation, or the Army, this ability to express oneself is perhaps the most important of all the skills a man can possess."[5]

A case in point **"Tele-woman"**

When something goes wrong in a supervisor's area, it frequently can be traced to a breakdown in communication. Someone said something to someone else, and the meaning was not understood. . . . During World War II, the writer was called to one of the large plants in Detroit to help on a problem-solving conference. The problem itself was stated simply. How could this particular factory speed up its production of a specific war material?

Most of the foremen at the conference agreed that the cause of the problem was "the stupid women who were coming into the shop." One man said, "Do you know what I caught one woman doing? I caught her using a micrometer for a C-clamp and trying to tighten it with a stillson wrench!"

We hadn't been working on the problem very long before one of the foremen said, "I had some pretty good luck on job training with one of those women last week. I took her over to the machine she was going to work on and said, 'You know how the dial on your Mixmaster works? The farther you turn it to the right, the faster it goes?' She said she did, so I said, 'This works the same way.'

"For everything on that machine, I tried to think of something in her home that worked about the same way, and what do you know? She caught right on!"[6]

The success of managers and supervisors depends upon the performance of their teams. This coordination necessitates efficient and accurate communication among all personnel. Much of this communication will be carried out by face-to-face or "ear-to-ear" speaking in interviews, informal talks, conferences, and telephone conversations.

[5] Peter F. Drucker, "How to Be an Employee," *Fortune,* May, 1952, p. 126.
[6] Arthur Secord, "How to Get Your Ideas Across," in *Leadership on the Job,* American Management Association, New York, 1957, p. 58.

The following case is a report from an employee about conferences held by his supervisor.

A case in point   **"Conference, anyone?"**

Mr. Q, the supervisor of our team of leadmen, was a demon for calling conferences. He never told us ahead of time about the conference, nor did he tell us what the subject of the conference was to be. Consequently we seldom had any of the special information that pertained to the problem to be discussed. We often wasted a lot of time going back to our labs to get figures and specifications that he needed for the discussion. Another time waster was that Mr. Q never made out a list of what he wanted to discuss, so that he spent a lot of time wandering around the mulberry bush and we would all be looking at our watches and thinking about all the work we had to do.

Sometimes Mr. Q would neglect to call in men from other departments who were needed to give information about the problem at hand, and we would have to wait while they were called by telephone to come, wait until they walked over from another part of the plant, and then have to consume more time bringing them up to date on what had already been said. Some men would be invited to the conference who were really not involved with the problem. They had nothing to contribute to the discussion, but they had to stay through the whole meeting anyway.

Mr. Q allowed too much wandering off the subject. Two guys would get into a sort of personal bull session about a particular point, and they would keep arguing and talking about it long after all the facts had been brought out. Mr. Q never seemed to sense when we had beaten a point to death and were more than ready to go on to the next. Most of the guys in my section felt that these conferences were a big waste of time.

The technical man communicates as a consultant

When an engineer goes the profitable and interesting route of the consulting business, his ability to communicate becomes an important tool for gaining clients and keeping them. He must be able to explain his service capacities and to sell his clients on the reliability of his work. The consultant uses designs, statistical charts, and working models; but interpreting the results of surveys, outlining causative factors in trouble spots, and presenting specified solutions will all require some talking. This technical data must be verbalized in such a manner that the client can understand simply and exactly the consultant's recommendation.

A client may ask the consultant to represent him before municipal, state, or Federal government groups in regard to large contracts. The client's economic progress may depend upon the consultant's power to inspire confidence and respect. The consultant's ability to speak well and conduct himself with poise when giving evidence or rendering his opinion will be a major influence in the decision of the governing group.

A case in point **"Zone defense"**

An important zoning case was up before the planning board of a large city. A realtor had hired a civil engineer as consultant. It was the duty of the consultant to explain the realtor's proposed change in zoning regulations so that the realtor could construct a large shopping center.

The residents of the area were incensed. They feared that a shopping center would decrease the value of their property. A committee of homeowners was to be present at the hearing before the city planning board.

The problem facing the civil engineer was to explain to the planning board and the protesting citizens that the proposed shopping center would be arranged so that it would not congest traffic nor degrade the landscape, and, in effect, to show how the well-designed, modern shopping center would add to the beauty of the neighborhood and the convenience of the homeowners.

The speech, facial expression, and physical actions of the civil engineer were disdainful and overbearing. His manner of speaking immediately prejudiced everyone in the room against him and his client. The case, although just, was a lost cause for the realtor.

The technical man speaks to the community

The technical man also has the responsibility of speaking to the community. Often the maintenance of smooth business operations and a satisfactory profit margin depends directly on sound public relations. A typical comment runs: "An engineer must do a selling job every day in his profession and to sell adequately, he must be able to speak well. Also an engineer must take part in civic affairs and this means that he must be able to make an effective speech. This subject cannot be stressed too much."[7]

A case in point "Mr. Chairman, Ladies and Gentlemen"

A large power company requires its top supervisory personnel, many of whom are engineers and technicians, to seek out speaking engagements with community groups to explain how the power company is contributing to the progress of the area. Pleas of, "But I was hired as an electrical engineer, not as a public speaker," are in vain. Opportunities for advancement with this company are seriously curtailed when the employee fails to gain respect for himself and his company during these speaking occasions.

The approach of this book

The path from the laboratory, drafting board, or blockhouse to the speaker's rostrum and conference table may be short and well beaten or long and rugged for the technical person. There is no royal road to becoming an effective oral communicator.

Good speaking is a unified act. The excellent oral communicator does not assemble techniques of gesture, research, voice control, language, etc., in certain specified proportions and emerge with the perfect formula for oral communication. Sometimes the best speakers cannot even tell you how they accomplished their excellent results. But just as a golfer tries to analyze the factors that make up

[7] Harrington, *op. cit.*

the perfect golf swing, so we divide oral communication into its component parts and try to help the speaker put them back together again in the combination most effective for him and for his different purposes.

Sometimes the speaker may want only to transmit information in the simplest form. Sometimes he may want to motivate others to act. Sometimes he may be building morale or inspiring others. Sometimes he may be merely conversing to show his goodwill.

The purpose of this book is to help the student acquire the techniques needed to give clear, accurate instructions; to organize and deliver reports of a technical nature; to be a good listener; to converse lucidly about plans, opinions, and advice; and to make an effective, forceful public speech. Actual cases are cited and theories are discussed. Assignments have been devised to meet the practical problems in speech that the technical man will face in his professional work.

Assignments and exercises

1. Each student will be paired off with a colleague in the class. Sufficient time will be allotted for interviewing each other. The students will be asked to introduce each other to the members of the class and the instructor. Each student will begin his introduction by writing the name of his fellow student on the blackboard. Tell about his educational background, his prowess in sports, his family, his hobbies, or his military record. Inform the group why he is interested in technical work or engineering. Try to include an anecdote or two that will make the introduction interesting to the group.

2. Explain to the class a communication problem which occurred on the job or in a past experience. Explain how the problem could have been avoided. Show what caused the problem and what resulted.

3. Give a talk in which you criticize a public speaker you have heard. Explain why you think he failed or succeeded in making his point.

4. Select an article or recent technical development from the science section of a periodical such as *Time* or *Newsweek* or from a recent technical magazine. Condense it so that you can communicate the ideas orally to the group in three minutes or less. You may use the blackboard for drawings if necessary.

5. Team up with another member of the class. One of the pair takes the role of a supervisor; the other, an employee. Act out a situation in which a communication breakdown occurs.

6. Select a procedure on your campus, in your profession, or in your daily life, such as registration, physical examinations, reporting an accident, and paying utility bills. Describe this procedure to your group so they can follow the needed steps successfully.

7. A member of the group or the instructor will suggest a topic of current interest as you step before the group. Speak in impromptu fashion for a minute or two about this topic; then answer questions about what you have said for two additional minutes.

8. Report on some meeting you have observed or taken part in. This can be a fraternity meeting, student council, executive group, safety council, etc. Did it accomplish its goals? Why? Why not?

2 LAYING THE FOUNDATIONS

Preparing to speak

A case in point **Kenney's sandstone lullaby**

Richard Kenney is a research engineer employed by the Oklian Oil Company. For the past two years he has been working on several projects related to waterflooding operations. He has conducted experiments to determine the causes of plugging when water is injected into sandstone reservoirs. Kenney's work, in cooperation with a production engineer, has saved his company many thousands of dollars.

Other engineers in the company felt they could profit from Kenney's research. It was decided to call a meeting of the major members of the staff who were directly involved in waterflooding operations. At this meeting, Kenney would present the results of his work and explain how such results could be applied to their operations.

More than twenty-five company engineers from all parts of the United States arrived at the meeting place and assembled in an auditorium, notebooks in hand, prepared to listen to instructions about the new technique.

Kenney began his discussion with a forty-five minute outline of the nature of petroleum production, telling how oil was produced from an oil field by pressure decline until such methods became uneconomical. He then reviewed the entire history of waterflooding as a means of recovering additional oil from such oil fields.

This review was old stuff to the assembled engineers. By the end of this elaborate presentation, some of his audience were

13

fast asleep; others were making elaborate doodles in their notebooks. In spite of the fact that Kenney's talk was illustrated by thirty beautiful slides showing apparatus, both pictorially and in scale drawing, the audience failed to show interest in his material. He concluded by saying that he would be glad to answer any questions concerning applications to field problems. A few minutes passed with no questions. The chairman of the meeting suggested that perhaps people would prefer to think things over and write Mr. Kenney concerning their questions. Mr. Kenney is still wondering why he has not received any letters!

In order to speak, you must have something to say. The frequently experienced nightmare wherein the dreamer is completely unprepared before a large audience has little basis in reality. People are seldom asked to speak publicly about subjects foreign to their experiences. If a technical man is in charge of engineering for a new type of metal forgings, he usually is required to talk about that project, not about the steel industry as a whole. In other words, a person usually is expected to talk about something with which he is directly involved.

The speaker needs to find answers to these questions: What do my listeners want to know about the subject? How much of the subject will interest them? How much background information do they have? How can I organize this information so that the listeners will understand? What method of presentation is best suited to this situation? What are some effective ways of maintaining the interest of my audience?

Kenney had overlooked the fact that everything he told the group in the first part of his speech either was already known by them or was available to them in periodicals and books with which they were familiar. Nor had he provided them with any new organizational framework.

The speaker should take the following steps when making an analysis of his communication problem:

Define the specific purpose of the communication.
Determine the scope and limitations of the subject matter to be presented.

Visualize the audience make-up and its probable feelings about the subject.

Assemble the data.

Polish the presentation to make it attractive and listenable.

Practice the oral communication for smoothness and assurance.

Specify the purpose

An oral communication may be an informal talk to the employees about safety in the machine shop or a formal report on the progress of the latest missile-guidance device. When an individual is asked to communicate orally, he should secure definite information from the person making the assignment.

Ask the following questions about the specific audience and subject matter to determine the specific purpose of the talk.

What does the listener want to know?

Do I expect the listener to take any action? If so, what action?

How do I want the listener to feel about this information? Confident? Encouraged? Aroused? Frightened? Relieved? Inspired?

Am I supposed to offer a solution to the problem?

Do I want questions, suggestions, or replies from the audience?

Am I trying to persuade them to accept this program or just informing them about our operations?

Then ask yourself, or the person making the assignment, questions that will determine the general purpose of the communication:

Is the purpose to inform, to lay all the facts before the listeners in the *clearest* manner, with no attempt to influence the hearers to act or believe in a given way?

Is the purpose of the communication to persuade the hearers to take some action, to believe in a certain policy, procedure, or theory?

Is the purpose to inspire? Is the speaker supposed to generate enthusiasm, to revive confidence, or to stimulate feelings of loyalty?

Is the purpose to entertain, to make the audience feel happy, welcome, at home, amused, or relaxed?

Often these purposes are combined. For example, the chief of production engineering may be reading a paper to the members of a professional society to enlighten them on the development of new types of plastics used in aircraft construction. He may also be striving to gain prestige for himself and his company. A supervisor may be reading an explanatory report on· the amount of experimentation conducted in his laboratory. He may also be aiming to persuade the listening vice-presidents to increase his operating budget.

Listed above, then, are the general-purpose areas for *aiming* the speech. Use these suggested purposes as check points when you prepare your communication. *Try to write in one clear sentence the purpose of the talk* to be given; for example: "To explain the Employee Insurance Benefit Plan in complete detail, including premiums, company participation, death benefits, disability benefits, and hospitalization." After writing the purpose in one sentence, feed it back to the person who requested the talk to be sure you have formulated it correctly.

Determine the scope and limitations of the subject

People who ask for progress reports, research summaries, result compilations, orientation talks, instructive lectures, briefings, etc., are sometimes vague, inaccurate, and nonspecific in their requests. "Say a few words about," "Just fill us in briefly," "You know what should be covered," and "Mention anything you think is essential," are expressions which should serve as danger signs for the speaker. Ask some very pointed questions to clarify what is expected. The following are sample questions:

Do you want detailed treatment of all experiments completed?
On which part of the business year should the report be based?
Do you want structure (shape, form, and dimensions) and/or function (the method and purpose of operation)?
Do you want theory (preliminary and final planning) and/or activation (completed product or process)?

Do you want a report on *all* discrepancies or only those affecting the John Doe Corporation?

If some items must be eliminated, because of time limitations, which items *must* be covered in the November 10 report?

Be realistic in coordinating the time allotted for the report with the indicated scope of the subject. For example, a vice-president once asked the technical man in charge of research to give his report on two years of experimentation in twenty minutes! This called for clear definition of what to include and what to omit.

Know your audience

"Who will be at the meeting?" is an important question in the planning stages of a speech. The answer to this question will determine the speaker's approach to his subject, i.e., the vocabulary, the kinds of examples, the depth of explanation, and even the jokes to be included for gaining attention.

A case in point **Who will be there?**

The following dialogue occurred when the members of a committee of U Corporation were preparing a sales presentation:

Joe: May I use these terms or do I have to break them down into more simple language?

Bill: Oh, all the men invited will be geologists. Don't worry. They'll understand the technical terms.

Fred: Wait a minute. Some of these men have been in managerial jobs for some time. They have been away from the everyday lab and field work of geology. You'd better simplify the language.

Who are the listeners?

The identity of the people in the audience will determine their relationship to the subject. The speaker should familiarize himself with the following facts about the listeners:

1. Job titles and positions of the listeners
2. Experience and training in connection with the subject
3. Probable orientation, assumptions, attitudes, and prejudices about the subject
4. Outside pressures on the listeners from groups or departments not present at the meeting

Be specific in your questions about the audience

The speaker may not be able to obtain all of the advance information from the person requesting the speech, but he should ask questions similar to these listed below:

1. Is the customer representative familiar with our inspection process?
2. How long have these people been with the organization?
3. Do the machine operators know the basic electronic theory?
4. Will a naval representative be present?
5. Will this report be given to our company family or will members of the holding company's executive board be present too?
6. Is management cold or warm about this project?
7. Has this group been oriented about safety procedures during the current year?
8. Did the customer have experience with our old model?
9. How much technical language can I use to this group?
10. Have they heard similar material before?

What are the feelings, attitudes, prejudices of my audience?

As a television cameraman adjusts the focus control on his camera to bring the picture on his viewfinder into a sharper image, the speaker needs to sharpen his knowledge of the audience's sentiments.

1. What questions will these listeners want answered?
2. What comparisons and analogies can be drawn from their experiences and applied to the subject for clarification?

3. Does the matter at hand affect the listener's job, salary, hours, recreation, or family?

4. Are the listeners familiar with the latest developments in the field pertaining to the subject?

5. What frame of mind will the audience be in? Apprehensive? Interested? Bored? Skeptical? Tired? Fresh?

6. Is there any common experience that can be used to draw the group or individual close to you? (Bad weather; income tax time; local, national, or international events in the news; community problems; or something that happened at the company picnic.)

7. Is there any way to obtain audience participation?

Assembling your ideas

Once the specific purpose has been determined, limitations of the scope established, and the audience target brought into clear focus, it is time to start gathering the ideas. The first process might be termed "individual brainstorming." This is a method of concentrating on the subject and allowing ideas to flow from the mind onto the paper without holding them up to criticism. The goal is to achieve a quantity of ideas and to encourage the creative process by accepting whatever comes to mind. Jot down these ideas as they come, in a stream-of-consciousness manner, no matter what they may be. An idea which might seem at first glance to be ridiculous may contain the clue to a valuable and practical thought.

Select and organize your ideas

After the first off-the-cuff ideas have been written down, you may have run dry of thoughts. These random ideas should then be surveyed critically. The ideas may be sharpened and molded by the following evaluative process.

1. Eliminate.

a. Repetitions. While brainstorming, you may have written some ideas twice in different words.

b. Vague ideas. Ideas which carry some germ of meaning, but which are too ill-defined for practical use should be omitted.

c. Unrelated ideas. All ideas should be matched against the specific purpose and the scope of the subject. If they do not relate closely and specifically, eliminate them.

2. Discriminate. Look for the big fish. Search out the most important, most basic ideas—the ideas which seem to represent the backbone of the talk. These will be the main ideas under which the more detailed thoughts will be grouped.

3. Classify. After the main ideas have been established, search out the subordinate ideas which seem to belong to them. Try to group the remaining ideas under the main thoughts to which they relate—the main points that they seem to support, explain, amplify, clarify, or describe.

4. Place in sequence. Arrange the main ideas in a logical progression. Decide which of the ideas comes first, which second, and which third. Establish a continuity of approach or a system of precedence for the points. For example, the order in which events occurred or the natural order of steps in accomplishing a project may serve as systems for arranging the ideas. The logic of the progression of ideas may be checked by asking: Does point 2 logically follow point 1? Does idea C naturally follow idea B?

Use logical order

1. Time order. Arrange ideas chronologically in the order that the events occurred. Example: How the Crash Occurred.

a. At 0700 the Smith Airlines plane was flying west at 8,000 feet.

b. At 0700 the Blake Airlines plane was flying east at 7,000 feet.

c. At 0705 the Smith Airlines plane descended to 6,000 feet to allow passengers to view Grand Canyon.

d. At 0706 the Blake Airlines plane descended to 6,000 feet for the same reason.

e. At 0707 the two planes collided in mid-air at 6,000 feet.

2. Space order. Arrange ideas from left to right, top to bottom, east to west, basement to penthouse. Example: The Construction of a Brick Bookcase.

a. Starting at the floor, place ten bricks side by side, in flat position, forming a straight line.

b. Lay a one-by-four white pine plank (exactly the length of the brick line) over the bricks.

c. Place ten bricks, as before, over the white pine plank.

d. Place a white pine stand-up frame (rectangle) over the bricks.

3. Process order. The natural order of steps in a technical operation may serve as a guide for arranging the explanatory material. Example: The Fabrication of a Transistor Amplifier.

a. Etch the junction bars to size.

b. Attach the base wires to the bars by fusion.

c. Attach the bars to the header.

d. Weld the header to the can.

4. Cause-to-effect order. Arrange the material to show how the main events or causes of a problem will have certain results or effects. Example: The Causes of Malfunction in Room Air-conditioning Units.

a. Failure to clean the filter periodically. (1) Air passage over evaporator coils is obstructed. (2) Air-conditioning unit ices over. (3) Unit fails to function properly.

b. Failure to check moisture drain periodically. (1) Drain becomes stopped with algae and other scum. (2) Moisture from evaporator coils is not drained away. (3) Unit fails to function properly.

c. Failure to clean condenser coils at least once a year. (1) Coils become clogged with dirt and leaves. (2) Air passage over condenser coils is reduced. (3) Unit fails to function properly.

5. Key-pattern or basic-scheme order. It is believed that some people understand best by seeing a basic pattern or fundamental principle which relates the parts to the whole and to each other. Search the subject to see if it contains such basic order. For example, the thorax of the human body can be visualized as a boxlike structure whose sides include the rib cage and spine, whose bottom is the diaphragm, whose top is the clavicular, scapular structures.

The outline

The vehicle for organizing the material for a speech is the outline form. One standard form uses Roman numerals for main ideas, capital letters for the subideas which support main ideas, and arabic numerals for examples and illustrations.

Sample outline for an informational speech

Title: "Water, Water Everywhere . . ."
Purposes: To inform a group of laymen about the need for new reservoirs for water storage
To outline the difficulties involved in the development of the necessary reservoirs

I. Introduction
    A. Quotation from "The Ancient Mariner"
    B. Anecdote about research man who was seeking "a cheap substitute for water"
Transition: "Oh, there's plenty of the 'wet stuff' around! But the major problem is capturing it and conserving it in an orderly way."

II. The storage and distribution of our water supply
    A. Reasons for reservoirs
        1. Flooding rivers
        2. Water supply for expanding population areas
    B. Verification survey for a large project
    C. Checks on rainfall and topography
        1. Visuals to show typical surveys
        2. "Take line" survey

III. The construction of a reservoir
    A. Plans and purposes for the dam
        1. To hold back the water
        2. To create electricity
        3. To distribute downstream water supply
    B. The slow job of land acquisition
        1. Setting up the real estate office for buying
        2. Engineering office for calculating and coordinating
        3. Property distribution

IV. Conclusion: A plea for laymen to keep themselves informed about water storage
    A. Industrial needs
    B. The needs of national defense

Prepare your ideas for oral delivery

After the main body of material has been put into logical order, the speaker should consider how to make his ideas attractive, forceful, and easy to understand. Many people fail at this point. The classical form of presentation is still a good one to use. Aristotle said: "Everything must have a beginning, a middle, and an end," or, in the phraseology of modern public speaking, an introduction, a body, and a conclusion.

The introduction

The first few sentences that the speaker utters must get the attention of his audience. If he does not capture them in the beginning he may never get their ears. A dry, uninteresting beginning may cause a considerable amount of mental drifting on the part of the audience, be it one person or many.

1. Humor.   Some speakers use humor as an introduction because it is universally appealing. But, and this is an important "but," the humor must be related to the talk. Sometimes a speaker begins with a hilarious joke, tells it well, receives well-earned laughter. Then he looks gloomily at his audience, picks up his manuscript, and announces solemnly, "But, seriously, now. . . ." His audience recognizes that the joke was a ruse to gain their attention. They may begin to put up some sales resistance at this point.
2. Direct reference to the audience.   This is one usable method for gaining attention. For example, a supervisor is facing an audience that is difficult to confront, a captive audience of employees herded together to hear the quarterly "safety speech." They are bored before the speech begins. They anticipate the worst. Sensitive to this situation, the speaker might say, "I know you fellows are probably bored, and you are thinking to yourselves, 'Oh, Lord, another talk about accidents in the machine shop,' but, I'm telling you, men, if you yawn today, you may be a mighty sleepy corpse tomorrow."

3. Vivid mental imagery. The use of vivid and unusual mental pictures in the first sentence is a method of gaining attention. For example, the supervisor might begin his safety speech in the following words: "The undertaking parlors in our community have received a shipment of beautiful, new coffins. Perhaps some of you men had better drop by after work and pick one out."

4. Visual openings. Visual aids are good devices for attracting attention. An engineer began a speech before a civic club by blowing up a balloon very slowly. As the balloon grew larger and larger, he gradually gained the attention of everyone in the room. Just before the bursting point, when the anticipation of the audience was keyed to a high point, he released the balloon and allowed it to blow itself all over the room. He then began his talk on "Progress in Aeronautics."

5. Sound effects. A tape recording of the beep-beep radio signal emanating from a satellite traveling about its orbit was a method used by a speaker to introduce a talk about America's entrance into outer space.

6. Striking statements. The use of striking statistics, provocative questions, unusually colorful quotations, and startling predictions are other ways of making the audience prick up its ears. Many a technical man has said, "How can I possibly find an interesting beginning to this paper on electronics?" The advice is: Find one or you may lose your audience.

Transition between the introduction
and the body of the talk

"Why should I listen to you?" is a question that the speaker should be expected to answer. It is essential that the reason for listening be made apparent to the audience. The guide for meeting this query lies within the purpose of the talk. The speaker might ask himself, "Why was I asked to make this talk in the first place?" An examination of the purpose should reveal the "you" value of the speech; that is, the aspect that bears directly upon the audience's concerns, hopes, and fears.

The following sentences are excerpts from speeches in which the speaker tried to show the audience that the talk was aimed at meeting their problems:

1. "Why should you be interested in the geochemical method of oil exploration? Because this method may be the only way it is economically feasible for your companies to explore the vast land spaces of Australia."

2. "Why should you give up your coffee hour to hear a discussion of the juvenile delinquency problem? Because $50,000 worth of damage to industrial plants in this area was directly attributed to juvenile delinquency in the past business year."

3. "If we don't find some way to reduce the accidents in the steam plant, we may face the cancellation of our employer liability policy, the only protection we have against damaging liability claims."

The body of the talk

Now that the speaker has gained the attention of the audience, and has told them why they should listen, he is ready to develop his points, that is, to go into the body of his material. The outline is the guide; the speaker should recheck his points to be sure that they are clear and palatable to his audience. At this stage, the example is the strong ally of the speaker. The illustration, the specific instance, the representative sample, the typical incident, are major avenues to understanding for some people. When a point is not completely clear, the audience will say silently, "For example?" "Give me a typical case," or "Let's see a sample schematic of this circuit." A blackboard drawing can be clarifying. A visual aid showing the operation, or a model, or a mock-up of the problem can aid understanding. When the speaker says, "I'll show you how this could work," the audience breathes a sigh of relief. The listeners know that they are about to see something concrete that they can seize and apply to their own experiences.

The conclusion

The last thing a person says is as important as the first thing he says. Few people seem to realize this fact, and the end of many communications is very often the weakest, vaguest, most uninspiring part. People seem to lack the energy to keep preparing and planning right through to the end. The end of an oral communication, like the end of a bayonet, should have a point. The conclusion of the speech must be more than an easy, harmonious goodbye. It must be more than a recapitulation of the reasons covered in the body of the speech. It must be more than a reminder of the general significance of the talk. It should answer the audience's questions: "Why did I listen to all this?" "Okay, what's the point?" "We know the situation is bad, but what can we do about it?"

Informal talks to small groups of employees might end with provocative thoughts that will stimulate questions and comments from the group. *Progress reports* might end with summaries of the most important projects accomplished and predictions about future goals. *Instructions on how to operate equipment* might end with suggestions for remembering key points or principles of operation. *Company policy talks* might be concluded by a succinct restatement of the main elements of the policies. *Orientation speeches on company organization* might end with a tracing of the flow chart of the chain of command (lines of operation) and the starring of important stations or key offices (departments). Mnemonic devices for remembering patterns of flow are also helpful. If *some kind of action* is the aim of the talk, the end might be an urgent appeal to the audience to write, to suggest, to wire, to vote, to buy, or to join. A *speech to inspire* or a *pep talk* is often well ended by a story which points up, projects, or illustrates the central idea. These stories should be vivid, interesting, and exciting. The following conclusion was made by the manager (a technical man) of an electric power company who was speaking to a service club in his community:

A case in point   **"Sit down in a storm"**

Central idea: The interests of the power company and the community go hand in hand. Let's all work together to advance our community.

The conclusion: "Two veterans of World War II hadn't seen each other for fifteen years. One was visiting the other. They talked until the wee hours of the night. Everyone else had gone to bed. They recalled their war experiences . . . Tarawa . . . Iwo Jima. . . . What were the names of those other islands? The one being visited went upstairs to his young son's room to borrow his globe map of the world. He tiptoed across the darkened room . . . got the globe and started back. Just as he reached the door, his little boy awoke. He jumped upright in bed, clapped his hands together and shouted: 'Dad, WHAT ARE YOU GONNA DO WITH MY WORLD?' This thought strikes us personally as an important question for you . . . for me. What are we going to do with our world . . . our nation . . . our community? Let's all work together . . . utilities . . . businesses . . . individuals . . . to keep our nation great . . . our community the best."

If you feel that you do not need a strong conclusion to your speech, keep in mind this ancient Chinese proverb: "To talk much and arrive nowhere is the same as climbing a tree to catch a fish."

Practice your oral communication

The best procedure in practicing the speech is to reproduce, as realistically as possible, the speech situation to be faced. If you will speak standing up, stand up while practicing. If you will speak without a speaker's stand to rest the notes on, practice standing alone holding the notes. If you will use blackboard drawings, maps, charts, models, or slides, be sure to include operation of these visual aids during the practice period. If you are acquainted with the room to be used for the conference, it will be easier to plan ahead how to handle, rest, or support the visual aids.

Get your notes in order

Number the pages. Be sure the notes are easy to read. Type or print plainly and triple space the lines so that it is easy to find any place in the notes at a glance. Make the notes neat with no markthroughs, strikeovers, wandering arrows, or complicated marginal comments. Don't create stumbling blocks.

Speak from notes

The extemporaneous method of delivery is preferred in most situations. (Techniques for reading a technical paper will be explained in Chapter 14.) Jokes, anecdotes, or stories should be told, not read or memorized. It is generally a good idea to write out the punch line of a joke. Tf you forget it, you are lost. For an anecdote, it is well to write out bits of dialogue as originally phrased. *Sample:* (1) Joke about Pat and Mike in the office building elevator shaft. "Watch out for that *first* step, Mike. It's a lalapalooza!" (2) Anecdote about young Abe Lincoln as a storekeeper. Lincoln: "If I ever get out of debt, I'll probably get right back in again."

Notes on main points of the speech should not be too detailed. They should contain just enough written symbols to stimulate your memory and to keep you on the track. *Sample:* Advantages of working for Allen Electric.

1. Better than average pay
a. Salary and raises
b. Christmas bonus
c. Profit sharing plan
2. Good working conditions
a. Air-conditioned labs
b. Up-to-date equipment
c. Safety precautions

Statistics and quotations should be written out completely and read to the audience. Material to be read should be practiced aloud several times. Underlining key words and the use of the / mark to indicate pauses will be helpful to the speaker. *Sample:* Quotation from a talk by J. Robert Oppenheimer: "The great testimony of history shows / how often in fact / the development of *science* has emerged in response to *technological* and even *economic needs* // and how in the economy of *social effort* // science / even of the most *abstract* and *recondite* kind / pays for itself *again* and *again* / in providing the basis for radically *new technological developments.*"

Rehearse the speech

Now that the notes are in order, the visual aids ready for use, you can begin your rehearsal. Check your watch before you begin. Audiences and program chairmen alike want a speaker to stick closely to the allotted speaking time. It is good practice to make a notation of the time after every major point. Talk aloud through the entire speech each time you practice. You may stumble and leave out some points the first time, but you should proceed doggedly through to the end. Like a corkscrew turning through a cork, you will bite off a little more of the talk each time you practice. Every time you complete the speech, refer to your notes or manuscript to see what you have left out and refresh yourself on any points that were difficult to talk about.

If you have any doubts about the use of a word or its pronunciation, consult a dictionary. If you experience any difficulty pronouncing foreign words or unfamiliar technical terms, say such words over and over until you can enunciate them smoothly. During the practice period, you may find that you will have to change your notes in places because the symbols you have written may not remind you of the required thought. The number of symbols and the types used are individual matters. Experiment and you will soon find the format which is most helpful to you.

Example: Rewards increase employee's motivation, or
Rewards—employee's motivation, or
Rewards————————motivation

Don't make changes in notes at the last minute; such changes may cause some concern if you have not had time to practice them. Some technical men have made the mistake of giving penciled notes to their secretaries for typing on the morning of a noontime speaking engagement. When one of these speakers faces the audience he is handicapped because the notes are unfamiliar to him in typewritten form. Practice with your notes until you are virtually free from them, so that you can speak with only occasional glances at them. This leaves your eyes free to establish good contact with the audience. *Nothing is so deadly for an audience as a speaker who talks with his head down and his eyes glued to his notes.* In such a case, the audience could leave quietly (and probably would like to), and the speaker might never know. Even during the reading of statistics, you should be able to pick out words or figures and then look at the audience to emphasize the ideas.

Summary

Fears arising from nightmares about being before an audience without having anything to say are strictly unfounded bad dreams. In reality, an individual will usually be asked to talk about something familiar and to inform the audience about ideas with which he is centrally involved. The speaker may have to fill in his general information with specific data, refresh himself concerning past experience with the subject, and bring himself up to date on any new developments.

The speaker will have to discover, as accurately as possible, what the audience wants to know and how he can best present this information for their interest, understanding, and acceptance.

Define the specific purpose of the communication.

Determine the scope and limitations of the subject matter to be presented.

Visualize the audience makeup and its probable feelings toward, and experience with, the subject.

Use individual brainstorming, allowing the ideas to flow freely into the mind. Afterward, apply the critical faculties to detect repetitions and irrelevant material.

Assemble the data and arrange the ideas in an orderly, logical progression.

Polish the presentation to make it attractive and listenable.

Practice the delivery for smoothness and assurance.

Assignments and exercises

1. Choose a recent technical development in your particular field. Go through the procedures of developing a talk explaining this process to (*a*) an audience of laymen who have little or no technical knowledge in the field; (b) an audience of "peers" whose knowledge of the process is highly developed. Turn in two outlines indicating differences in introduction, vocabulary, and examples.

2. Report on a talk you have heard or read recently. Was it slanted toward the audience? Did the speaker catch immediate attention? Was there clear-cut progression of ideas? Did it conclude forcefully?

3. Visit a plant in your vicinity. Interview the safety director and obtain material for a talk on safety regulations. Adapt this material for a talk to your classmates, keeping in mind their lack of specific knowledge.

4. Team up with a colleague for a role-playing exercise, one student to be a supervisor; the other, a key employee. The supervisor asks the employee to make a progress report. The employee asks the supervisor questions to make clear the purpose and scope of the talk.

5. Choose a real audience to speak to, either on the campus, on the job, or in the community. Interview a member of this group to discover what their interests are and what they would like you to speak about. After choosing a subject, use individual brainstorming to create your ideas. Choose the proper sequence in which to arrange the progression of your ideas. Formulate an attention-getting introduction and a satisfying conclusion. Deliver this talk before the class. Identify the audience for the class. Ask them to criticize your ability to hit the target audience.

3 PERSON TO PERSON

*The use of body and voice
for a direct speaking style*

A case in point **Words are not enough**

Leonard Stall got up to address a group of fellow science teachers. His legs were wobbly and his knees seemed to be bent. His head was lowered over his notes. He peeked furtively at the audience from underneath his brows. His elbows jutted out at awkward angles, and his fingers plucked nervously at his sleeves. When he began to speak, his voice was low and almost inaudible. His body draped over the stand and his facial expression was fixed in a defensive half-grin. As his colleagues looked at Leonard, they thought, "Whatever he has to say could hardly be very important. Obviously, the poor guy doesn't want to say it."

How to use your body effectively

Gestures and bodily movements arouse feelings of empathy within an audience. We tend to imitate observed action to which we are attentive. Start yawning in front of a group and you will find echoing responses on the part of the audience. Some will yawn overtly; others will feel their muscles imitating the yawn covertly and will only control overt behavior with great effort. Lean to the right in front of a group. In a little while you may note a physical reaction on the part of members of your audience as they tend to lean in the same direction.

If a speaker uses listless and vague motions throughout his oral communication, the tendency on the part of his listeners may be toward listless and vague listening. A tightened physical appearance may bring about tension on the part of the audience. Do you want your listeners to enter into your feelings and ideas? Then your motions, bodily movements, and gestures should give them patterns to follow that will echo and emphasize the content of the speech.

Mention the term "gesture." Usually listeners will involuntarily move their hands or fingers. The arms and hands are important in the formation of movements that emphasize certain points, but the major idea is to let the *whole* body join the voice in expanding the meanings expressed by the words. When it is necessary to add stress to a point, the whole body leans toward the audience. When the hand is clenched for emphasis, the whole body tightens to reinforce the motion of the hand. When the index finger points in accusation, the shoulder and the torso move forward with the finger. When Mickey Mantle hits a baseball or Arnold Palmer drives a golf ball, they put their whole bodies into the swing, not just their hands and arms.

You are "speaking" from the time attention is first called to you until someone else has grasped the attention of the group. Be careful to control your body while you are being introduced. The audience may be looking critically at your sitting position, your facial expression, or at what you are doing with your manuscript or notes. As you rise to your feet and approach the platform, all eyes follow your progress. Your approach must be one of quiet confidence. Sometimes it is wise to map out your path to the speaker's platform in advance. Note a wire to be avoided, a chair to be moved, a light to be adjusted. A stumble, or notes sliding to the floor, may ruin your opening. Your exit from the stand or the front of the room should be planned. Robert Benchley got his biggest laugh at the conclusion of "A Treasurer's Report" by running into the wall of the proscenium. Usually you are not bucking for a laugh.

Basic principles for gestures

1. The need for integration and coordination (timing). The hand movement must be coordinated with the verbal material.

If you would like to experience a truly comical effect, try making an emphatic hand gesture just *after* the emphatic word is expressed. Sometimes it is effective to begin the gesture before the words are expressed, but rarely should the movement come later. For graceful movement, start your hand gestures from the shoulder and follow through to wrist and fingers.

2. The need for variety. Psychologists have continually pointed out that attention is rarely fixed for more than a few seconds at a time. Unless change occurs, attention moves toward inward thoughts or extraneous external conditions. Variety of gesture and movement will help create attentiveness on the part of the listeners. The constant use of a single gesture or movement is monotonous. Some speakers enjoy a single gesture such as pointing, slapping the table top, or waving vaguely with one hand. Avoid using a gesture or movement that develops into a mannerism.

3. The need for reserve. Usually the number and vigor of your gestures will depend on the audience, the type of material, and the general purpose of your talk. If the audience is small, and the ideas routine, broad vigorous gestures might seem ludicrous. If the audience is large, the gestures or movements may be expanded. As the emotional content of the spoken material rises in intensity, so may the various bodily movements and gestures. The speaker should control his hands and body to fit the occasion and the audience. Always keep in mind that the body and hands must echo or emphasize the verbal message.

Types of gestures

1. Enumerative. For beginners, the easiest type of gesture may be the *enumerative*. When you mention a number from one to five, you emphasize the idea by raising the appropriate number of fingers. "There are *two* (raise two fingers) ways to solve this problem." "Now I come to my *third* (raise three fingers) major point."

2. Descriptive. Another type of gesture that may be learned easily is the *descriptive*. "The insulators used in this device are comparatively small. Actually they are rarely more than *3 inches* in length." (The thumb and forefinger approximate a 3-inch length.) "My colleague on this particular job was a lot shorter than I am. He stood only about *this* high." (Show his approximate size with hand raised and away from your body.) "The jet took off at a 45° angle." (Raise the hand and move it upward at approximately the mentioned angle.)

3. Locative. As the name implies, you locate a particular object or area. "Twenty thousand miles *above* the earth's surface . . . ." (Your hand and face move upward.) "Behind me on this flow chart, you will note . . . . (Indicate the chart behind you with your right thumb.)

4. Symbolic. A more difficult type of gesture is the symbolic or suggestive. Here bodily motion conveys an abstract idea to the audience to reinforce the words. We raise our heads and look toward the heavens to indicate reverence or solemnity. We swing an arm in front and across the body to wipe out an idea or thought repugnant to us. We may push our hands outward with palms up in pleading for assistance. "The stress at this moment becomes more and more powerful. . . ." (The two hands clenched in front tighten and bend downward as though they are breaking an iron bar.) "The electron flow becomes more and more rapid. . . ." (Either hand may churn the air in a circular motion, becoming faster and faster.) "Cooperation in this effort is most imperative. . . ." (The hands may clasp in front with fingers intertwined.)

5. Emphatic. A definite movement of the hand and arm will emphasize certain words or phrases. Bending forward **or** taking a step toward the audience adds importance to an idea. The clenched fist is a strong gesture of emphasis. It is reserved for the strongest feelings only and may be used with great effectiveness. "Thus the bit, as it works through these formations, encounters *greater* and *greater* resistance. . . ." (The hand emphasizes the underlined words with strong downward motions.) "In order to put this project through on schedule, we'll need the cooperation of every *draftsman,* of every *designer,* of every *model builder* . . . of *every man* in this whole section." (Use a strong pointing gesture for each and a clenched fist to indicate the whole group.)

Your posture

When talking to a group, you should be at ease. At least you must convey this impression to your audience. It is wise to stand tall with shoulders up and chin (or chins) parallel with the floor. This does not mean the military posture of attention. Although there is no one posture that fits every person and every occasion, most observers seem to agree that a man who stands with his feet about 8 to 10 inches apart—one foot slightly behind the other with weight on the back foot—seems to look at ease. From this neutral posture he can make variations easily. Be able to move gracefully when the occasion calls for it. Don't seem glued to the floor. You may move about, but stay erect while moving. Don't slump or lean. Don't prop yourself up on table, lectern, chair, or wall.

Try to keep your hands at your sides when you begin. Show the audience that you *can* keep them at your sides if *you* desire to. Your hands may feel like a couple of bunches of bananas at first, but later gestures will be more effective if you proceed from this neutral hand position. Avoid the all-too-frequent platform mannerisms that call vigorous attention to themselves. Some of these habits are displayed by the following:

1. The Caged Lion. He walks in measured tread back and forth on the platform. At least he "moves" his audience! Their heads move back and forth as their eyes follow him. The listeners remind you of a crowd at Wimbledon watching a tennis match. This is a good way to lose the match before you begin.
2. The Pinball Machine Player. This fellow grasps the podium with both hands and leans over it. You expect him to draw back the lever and let the first ball go. At any moment a member of the audience may yell, "tilt!"
3. The Money Man. He is completely absorbed in a few coins in his right-hand pants pocket. (Or they might be keys.) So is the audience absorbed, in a few moments. They can't hear what he says over the persistent jingling.

4. The Teeter-totter. He rocks back and forth, heel and toe, heel and toe. You'd like to enter him in the 50,000 meter walkathon.
5. The Chalk-chucker. This man is usually silhouetted against a blackboard. He continuously tosses his chalk up in the air and catches it, or he breaks the chalk up into little pieces and chucks it into the tray.
6. The Hitch-hiker. He keeps hitching up his britches with his forearms. You want to buy him a new belt.
7. The Face-rubber. He seems to be bored with what he is saying. He continually rubs his eyes and forehead with studious concentration. Variations on this fault are the nose-nudger, the mouth-mauler, the ear-puller, and the cuticle-cutie who inspects his nails repeatedly.
8. The Fig-leafer. He clasps his hands in front of his body. Phidias' statues are fashioned more gracefully.
9. The Dresser-upper. This fellow waits until he reaches the platform before he checks his necktie, buttons his coat, and makes sure his cuffs are the proper length from coat sleeves.

Women speakers betray their own distinctive platform idiosyncrasies. Obvious examples are the bead-pullers, the hair-patters, the girdle-hikers, the nail-biters, the ring-turners, the eyeglass-twiddlers, the makeup-menders, and finally, the huntress who, before, and during her talk, hunts her lingerie straps in the neckline of her blouse.

Eye contact with the audience

The audience should not be a blur of faces to the speaker. Select some individuals with whom to establish a firm eye contact so that as a speaker you can observe their facial reactions. Do not look over the heads of the audience. See the faces in front of you. You should not be so preoccupied with your notes that you are constantly looking down at your material.

You cannot look directly into the eyes of every member of your audience if it numbers more than a handful. But do not neglect any large segment. First, glance at the center of the audience. When you thank the person who introduced you, look toward him. Then move your head down left, then to the right and slowly past the center. Don't dart your eyes but look firmly before you move on.

Your speaking voice—what the audience hears

He ceased; but left so pleasing on the ear
His voice, that list'ning still they seemed to hear.

(Homer, *The Odyssey*)

Many auditors are impressed not only by what a speaker says but by the tonal qualities of his voice. These first impressions are powerful. If a man speaks with a thin, weak voice, his listeners automatically conclude that all his other characteristics are weak and flimsy. If his voice has overtones of harshness and hoarseness, they feel he is brusque and overbearing. If his voice is soft and high in pitch, his listeners question his vigor and strength. The voice can be adjusted to reflect the effects for which the speaker is striving. Some effective speakers have had unimposing voices (President Lincoln) but other qualities were strong enough to overcome this serious handicap. Most voices can be greatly improved by instruction and practice. Voice training is important in achieving this end.

The first task is to study your own voice by listening to tape recordings until you are used to hearing your particular tone and style. You may have an idealized version of your voice. It is similar to the idealized version you have of your face. How often have we observed someone looking at his own photograph and remarking: "That doesn't look like me at all." Even while listening to a high-fidelity recording of his own voice, the listener is apt to feel, "That doesn't sound like me."

After listening to tape recordings, it's time to ask a competent instructor to point out weaknesses that can be corrected. Then comes the time of tedious practice. You must remember that if changes are indicated, it means trying to break habits formed many years ago. When you speak in your everyday life situations be aware of the changes that should be made in your vocal pattern. If a competent instructor points out techniques for making these changes, be aware of these new patterns, not only during speech training, but every waking moment of the day.

Breathing

In order to make normal speech sounds, the speaker must first inhale. He then exhales under pressure, and vibratory motion in the larynx (adam's apple) sends sound waves out through his mouth and/or nasal apertures. The sounds are amplified, or resonated, in the cavities of the mouth, pharynx (throat), and nasal passages. The various patterns that distinguish individual sounds are formed mainly by the tongue, the hard and soft palates, the gum ridges, and the teeth. The first step, obviously, is breathing. Advice here is simple. Just continue the process you have been using all your life. It is unnecessary to use any trick methods, or worry about whether you are using diaphragmatic or thoracic breathing. Exercises in breathing are rarely needed for a good supply of out-going, pressurized air to start the speech process.

Stand straight and tall so that your full chest area may be utilized.

Before you begin to speak, be sure you have a good supply of air in the lungs. Inhale slowly when you first look at the audience.

Breathe frequently during your speaking.

Break up your speech material into small segments so that you don't run completely out of air before you take the next breath. A speaker talks in breath-group phrases instead of sentences.

Your optimum pitch

Generally a man's pitch should be close to 125 cycles per second (C below middle C on the piano) and a woman's an octave higher. Every voice, however, has a particular pitch which is most desirable. See Appendix A for methods used in locating optimum pitch.

Resonance and power

The parts of the vocal mechanism that furnish resonance for the vocal tone are the mouth cavity, the nasal cavities, and the back of the mouth (pharynx). Open your jaws when you talk, moving your lips with vigor. Keep your tongue well forward in your mouth and handle the sounds *m, n,* and *ng* with precision to avoid over-nasality.

It is annoying to an audience of one or one thousand if the speaker is too loud, but, since the communication is completely valueless if the auditors cannot hear the speaker, you might err a little on the side of too much volume rather than too little.

If electronic equipment is used, test the equipment before you begin. Prestige is lost, and any effect of a good beginning is dissipated, when a speaker blows into the microphone and then begins his speech by shouting, "Testing—one, two, three . . . can you hear me out there?"

Watch the audience carefully. Look for signs of inattention. When you are mentioning proper names or technical terms that may be unfamiliar, be sure to project them as though they were underlined on your manuscript.

Rate or speed

Normally the speed or rate of effective speaking varies from about 125 to 185 words per minute. If the material is highly informational, or you expect your audience to take notes or copy certain statistics, talk slowly and with frequent pauses. If you exhort a group in a pep talk, the words might be expected to flow at a faster rate.

Flexibility

Many of us have been lulled to sleep on Sunday mornings by a minister who has developed a single pitch pattern within each succeeding sentence. These sentences may all end with a slightly rising inflection. The general effect is that of soft waves rolling slowly on a gently sloping beach. This is highly soporific and may account for the many jokes about slumbering worshippers.

Some sentences should end in a sharp downward inflection. This adds a note of finality to the particular thought. On occasion, level pitch, held for a series of words, adds suspense or equality to a group of thoughts. Sudden changes of pitch are appropriate if they add interest to the words. Try to achieve similar flexibility with loud and soft, fast and slow delivery.

Vocal variety is the best antidote for monotony. Pausing between separate words in a phrase is a device for showing relative importance. Pauses between sentences or ideas have valuable effects. A pause allows the listener to consider, anticipate, and classify the information being received. It heightens the suspense concerning what is coming next. It acts as "white space" around the sounds you are uttering, emphasizing the contrast or equality of thoughts in a sequence.

However, beware of the vocalized pause. Beginning speakers fear any break in the rapid flow of words. When they pause, they feel they must fill in the silence with "uh," "well," "ah," and other meaningless syllables. This destroys any possible period of rest or reflectiveness for the listeners. A pause seldom seems as long to the audience as it does to the speaker. If a speaker has perfect command of his material and pauses thoughtfully and appropriately, his speaking will gain greater respect, rapport, and attention. If he rides roughshod over his material, throwing in meaningless grunts and words, he will lose the respect of his auditors, and their comprehension will suffer correspondingly.

In relating an anecdote, flexibility will help you to imitate the different voices in the dialogue.

Assignments and exercises

1. Write a sentence to illustrate each of the following gestures. Deliver each sentence before the class, coordinating the gesture with the words.
   a. Index finger points
   b. Clenched hands pound table
   c. Palm thrusts forward in rejection
   d. Palm moves downward to suppress
   e. Palm opens in supplication
2. Select a gesture to reinforce the following sentences. Deliver the sentence and execute the gesture before the class.
   a. We must suppress *communism!*
   b. Medical-training costs are growing higher and higher.
   c. Rising inflation affects *you!*
   d. It is simply a question of ideologies: on the one hand, democracy; on the other, totalitarianism.

e. The antimissile missile found its mark with a terrible *crash!*

f. The bombed aircraft carrier sank stern first into the ocean.

g. We must reorganize this company from the ground up.

h. I reject the idea that further research is useless.

i. The increased "g" loading caused the aircraft to buckle in the middle of the fuselage.

j. AM transmitters modulate the length of the radio waves. FM transmitters modulate the frequency of radio waves.

3. Talk about something that makes you angry. Talk about your pet peeve or favorite gripe. Gesture freely. Use suggestions from the instructor and class concerning your use of gesture for emphasis and reinforcement.

4. Describe an exciting or dangerous experience that you have had. A serious automobile wreck would be a suitable subject. Use your hands to indicate shapes, sizes, forms, directions, and speeds.

5. Read a selection to the class. The instructor will move most of the class to the back of the room. Ask anyone to raise his hand or say "stop" when you cannot be heard.

6. Make a speech to the class in which you recommend a plan, procedure, design, or product. Record the speech on tape. Check your use of vocal stress in emphasizing the important words. Do you emphasize the wrong words? Do you omit necessary emphasis?

7. Read a selection to the class. Ask them to stop you any time your voice becomes a monotone.

8. A sound movie of each student is a helpful tool for analyzing appearance, gestures, bodily action, and voice. If this is unavailable, use an 8-millimeter film of the student as he makes a speech.

9. Work on part of an oral communication you have found in a magazine, pamphlet, or newspaper. See if you can deliver it to the group with good vocal variety and with effective bodily action.

10. Make a critical report concerning the use of voice and body by a speaker on television. Turn the sound off and concentrate on his use of gesture and bodily movement. Then turn up the sound and take your eyes away from the screen and concentrate on the voice.

4

THE BLUEPRINT TAKES FORM

Support for your points

A case in point **"Flesh up the bones"**

John Masterson was manager of the Western Power and Light Company in Highland City. He was required by top management of this statewide power company to make speeches, whenever he was asked, in order to improve public relations for the company. Masterson was asked by the Highland City Civic League to make a speech at the regular weekly luncheon meeting. The program chairman said it would be permissible for Masterson to speak about the Western Power and Light Company since a large number of new families had moved into the community and would like to know about the conveniences and services provided by the company.

Masterson began his speech by saying that he was a Highland City hometown boy. Unfortunately he did not explain this in a very interesting way. He made a halfhearted joke about being born there: ". . . but there is no plaque commemorating my birth. Instead there is now a bowling alley and a supermarket located where my old homestead used to be." This sad little half story, half commentary didn't get any laughs or even grins from the audience. Masterson didn't put enough thought into supporting the main idea of his introduction: "I am a hometown boy." He had been a football hero at Highland City's high school. He had worked at a corner drugstore where the old gang had congregated after school. He had been elected president of his senior class and had been cast as the lead in the senior play. From all these experiences he could have woven vivid or humorous anecdotes that would have gained the attention of the audience, and, at the same time, supported the main idea of his introduction.

Masterson then launched into his first major idea, the growth and development of the Highland City Power and Light Company. This was a brief history showing how the company had developed from a small, one-dynamo operation into the present power plant which served a city of 50,000. He lost part of his audience, however, by failing to define some technical terms. He talked about "10-kw outputs increasing to 1,000-kw outputs." There were some people in the audience who didn't know what "kw" referred to. To show that his company was progressive, Masterson asserted that the research division was conducting experimentation, along with a chemical products company, to refine tar and lignite derivatives. He merely stated this, without giving any examples to show how such experiments were related to the advance and development of electric power service. He also said that his company, along with two other power companies and the state university, were experimenting with atomic energy, but he did not describe or tell the purpose of the experiments. A comparison of atomic energy for generating electricity and present methods could have been made.

John Masterson's speech was dull and vague. He failed himself and his company in this speech situation. What was his problem? About all Masterson had for a speech was a series of statements. He had a skeleton outline of a speech, but he did not flesh up the bones with supporting material that would amplify, explain, and emphasize his points. John Masterson entered a speech situation with about one-tenth of his preparation completed.

After outlining the main ideas of the speech, search for means of amplifying and clarifying these ideas. Some sources of support for main ideas are factual information, statistics, definitions, examples, comparisons, analogies, descriptions, quotations, testimony, stories, and visual aids.

Factual information

When a speaker talks in vague generalities, the listeners suspect that he does not have the basic information in hand. Start with all the information you already have about the subject. Then turn to reliable references. Find out about the experiences of others through interviews and conferences. Search in books, newspapers, and other publications. Verify that your source is qualified, dependable, and current. When in doubt, find out. Knowing the facts gives the speaker confidence and authority. (See Chapter 8 for research techniques.)

Statistics

Audiences are impressed by statistics. But there are inherent dangers in their use. Examine the following do's and don'ts: *Don't* include more statistics than the audience can comprehend by listening. Remember that the hearers are not reading. They are *listening. Don't* make statistics too complex. Round numbers and approximate figures are preferable because they can be perceived immediately. "About 60 per cent" is preferred to "fifty-nine, point nine, nine, nine." *Do* give the audience some standard of comparison for judging the significance of the statistics. For example, a speaker says that in the event of an atomic bomb striking Middletown, the overflow to Centerville, 15 miles away, would be 1,300 roentgen units. These figures are not meaningful unless the speaker explains that 75 roentgen units would kill everybody in Centerville. *Do* help the audience visualize your statistics. A speaker says that a television antenna is 1,500 feet high. He can make the effect sharper by saying that if the antenna rested on the ground it would reach from the town hall to the high school building. The "laid-end-to-end" kind of phrasing helps to make the statistics more visual to the audience. *Do* use visual aids. It is helpful to the audience's memory and reference if the statistics are written on the blackboard, or if some other visual aid is used to place the figures before the eyes of the audience during the presentation.

The speaker who most successfully provides his audience with information is not the one who exposes them to the largest quantity of facts and statistics in a given length of time. The most successful speaker is the one who makes a reasonable amount of information clear, vivid and significant in the amount of time available to him.

Definitions

Many communications are beamed at lay groups who are not familiar with technical terms and shoptalk. Even when the speaker is addressing other technical men, it is well to define some technical terms, for it has been discovered that the meaning of words varies among scientists and engineers. Words for tools, processes, and equipment vary from plant to plant and from one part of the country to another. Be sure that you and the members of the audience have the same meaning for a word. Use a definition. The following types of words generally require definition:

1. Abstract words whose meanings are fuzzy and nonspecific. Examples: fair wage, artistic, functional, liberal, conservative, democracy, precision, accuracy
2. Technical terms used in a particular branch of science, engineering, medicine, or industry
3. Words used in any specialized activity, such as a division of the armed forces or a police department
4. Slang used by provincial groups, age groups, or professional groups
5. Archaic terms which are now outmoded and no longer in general usage
6. Esoteric, foreign, or unique terms

Examples

Teachers, counselors, industrial training officers, and ministers agree that the example is one of the best ways to clarify and emphasize a point. The members of these professions are in the position of explaining concepts, methods, precepts, problems, rules, and procedures on an everyday basis. They have found that the example is a sure way to make some people understand. Typical incidents, representative cases, and sample problems are concrete aids to clarity. Examples may be used in the content of the speech as follows:

To serve as sample problems when a solution or method of procedure is being explained

To show how a rule or principle may be applied in a specific case

To show cause and effect relationships

To explain the application of theory to practice

To support a recommended course of action

To show how something has worked in the past

To show how certain mistakes, discrepancies, or wrong methods can affect the present situation

Comparisons, contrasts, analogies

A cardinal rule in making information clear is to explain the *unfamiliar* in terms of the *familiar*. Comparisons, contrasts, and analogies are good devices for implementing this rule. By putting elements side by side to show their relative values, likenesses, and differences the new and strange may be held against the familiar and old to establish a bridge from the known to the unknown.

Comparisons should meet certain requirements to be practical and effective: (1) the items compared should be similar enough to project logical likenesses; (2) the item to be used as the vehicle of comparison should be familiar to the audience. A speaker can explain the soundwave theory by comparing it to the ripples made in a pond into which a stone is dropped. The phenomenon of the sonic boom can be likened to the action of a person walking through a field of tall grass. The walker displaces and piles up the stalks of grass as the jet plane compresses and stacks up the molecules in the air wall.

Contrasts emphasize differences rather than likenesses. An engineer, recommending a new assembling system for an industrial plant, can contrast the new system with the old, showing, point by point, the differences between the two. He can use familiar aspects of the old system to explain points of the new system.

Analogies are extended comparisons. By the use of some device or process which is known to the audience, a new idea can be explained in terms of the familiar. For example, the operation of a water distribution plant can be made analogous to the operation of a bank account. A man deposits a check for $100 in his bank account each week. He draws out $14 each day to meet daily expenses. A pump, operating only once a week, pushes 100,000 gallons of water into a standpipe. The standpipe releases **14,000** gallons each day to meet the daily water demands of the community. Once a week the man deposits enough money in the bank account to meet his financial needs for a week. Once a week the pump raises enough water in the standpipe to meet the water-supply needs.

Description

Words create a mental image in the minds of the audience. Using words within the limits of your listener's vocabulary, talk about sizes, shapes, and dimensions. Use the most accurate and graphic language you can as you paint the general impressions first, then proceed to describe the component parts or specifics.

Quotations

To quote is to select the words of authoritative individuals, groups, agencies, or publications particularly suitable for supporting and clarifying the point in question. Quotations may be used as follows:

1. To set forth statistics, definitions, and examples which help to clarify a point
2. To utilize the opinion of an authority whose experience and integrity is respected by the audience
3. To phrase the purpose, theme, or conclusion in memorable, colorful words
4. To state evidence which will support the speaker's cause
5. To show a variety of reactions, both pro and con, to the point in question
6. To bring before the audience stories, anecdotes, and humorous commentary which will attract attention and hold interest

As with other forms of support, we must test the reliability and propriety of quotations we use. Is the quotation pertinent to and expressive of the point? Does it strongly support the point? When the quotation is lifted from its original context and placed in the context of the speech, does it apply practically and honestly to the matter at hand? Is the source of the testimony, evidence, or assertion respected for its accuracy and integrity? Is the source up to date, taking into account new developments and discoveries in the field? Is the source prejudiced? Is there any special obstacle that prevents the source from being objective? Is the source slanted? Is the material stated so that the truth of the matter is twisted to support a particular viewpoint?

Stories, anecdotes, jokes

Stories are suitable for clarifying and emphasizing a point as well as for arousing interest. The audience may believe an assertion, but they will remember it longer if it is illustrated by a story. For example, a safety engineer making the usual safety talk may really impress the audience if he tells the story of a man who used the equipment carelessly and was injured painfully, hospitalized for a long period, and caused worry and economic distress for his family.

Stories add a personal and dramatic touch. In general, listeners are more interested in specific people than they are in "consumers," "steelworkers," and "farmers." If factual information can be placed in story form, showing the effects of the problem on people as individuals, the point will be more applicable to the audience. It is difficult for the audience to empathize with the "$1\frac{1}{2}$ workers" of a cold statistic. It is easier for them to feel close to John McGee who is twenty-eight years old, is married, has three children, and has similar working conditions, wages, and family problems to those of the guy next door.

Stories are frequently used to obtain attention in the introduction; to add emphasis to the conclusion. They are invaluable when a speaker wants to emphasize the function and application of rules, regulations, and specifications. In choosing a story, we must test its quality and suitability. Is the story suitable to the background and experience of the audience? Does the story appeal to you personally? Can you tell it with enthusiasm and animation? Is the story effectively organized? Are the characters introduced and identified? Does the plot line have a rising curve of interest? Does it have a payoff or climax? Is the punch line phrased for maximum effect? Is the story brief? If the story is too long and complicated the audience may forget the point that you are illustrating.

Visual aids

The projection of statistics, schematics, drawings, charts, maps, and graphs to accompany your words, makes explanation facile and accurate. Visual aids and their uses are explained more fully in Chapter 6.

Assignments and exercises

1. Read or listen to an oral communication. Isolate one of the major points. Explain to the class how the speaker has supported this point. Identify the types of support used. This may be written or reported orally.

2. Isolate the major point in an editorial or in a letter to the editor of a newspaper or magazine. Show how the writer supported his point.

3. Build a short talk (about three to four minutes in length) around an analogy, either factual or hypothetical.

4. Support one of the following points by quotation and testimony:

a. Television has reduced the amount of reading in the United States.

b. Religion is growing in force (or fading) in the United States.

c. A man is a part of everything he sees and reads and hears.

d. Alcoholism is now one of the nation's leading problems.

e. It is more important that we send loaves of bread around the world, than missiles into outer space.

5. Use an anecdote to illustrate one of the following ideas:

a. Hypnosis can reveal the brains that most people have but have not used yet.

b. If race drivers drove the way people do on the highway, there would be no more auto races.

c. Every student needs a course in college mathematics.

d. The best conditions for scientific research exist in the United States.

6. You are a technical man working as liaison between the sales department and the production department. Some new salesmen with little technical background have been hired. Explain to them the functional capacities of a piece of equipment they will be selling. Use techniques mentioned in this chapter.

7. Instruct a student group in the use, care, and maintenance of some new equipment on the campus, such as television, stage lighting, radio, projectors, air conditioning, and public address. Use as many of the supporting methods mentioned in the chapter as you can.

5 ONE MILLION UNITS OF RAW MATERIAL

Language—the structural material of speech

Man's dominant position among the living creatures of the earth is attributed to his unique ability in the use of symbolic language. Animals utter cries, seem to signal each other in a crude fashion, but man alone has mastered the complicated use of symbols for accurate, purposeful communication. Human beings have learned to transfer sounds to visual form (writing, printing, braille, etc.) and obtain meaning by seeing these forms or tracing them with the fingers. But, normally, human beings do much more talking and listening than reading and writing.

Articulation

A speaker must have ability in handling the spoken symbols of his language. We are not favorably impressed by careless, sloppy speech. Most hearers suspect that such speech indicates sloppy thinking. The golden mean requires vigorous use of the articulators without overprecise, pedantic enunciation of words.

A case in point "What kind of jet"?

A group of technical men had just finished a long meeting in which air transportation was the main topic of discussion. The new jet age had made distances so much shorter in time that new travel schedules were essential. Greater areas for the various consultants to cover were being assigned. The group was deep in troubled thought about the ways in which faster planes had affected their jobs. Another of the executives had just arrived.

He had not been present at the deliberations. After a few quick words of greeting, he looked at the clock behind him. Then he announced to the group, with upward inflection, "Jeet jet?" There was a puzzled silence. "What kind of a plane is that?" asked one of the participants. This completely confounded the executive. "Are you kidding me?" he asked. It took a little time before the astonished group realized that the original question had been: "Did you eat yet?" The general hilarity did not raise the prestige of the officer of the company.

The smallest segment of language is the individual sound, or phoneme. The sounds of our language are usually classified in three major groups: vowels, consonants, and glides (or diphthongs). Speakers have less trouble in articulating the vowel sounds. They may say "git" instead of "get" or "boin" instead of "burn," but these may be classified as problems of pronunciation, usually stemming from imitation of the style of a particular area of the country. Proper articulation of the vowel sounds requires an open mouth and a free-moving set of jaws. If the tongue is kept well forward so that the back of the throat is open when the vowels are formed, the vowels can be emitted clearly and heard easily.

The consonants carry the major portion of meaning in our language. Try to decipher the following sentence which shows only the vowels. The dots indicate each missing consonant.

..i.i.. o. .i.e.. .i..ou. .e.o.i.. .o.oo.i.. .u.. .e e.i.i.a.e.

The sentence using only consonants reads as follows:

Dr.v.ng .f r.v.ts w.th..t r.m.v.ng c.c..n.ng m.st b. .l.m.n.t.d

The sentence, "Driving of rivets without removing cocooning must be eliminated," is much easier to read in the second form, showing only the consonants. Perhaps only the technical word *cocooning* gave you any trouble at all.

Improper enunciation of consonants seems to be the major articulation fault. Sometimes consonants are omitted from the interior of a word in such examples as *government, length, recognize, picture, actually.* The word becomes a mumble, and clarity is reduced. Sometimes consonants are added in opposition to accepted usage such as in the words *once*(t), *twice*(t), *drowned*(ded), and *attacked*(ted) Sometimes the consonants are inverted as in *lantern.*

(lantren), *hundred* (hunderd), and *modern* (modren). Sometimes a speaker is confounded by a cluster of consonant sounds: *asks, clothes, strength, insists, facts, taxed,* etc. The speaker must try to achieve great flexibility of the tongue and lips for clear-cut rendition of consonant sounds.

The glide sounds of American English include *ow,* as in *how now, brown cow; i* as in *high time; o* as in *row boat; oi* as in *boil the joint; ew* as in *new tune.* The two main offenders seem to be the *ow* and the *i.* Both these sounds start with an approximation of the sound *ah.* After this sound is established, the *ah* glides to *oo* in the case of *ow* (ah-oo); the *ah* glides to *ee* in the case of *i* (ah-ee). The glides are rapid but they should be fully voiced. Thus in articulating the word *town,* the sounds in succession are *t-ah-oon;* when voicing the word *pine,* the sound progression is *p-ah-ee-n.* If you have trouble with these sounds, underline them when they appear in your manuscript or notes. Make an exaggerated effort to articulate them in a fashion acceptable to your critics.

Pronunciation

American English is a difficult language to pronounce correctly. Ask any foreigner who tries to learn our language. With our twenty-six letters of the alphabet, we must form approximately fifteen vowel sounds, nine glides, or diphthongs, and twenty-five consonant sounds. The letter "a" alone is pronounced quite differently in the words *at, ate, arm, awe, sofa, beat,* etc. The sound "sh" may be spelled in various ways: *ship, anxious, ocean, auction, chagrin, sugar, conscious, schist.* Pronunciation involves the sounds you make, the syllables you accent, and the combinations of these sounds formed into words to conform with the generally accepted pattern used by educated speakers in a particular region. In the United States there are three distinct regions with distinctive pronunciation patterns. Within each region there are local enclaves with their own patterns. Furthermore, certain industries and even companies have adopted certain pronunciation patterns and guard them zealously.

The dictionaries, supposedly, record the pronunciations in general usage by educated speakers. Lexicographers consider themselves describers, rather than prescribers, of correct pronunciation. Since the patterns are in a state of flux, it is difficult to discover whether the dictionary pronunciations are current or out-of-date. The man who points in a superior manner to the dictionary as the arbiter of *his* pronunciation may actually be indicating a form that is passing out of favor. The various forms indicated in the dictionary are (or have been) cited because the editors have some proof of their usage. However, all forms listed are equal in correctness. Normally, the best pronunciation attracts the least attention. Thus, speech should not be too local in nature, but must be highly adaptable. If the personnel of the plant in which you are employed say "status reports," pronouncing *status* as though it rhymed with *lattice,* use that pronunciation rather than *status* as though it were *state us.*

People establish pronunciation. The lexicographers record the pronunciations of the educated people in a given area and note variants in the pronunciation. If any of the variants are in frequent use, they will be recorded in the dictionary. In this way variant pronunciations become equally respectable ways of pronouncing a word. The dictionary is our most useful reference book on pronunciation. No other authority exists or is so widely recognized. You must be thoroughly familiar with the diacritical markings or phonetic symbols used by your particular dictionary so that you can tell at a glance what the word sounds like and where the stress falls. Every dictionary has its own phonetic symbols. Memorize carefully the symbols used by your particular choice. (See Appendix B for diacritical markings.)

The value of a good vocabulary

There seems to be a high degree of correlation between what is known as intelligence and size of vocabulary. When a person can name objects around him, when he can call abstract ideas by name, when he can put his thoughts into accurate language, he probably has better recognition and discernment of the perplexing problems that beset us in our social, political, religious, and business worlds. The unabridged dictionary carries about a half million entries. It has been estimated that if all technical words and variants were listed, the number of words would be increased to one million for the English language.

There is a definite relationship between the number of words at your command and your ability to express yourself more precisely, distinguish between finer shades of meaning, grasp more firmly new or complex concepts, and recognize ideas more rapidly and accurately in your reading and listening. Language conveys little meaning unless it stirs ideas and emotions in the mind of the hearer. Use known words, well within the vocabulary of the audience. Unfamiliar or unusual words may be used to express a new concept or precise shading of meaning. But unfamiliar words must be defined or explained sufficiently in the context of the talk. It is unwise to act superior when presenting a new word or phrase, indicating to your listeners, "Oh, you don't know the meaning of the last six-cylinder word I just used. Let me explain to you ignoramuses just what I meant by it." If you preface your definition with "of course you all recognize . . . ," it may be more palatable to the audience and the new word will be acceptable to the group. (See Appendix C for a vocabulary test.)

A more meaningful vocabulary

Intelligible and sensitive communication depends upon your skill in using words. Language is a pattern of words. Ask yourself: "Do I really succeed in making myself understood? Does my speech invite attention or does it turn ears aside? Do I have enough verbal range and flexibility to speak as well on special occasions as I do in casual conversations? Or do I just get by?" A word is only a symbol for shared reality. To be effective you must be sure not only that your language is understood, but that it *cannot be misunderstood.*

Chop out the deadwood

Eliminate such phrases as "See?" "I mean," "Well-uh," "Don't cha know?" etc. Avoid such worn-out phrases as "According to our records." Why not say, "We find"? "We are carrying on research along these lines" is a meaningless phrase. Try to eliminate long-hackneyed phrases and substitute short, plain words. Substitute "soon" for "at the earliest possible moment"; "about" for "on the order of magnitude of"; "since" for "in view of the fact that"; "complete" for "absolutely complete."

Use familiar words

Don't use a lot of high-sounding verbiage (verbal garbage) just to make yourself sound good. Remember that you are trying to communicate. Use the word that is familiar to the audience and that will carry the meaning quickly and directly to them.

Cases in point   **"Words, words, words"**

During World War II the Office of Civilian Defense ordered Federal buildings to secure "obscuration either by blackout construction or by termination of the illumination." President Roosevelt rephrased the order in the following fashion: "Put something across the windows or turn out the lights."

Editor Brown of the *London Observer* feared that some future translation of the Bible would delete the phrase "Heal the sick" in favor of "Rehabilitate those victimized by psycho-somatic maladjustment."

In December of 1944, the 101st Division of the United States Army was surrounded by the Germans in the Battle of the Bulge, and the American commander found himself having to reply to a lengthy demand for the division's surrender. There was no mistaking the message sent out by the commander, General McAuliffe. His reply was brilliant communication, inspiring his men, amazing the world, and astounding the bewildered Germans. No meaningless words were in this message. It consisted of a single word: "Nuts!"[1]

[1] John B. Haney, "Colonel Blunderbuss' Battle Cry," *Journal of Communication*, vol. 7, Spring, 1957, pp. 24–28.

Use precise words

We may say that a man is firm in his belief or that he is obstinate. What is the exact difference? At what point does firmness become obstinacy? Obviously, a man is *firm* if we agree with him or admire his stand, but he is *obstinate* if we disagree with him and believe he ought to change his mind. The difference between the words *firm* and *obstinate* does not appear in actual definition as much as in our attitude toward the person to whom the words are applied.

The precise word carries connotations that reflect not only dictionary meaning but attitudes of the speaker toward other people and toward the particular situation involved. A *thrifty* man is one whose saving of money meets our approval, but a *stingy* man is one whose saving of money arouses our disapproval. In both cases any difference in the actual quality for which the words stand—careful use of money—is difficult to detect. But the difference in our attitude toward the person who possesses that quality is obvious to our auditors.

A case in point **The "sneak" of Araby**

In the middle of a conference on the progress of a new building project at the Arabian Chemical Plant, the door opened suddenly and one of the engineers involved in the planning conference came in to take his place at the table. He was late, and his presence was remarked on by the chairman in the following manner: "Well, I see Don just sneaked in." Don was infuriated. "I did not *sneak* in," he retorted. "What do you call it, then?" asked the chairman. "Just say I *entered quietly*," Don shot back. Luckily, this little interchange dissolved into a roar of laughter in which Don and the chairman joined.

Beware of jargon

The technical man's talk is filled with highly technical words and phrases. If his audience has had experience with the reality symbolized by this language, meaning is transferred. However, if the language is so highly specialized that meaning is obscured, this jargon becomes a stumbling block on the road to understanding.

A case in point **"Cutie-pie"**

Some of the members of a Junior Chamber of Commerce were complaining recently about the talks they had scheduled for their meetings. "We are all interested in atomic energy," said the program chairman, "Especially since our major local plant is engaged with several others in the nation in experimenting along the lines of using this power for domestic use. So we try to get one of the scientists to tell us about progress. But they use so many specialized terms, we become completely confused and bored when listening to them. Why can't they translate the phrases to *our* language? The last meeting got a lot of laughs but little comprehension when the speaker kept talking about an instrument he called a "cutie-pie." It was only *after* the meeting that he explained to me that a cutie-pie meant a "portable instrument equipped with a direct reading meter used to determine the level of radiation in an area."

Lay groups or workers uninitiated into the mysteries of the peculiar language used by a certain profession or business may be amused or mystified by the strange words that pour forth so glibly from the user of jargon, but they are also irritated at the loss of meaning. The following are examples of shoptalk that result in muddy communication outside the shop.

A tickler: a finned steel rod in the sodium discharge pipe of a sodium (metallic) cell to collect calcium chloride.

A frying pan: a slip blank made of flat metal to be bolted between flanges in a pipe.

A squeeze job: perforations in cement to stop waterflow.

Bury a dead man: to cover the concrete supports used for guy wires.

Cases in point **"Come again"?**

One construction supervisor in a large steel company sent his new assistant for "the old man," which in shop talk means a large drill press. In a few moments the assistant returned towing the bewildered elderly gentleman who operated the tool room.

A judge heard the following testimony from a railroad man: "I looked out the smutty and saw the spark. So I pulled the monkey tail and the hogshead threw it in the ditch." After some questioning the judge received the following translation: "I looked out of the caboose window and saw a hotbox on one of the wheels. I pulled the emergency cord and the engineer put full air on the brakes and brought the train to a sudden stop."

Select appropriate words

Suit your words to the subject, the occasion, and the audience. Most of the time you will be using colloquial language. This does not mean that you will descend to substandard provincial talk, but it does mean that most speaking should avoid formal literary language. In speaking, you can make great use of personal pronouns and contractions that might seem too informal when written. However, don't talk down to the audience. It was Raymond Clapper who once stated this basic rule: "Never underestimate the intelligence of your audience; and never overestimate its information."

If your precise meaning can be expressed only by a long or unfamiliar word, and you can explain it by context or redundancy, then use it. There is no need to assume that your listeners have the intelligence of ten year olds unless they are ten year olds. Keep in mind the occasion, too. When you are explaining a process to the cub scouts in the Beaver Den, your language will be simpler than when you are reading a paper to trained technical personnel.

Use specific words and phrases

Use specific and concrete words rather than general and abstract words. An abstract term is one referring to a quality or idea that does not have physical substance. A concrete term denotes something that can be perceived through the senses—something that can be seen, heard, touched, smelled, tasted, or felt in the muscles or organs. "Highway casualty" is abstract; "Janie Caldwell, age seven, lying dead in the road" is concrete. "A relatively tiny increase in the number of bone cancers and leukemia victims as a result of radioactive fallout" is abstract; "little Sonny Fraiser celebrating Christmas in August because he will be dead of leukemia long before December 25" is concrete.

Eliminate ambiguous or vague words. Would you say that the general manager was *cool* to a proposal? Or would you say that he was frosty, frigid, gelid, icy, glacial, unreceptive, apathetic, opposed, indignant, resistant? The following talk illustrates the vague language we sometimes hear at luncheon clubs. Do you understand exactly what the speaker is talking about? Has he charted out any course of action?

A case in point   **A speech for any occasion**

Mr. Chairman, Ladies and Gentlemen:

It is indeed a great and undeserved privilege to address such an audience as I see before me. At no previous time in the history of human civilization have greater problems confronted and challenged the ingenuity of man's intellect than now. Let us look around us. What do we see on the horizon? What forces are at work? Whither are we drifting? Under what mist of clouds does the future stand obscured?

My friends, casting aside the raiment of all human speech, the crucial test for the solution of all these intricate problems to which I have just alluded is the sheer and forceful application of those immutable laws which down the corridor of Time have always guided the hand of man, groping, as it were, for some faint beacon light for his hopes and aspirations. Without these great vital principles we are but puppets responding to whim and fancy, failing entirely to grasp the hidden meaning of it all. We must readdress ourselves to these questions which press for answer and solution. The issues cannot be avoided. There they stand. It is upon you, and you, and yet even upon me, that the yoke of responsibility falls.

What, then, is our duty? Shall we continue to drift? No!! With all the emphasis of my being I hurl back the message no! Drifting must stop. We must press onward and upward toward the ultimate goal to which all must aspire. But I cannot conclude my remarks, dear friends, without touching briefly upon a subject which I know is steeped in your very consciousness. I refer to that spirit which gleams from the eyes of a new-born babe, that animates the toiling masses, that sways all the hosts of humanity past and present. Without this energizing principle all commerce, trade and industry are hushed and will perish from this earth as surely as the crimson sunset follows the golden sunshine.

Mark you, I do not seek to unduly alarm or distress the mothers, fathers, sons, and daughters gathered before me in this vast assemblage, but I would indeed be recreant to a high resolve which I made as a youth if I did not at this time and in this place, and with the full realizing sense of responsibility which I assume, publicly declare and affirm my dedication and my consecration to the eternal principles and receipts of simple, ordinary, commonplace justice.

For what, in the last analysis, is Justice: Whence does it come? Where does it go? Is it tangible? It is not. Is it tactual? It is not. Is it visible? It is not. Is it ponderable? It is not. Justice is none of these, and yet, on the other hand, in a sense it is all of these things combined. While I cannot tell you what justice is, this much I can tell you—that without the encircling arms of justice, without her shield, without her guardianship, the ship of State will sail through uncharted seas, narrowly avoiding rocks and shoals, headed inevitably for the harbor of calamity.

Justice!—Justice!!—Justice!!!—To thee we pay homage. To thee we dedicate our laurels of hope. Before thee we kneel in adoration, mindful of thy great power, mute before thy inscrutable destiny. . . . [2]

An enriched vocabulary

You will want to grow in your knowledge of words so that they may serve you better in receiving and communicating information and ideas.

[2] A. Parker Nevin, "An Address for All Occasions," *The Princeton Alumni Weekly*, 1936.

Use the dictionary

Be sure to have a good desk dictionary handy for immediate reference at home or at work. The moment you note an unfamiliar word or have need for a synonym use the dictionary. Too many times, individuals make *mental* notes of the need for more verbal information. They have good intentions. They say to themselves, "When I lay up a store of needs, I will move across the room to the bookcase, or open up that desk drawer to get the information I want." In a few moments the necessity is forgotten. Had the dictionary been in immediate range, an addition to the bank of phrases and vocabulary might have been made. If you meet an unfamiliar word in your reading or listening, and no dictionary is available, write it in a small pocket notebook. Look it up as soon as possible. Even if you can guess the meaning of an unfamiliar word, you had better look it up to be sure.

Use the new word

Make this new word a part of your own vocabulary. Fix it firmly in your mind by relating its root, prefixes, suffixes, or synonyms to words you already know. Pronounce the word aloud several times. We hesitate to use a new word whose pronunciation has not been fixed by oral use. One student who had learned the word *dais* and knew its meaning well, tried to use it on a group. He had not tried it out loud. His statement ran something like this: "As I stand before you on this . . . daze . . . I mean day . . . uh dass . . . uh, PLATFORM. . . ."

Try the new word or phrase in sentences. Make up various sentences in which the new addition to your vocabulary may appear. Say them aloud. Use the new word in speech and writing. This will help to establish it in the bank of active words at your command.

Learn the commonly used roots, prefixes, and suffixes that have been incorporated into our language from Latin and Greek. Some educators argue that a good background of Latin is valuable for learning English. The same case could be made for Greek. Since few students these days take up an extensive study of these two ancient languages, conscious study of the important roots, suffixes,

and prefixes will help you to recognize meanings of unfamiliar
words. See Appendix D for lists of prefixes, suffixes, Latin roots,
and Greek word elements. Check over the lists of these roots and
try constructing a few examples beyond the ones mentioned in the
Appendix.

Errors in grammar

A single grammatical error may destroy the prestige of the speaker
and reduce his effectiveness. This is especially true if members of
his audience know better. An exhaustive study of grammar is outside the range of this book, but some of the more frequent and
noticeable errors are listed below.

1. The nominative pronoun as an object
Wrong—They gave Jim and *I* the complete report. (Use *me*)

2. "Myself" as subject
Wrong—The other two men and *myself* examined the plan.
(Use *I*)

3. Plural nouns with singular verbs (or vice versa)
Wrong—The members of the group *was* in complete agreement.
(Use *were*)
Wrong—A single individual of the working group *haven't* the
ability to lift this apparatus. (Use *hasn't*)

4. Plural modifiers with singular nouns
Wrong—These kind of plans will not work. (Use *these kinds*)

5. Confusion of adjective and adverb
Wrong—He worked fast and *furious* at the job. (Use *furiously*)

6. Confusion of comparative adjectives or adverbs
Wrong—After trying both plans, he decided that the first was
the *most* economical. (Use *more*)

7. Double or superfluous negatives
Wrong—We *can't* hardly hear you. (Use *can*)

8. Who, which, and that as relative pronouns
Who as a relative pronoun refers to persons; *which*, to things.
(Use the man *who* studies these specifications, the engineers
whom I invited to the meeting, the machinery *which* I saw.)

The relative pronoun *that* is unlimited in its reference and may refer either to persons or things.

9.   The redundant use of the pronoun
Wrong—Jim, *he* went to the meeting. (Eliminate *he*)

Language and the human being

All day long, and perhaps through the night, too, human beings must react to the phenomena of the world about them and to the other human beings that make up that world. For the most part, we evaluate these events through our senses and store these sensations in the form of symbols called words. In transmitting reactions from one person to another, we must use the words (symbols) we have evolved and learned.

These symbols have powerful influences on the actions of others. Certain types of language draw people together, give them a feeling of oneness and cooperativeness; other types force them apart and build up feelings of hostility. As Abraham Lincoln once said: ". . . assume to dictate to his judgment, or to command his action, or to mark him out as one to be shunned and despised, and he will retreat within himself, close all the avenues to his head and heart; and though your cause be naked truth itself, transformed to the heaviest lance, harder than steel, and sharper than steel can be made, and though you throw it with more than herculean force and precision, you will be no more able to pierce him than to penetrate the hard shell of a tortoise with a rye straw. Such is man, and so must be understood by those who would lead him even to his best interests."

By sparing the individual's self concept, you may avoid giving him the impression that you are attacking his ego or attempting to dictate his behavior. Let us list a few general uses and misuses of the thousands of words that cross our lips daily.

Words that unite you with your fellow man

1.   Words of affability. In a country where a president was elected to two terms of office under the slogan, "I like Ike," it is obvious that you should make every effort to sound pleasant. "The person who would commend himself to Americans in particular, who rate ability as naught without affability, will see to it that his manner of writing (or talking) comes from a genial nature and one that has the reader's (listener's) entertainment as well as enlightenment at heart. A feeling of warmth and kindness toward any audience will supply a resilience of spirit which no brilliance of mind can make up for. Peevishness can be detected as easily as a glaring error in grammar."[3]

2. Words of common experience. By indicating that the listeners have shared his experiences, the speaker expedites their reception of his ideas. Thus we may sprinkle our speaking with such phrases as: "Just as we have agreed before . . . ," "As you all know from experience in this type of work . . . ," etc. A safety poster showing a tool lying on the edge of a scaffold illustrated this style of speaking. The caption read: "*You* know better than this. When the *other fellow* doesn't, tell him."

3. Words of respect. Words that acknowledge the thinking ability and high moral purpose of your listeners will draw you to them. The President of the United States, announcing the fact that no tax cut would be forthcoming during the following year, said: "This Act was written with the confident belief that the great majority of business men are ready to cooperate with their fellows and their government." Other phrases exemplifying this use of language might be: "You folks will, of course, draw your own conclusions on this proposition"; "Thoughtfulness and watchfulness are characteristics of intelligent people. That's why . . ."; "You are the busy people, the ones that get the job done. Now you are being called on again to . . . ."

4. Words of prestige. You may convey the feeling that your ideas are accepted by other persons or have tradition behind them. Phrases such as the following may prove helpful: "It is generally conceded that . . ."; "The executives of many

[3] Charles F. Ferguson, *Say It with Words*, Alfred A. Knopf, Inc., New York, 1959, p. 102.

leading firms in this nation are ardent supporters of . . .";
"These theories are accepted by leading physicians throughout
the nation."; "Throughout the history of our company we
have always . . . ." Abraham Lincoln opened his famous address with, "Four score and seven years ago our fathers brought
forth on this continent a new nation . . . ."

Words that isolate you from your fellow man

1. Black and white words. A few areas of life can be divided
into two dimensions: life and death, east and west, will do or
won't. But most areas of existence have a multivalued orientation. That is, between the opposites you find any number of
gradations. If a speaker makes a habit of forcing a listener
to choose between black and white, all or none, *my* way or
the *wrong* way, he frequently blocks acceptance of his ideas.
Is a given act good? or evil? Some people react to the playing
of instrumental music in a church with the word "sacrilegi-
ous!" Others react to the same experience with the word
"spiritual." Be careful not to let your words force you into
clinging to an untenable position, like a painter who paints
himself into the corner of a room.

2. Time-freezing words. People who use words in this manner
have forgotten that our lives are dynamic and everything we
know about is in a constant state of flux. A short time ago a
United States atomic-powered submarine was denied entrance
to a harbor by a country that feared the whole harbor would
be "atomized" by the submarine. They had failed to keep up
with the times. They did not know that new methods of shield-
ing had been discovered to make the atomic reactor harmless.
Imagine the thinking of those responsible for denying the submarine entrance. "The atomic bomb killed people. This submarine is atomic powered. Therefore, it will kill people."
Your language should be specific as to *date* and *time;* it should
take into consideration the changes that occur as time marches
on. An elementary science class only a few years ago would
have had students committing to memory the definition: "An

atom is the *least divisible portion of matter.*" This bit of "scientific information" is hardly acceptable today.

3. Kaleidoscope words.   We all remember the childhood toy called the kaleidoscope. When you turned it ever so slightly, the little colored pieces of glass formed an entirely different pattern before your amazed eyes; you handed it to a friend, and as it turned over in transit from your hand to his, an image different from the one you saw greeted his eyes. So it is with the use of words. You select a word to use, and when your listeners hear it, they may react in a way that surprises you because they attach a different meaning to the word. Make sure you have chosen terms whose meanings coincide with the interests and previous experience of the listeners.

4. Kimono words (euphemisms).   We cover our bodies hastily with a kimono or dressing gown in order to keep from revealing nudity. Polite social usage demands this behavior. Sometimes a speaker is so delicate in his choice of words that the listeners fail to recognize the true meaning under the protective clothing. It is often necessary to call a spade a spade. If we need to *work overtime* to get a job done, don't say: "It would seem obvious that the time given to this task may exceed normal working conditions so agreeable to our wives and families."

5. Label words.   A lot of arguments and communication breakdowns occur from using words as labels instead of using objective descriptive language. "John is *lazy*" is really not a very scientific report. The statement doesn't tell us much about John. "John walks and talks slowly" would say a bit more. When the label "lazy" is applied to John, a judgment is expressed, but no facts are given. A discussion between two chemists concerning one of their colleagues ran something like this: No. 1 says, "You know, Bob, that guy is just plain stupid." No. 2 says, "Heck no, he is brilliant!" Well, which *is* he?

So many violent and fruitless arguments arise from this casual use of the word *is* followed by a label. "The outlook is good," "That girl is beautiful," and "This steak is overcooked" are statements that describe the speaker's reaction.

The use of vocabulary for imagery

Words may be used to arouse sensory impressions within the listener's mind.

The imagery of sound

An audience will hear not only what you say but the very sounds
you are describing. The following selection is an example of auditory imagery: "Nowadays as we seek the sweet silence of home, a
devil's crew from Vulcan's workshop descends upon us. Even beyond the expected jarring ring of the telephone or the nervous peal
of the doorbell, there is the constant hum of the vigilant refrigera-
tor, the strangled squawk of the television set, the relentless tick-
tock of the clock, the commanding drone of the deep-freeze, the
triumphant whirr of the kitchen mixer, the plaintive pop of the
toaster, the throaty rasp of the orange-squeezer, the gloating gur-
gle of the coffee-maker, . . . Ah, Mr. Edison, what dins are com-
mitted in thy name."[4]

The imagery of sight

Make your audience "see" the objects and events you are describing. Mention size, shape, color, movement, and the relative position
of one object to another. Thornton Wilder's play *Our Town* is
staged without any scenery. The stage manager describes the setting
for his audience: "The name of our town is Grover's Corners, N.H.,
just over the line from Massachusetts. . . . The first act shows a
day in our town. The date is May 7, 1901, just before dawn.
(COCK CROW off-stage) Aye, just about. Sky is beginnin' to
show some streaks of light over in the East there, back of our
mountain. (Xing half of C.) The mornin' star always get wonderful bright the minute before it has to go. (Stares up off L. at star a
moment.) Well, now I'll show you how our town lies. (Xing up C
into Main Street.) Up here is Main Street. Cuttin' across it over
there on the left is the railroad tracks. Across the tracks is—Polish

[4] William Fadiman, "The Phoenix Nest," *Saturday Review*, Aug. 20, 1960,
p. 6.

Town. You know, foreign people that come here to work in the mill, coupla Canuck families, and the Catholic Church. (Xing few steps down, pointing off L. with pipe.) The Congregational Church is over there; the Presbyterian's across the street. Methodist and Unitarian are over there. (Off down R.) Baptist is down in the holla (out front)—by the river. (Xing up C. again.) Next to the Post Office there (off L.) is the Town Hall: jail is in the basement. Bryan once made a speech from those steps there . . . ."[5]

The imagery of taste

Get your audience to imagine the tastes you describe. Example: "There is no flavor comparable, I will contend, to that of the crisp, tangy, well-watched, not overroasted crackling. It is well-called— the very teeth are invited to their share of the pleasure of this banquet. Fat and lean so blended and running into each other that both together make but one ambrosian result—too ravishing for mortal tastes."

The imagery of smell

Make your audience smell the odors connected with the situation you describe. Example:

> Nose! Smell again the early-morning smells:
> Congealing bacon and my father's pipe;
> The after-breakfast freshness out-of-doors,
> Where sun had dried the heavy dew and freed
> Acres of thyme to scent the links and lawns;
> The rotten apples on our shady path;
> Mint round the spring and fennel in the lane
> And honeysuckle wafted from the hedge;
> The Lynam's cesspool, like a body blow; . . .[6]

[5] Thornton Wilder, *Our Town.* Reprinted by permission of Harper & Row, Publishers, Incorporated, New York, 1938, p. 10.
[6] John Betjeman, "Summoned by Bells," *The New Yorker*, Aug. 27, 1960, p. 34. Reprinted by permission of Houghton Mifflin Company, Boston.

The imagery of touch

We can describe shape, texture, and pressure. Example: A hand touched mine in the dark, and fingers came feeling over my face; other hands behind me plucked at my clothing.

The imagery of muscle strain

Get your audience to feel the pull upon muscle and tendon. Examples: All muscles became great hard knots; the sweat stood on their foreheads; it seemed as though their backs would break with the effort; by not a fraction of an inch would it move.

The imagery of the internal organs

Hunger, nausea, dizziness—there are times when an image is not complete without details relating to the inward feeling. Example: That climb seemed interminable to me—a deadly nausea came upon me. Several times my head swam, and I felt all the sensations of falling.

The sense of temperature

Language can bring vivid feelings of heat or cold to the listener. Example: "It was hot—unbearably hot! Beads of perspiration gathered on my forehead; they swiftly gathered together and formed little rivulets as they rolled down my face. The sun was a white-hot globe of molten steel radiating waves of kinetic energy. Oh, how I longed for one sweet draught of cool, cool water."

Assignments and exercises

1. Report on a field with which you are *not* familiar. You will encounter new words. Learn the meaning and pronunciation of these words. Use them in your report. The following topics are suggested as possibilities:
   a. The function of blood pressure
   b. Binaural hearing

c. The New York Stock Exchange

d. Whaling in the 1960s

e. The human nervous system

f. Techniques in commercial printing

g. Appreciation of classical music

h. Learning to like progressive jazz

i. Rock hunting

2. You may use the above assignment to talk about a new hobby that you have recently taken up or you may explore some area that you have been wanting to look into.

3. Select as a topic a new course that you are studying. Explain the purpose of the course and one of the central theories discussed in the course. Familiarize yourself with meaning and pronunciation of special terms.

4. Assume that you are being interviewed by a prospective employer. You would like to work for this company. Recommend yourself for employment. Explain your education and background in accurate, succinct language. Be sure to eliminate slang, grammatical errors, and vague terms from this presentation. Know the meaning and pronunciation of all words.

5. Analyze the slang now in vogue or report on differences in vocabulary and pronunciation in the speech of people from different parts of the country.

6. Give a talk, about four minutes in length, using as your theme a single short quotation. You may use one of your favorites. Be particularly attentive in choosing words that will be effective.

7. Make a report (written or spoken) on the language of a speech you have heard or read. Was the language of the speaker appropriate for his audience? Did he clarify unusual words or phrases? Did his words strongly affect your senses of sight, smell, kinesthesia, etc.?

8. Choose at random five words in the dictionary which you have never spoken out loud. Build a three-minute talk around these words and deliver it to the class. This will tax your ingenuity!

9. Make a talk to the group in which you purposely quote from literary or technical sources that contain difficult language. Make your audience understand and appreciate everything you say.

10. Compose and deliver a talk about some process in your field that is being developed in a foreign country. Use some foreign words or phrases, being sure to make the meanings clear to the group.

6 THE EYES HAVE IT

Gaining attention and clarity through visual aids

A case in point **Tragic farce**

Ed Burnett enters Regan Hall of Craigmont Junior College. Ed is an electrical engineer with Lawther Radio Corporation. He was recently attached to the sales department and has just assisted in his first sale, an audio setup for the speech and drama department of the college. The equipment has been installed, and Ed has come to the school this morning to make a little talk about the operation and maintenance of the equipment.

Ed is about five minutes late and he is carrying a microphone, a rolled-up cardboard chart, a phonograph record, and two pictures mounted on paperboard. He arrives at room 203 rather breathlessly and is met by Dr. Spiegel, the president of the college, who introduces him to a larger audience than Ed had expected. These people are seated in a large classroom which is equipped with a blackboard and a lectern with the typical slanted top. Present are Miss Thompson and Mr. Greer of the speech department, and Mr. Matson who has charge of audio-visual aids at Craigmont College. In addition there are two teachers, prospective customers, from a nearby college. Ed has invited them to inspect the new equipment. Several members of the radio club and the student council, who helped to raise the money to buy the new equipment, are present. This turns out to be a formidable group.

Ed is led to the lectern by Dr. Spiegel, who introduces him and allows him to take over. Ed looks around for a table on which to place his material, but there is none. He asks two students to move out of the front row so that he can use their chairs for a table. The armchairs work pretty well as a table, but the chart keeps rolling to the floor. This makes Ed nervous. In desperation, he decides to let the rolled cardboard stay on the floor and launches into his lecture.

Ed's lecture

"President Spiegel, members of the faculty, and students, I am very glad to be here this morning . . . and to talk to you about this wonderful audio equipment . . . that has been installed for the betterment of education in the department of speech . . . and the audio-visual field. First, we shall take up the microphone. (Ed picks up the microphone, a small saltshaker type. The microphone cord, which should have been removed previously, coils around his arm like a serpent. Ed tries to uncoil himself; finally does, but not without a few chuckles from the audience.)

"Some people never learn to wind an audio cord! (Ed is referring to his assistant, Tom Josey, back at the plant.) Yes, the microphone . . . a very sensitive instrument which should be handled with care. Now the principle upon which this microphone operates . . . a thin corrugated duralumin ribbon is suspended between two poles of a strong magnet. When the ribbon is set into motion by sound vibrations, small electric currents are developed which are then amplified by the audio equipment. There are, of course, other types of microphones . . . but this is the one you are using. I shall remove the case and show you the ribbon which reacts to the sound waves. (Grasping the microphone in both hands, Ed struggles to unscrew the top half from the lower half. Nothing happens except that Ed gets red in the face.)

"Seems to be stuck. (Taking out his handkerchief, Ed fights manfully with the mike, but to no avail.) H'mm . . . that's funny. It came off easily enough last week. Oh, well . . . . (He lays the mike on the slanted top of the lectern.) I have a chart here that will show you just as clearly. (Ed bends down to pick up the chart from the floor and there is a resounding crash as the round mike rolls off the angled lectern.)

"Oh, no! That mike cost . . . . (The rest of Ed's remarks, probably unprintable, are lost under his breath. Adjusting himself to the $65 coming out of his salary, Ed gets back to the lecture. At least, the crash got the attention of the audience. Ed picks up the rolled chart and tries to remove the tape that has kept it rolled tightly. This chart has been rolled up for some time and has a tendency to roll right back up again after Ed unrolls it. He struggles with it for a moment and then, being resourceful, decides to pin it to the wall in order to keep it flat. Moving to the wall near the blackboard, Ed remembers that he didn't bring any thumbtacks, cellophane tape, or masking tape. However, he remembers the tape that kept the roll together. He tries to remove some of this. It flakes off in small bits. Finally, he gets some off and puts two strips on the top of the chart and two strips on the bottom, thus sticking the chart to the wall.)

"There!" Ed says to get attention. "Now as you can see. . . . (At this moment, the tape on the chart gives way and it rolls up like a coiled spring as it falls to the floor. The people in the audience are beginning to feel sorry for Ed.)

"Oh, well, I have some pictures here of the dynamic type of mike and the velocity type . . . these pictures are probably more accurate reproductions than those on the chart, anyway. (The pictures to which Ed refers are photographs clipped from a technical manual and pasted on stiff paper. Unfortunately for the people past the second row, the magazine-size pictures are designed to be seen from a distance of 18 inches, not 20 feet. Ed is pretty flustered now. He flips the pictures up and down swiftly with a shaky hand so that they become a blur to his audience.)

"Now, this is the dynamic mike with the diaphragm-type of operation and this the velocity mike with the ribbon-type of operation. (Ed didn't really think the teachers would understand the operating principles of the microphones, anyway. But he thought he would include this material just to be impressive.)

"Well, so much for that! I'll use the blackboard for illustrating the rest of the equipment. (Ed has not told Dr. Spiegel that he would need to use the blackboard. No preparations have been made. There is no chalk. There is another embarrassing pause while Dr. Spiegel dispatches one of the students to get some chalk. Ed doesn't feel up to any more impromptu speaking. He spends the time looking at his notes. The audience is holding whispered conferences. Ed wonders what they are saying. The student finally appears bearing three long, fresh pieces of chalk. Ed begins again.)

"The control board has often been compared to the painter's palette. (Ed faces the blackboard and begins to draw the control board, his back turned squarely to the audience.) For, as the painter uses his palette to blend his colors, the control board operator blends the human voices, the music, the sound effects. (Ed is voicing one of his favorite analogies, but few of his audience hear it because Ed is talking directly into the blackboard. Ed now points to three dials in his sketch with the hand toward the audience, and his body covers the part of the drawing to which he is pointing. Ed speaks rapidly.)

"This control board has three main dials. The first dial controls the mike; the second controls the sound from the turntables; and the third, the tape recorder. The dial controlling the mike should be turned to about 24 for a point of reference; the dial controlling the turntables to about 26; and the dial controlling the tape recorder to about 8. (Ed flicks his hand quickly and loosely over the drawings so that no one is sure to what he is pointing. Since he has failed to label the dials, it is impossible for the audience to keep up with him.)"

When Ed finished this lecture, he was exhausted, and so was his audience. The audience had learned very little about the equipment, but they learned a lot about how *not* to use visual aids.

The necessity for visual material

The best way to know reality is to experience an event. But this is not always feasible. Not everyone can make a safari through the wilds of Africa. Mere words about this experience are a poor substitute. But pictures can make the abstract description of an experience more concrete. One study showed that telling alone produced an audience recall of 70 per cent of the material three hours later; only 10 per cent after three days. Showing alone produced 72 per cent recall of the material after three hours; 20 per cent recall three days later. But telling and showing *together* produced 85 per cent recall after three hours; 65 per cent after three days.

Military leaders claim that 40 per cent of instruction time is saved by the use of visual methods. Psychologists say that 85 per cent of human knowledge is absorbed through the use of sight. Material that is *seen* is remembered 55 per cent better than material that is only heard, according to research in reception through the senses. A 160-page government report was condensed into six simple visuals. These visuals were presented at cabinet level and their message absorbed and approved in less than fifteen minutes.[1]

Visual aids must assist the speaker, not replace him. Sometimes, inexperienced speakers use novel or complex devices that are distracting. When this occurs, the visual is no longer aiding; it is sabotaging the speaker. Whatever the aim of the speech, the attention of the audience should always be on the speech and the speaker. If the visual material is more effective than the speech, perhaps the speech is unnecessary. Don't present visual material merely to be admired, to be funny, or to be dramatic.

Classes of visual aids

Devices that further communication through visual impressions are classed as visual aids. They may be identified under the following headings:

Real objects

Actual objects help make ideas more concrete in the minds of a listener. When speaking about the uses of lignite, bring a piece of the material with you. Exhibit it to your audience. One speaker had finished a lengthy description of the uses of oil-well cores in determining the strata of geological formation and the value of

---

[1] Francis J. McHugh, *Graphic Presentation*, Tecnifax Corporation, Holyoke, Mass., 1956, p. 9.

these cores in predicting the presence of petroleum deposits. He was dumbfounded when a member of his audience naïvely asked him, "But what does one of those cores look like?" At the next meeting of the group, he produced a gunnysack. Extracting a number of the cores from the sack, he put them into the hands of the members of the group. "Here," he said, "are the oil-well cores. Feel them! Smell them! Taste them! Now do you know what they're like?" They did!

Reproductions

Replicas, mock-ups, models, and plaster casts used in explaining anatomy are examples of this type of aid. One speaker convincingly proved a point about proper hinging by using a pair of miniature refrigerators. Breadboard models or cutaway mock-ups make valuable training aids.

Pictorial reproductions

Sketches, pictures, and photos can be displayed on an easel or attached to the wall. Pictures may also be attached to a flip chart (described later in the chapter). Films may be projected, and small pictures may be transformed into 35-millimeter slides and projected to any size.

Pictorial symbols

Diagrams, graphs, charts, maps, important words, phrases, and paragraphs may be projected or they may be displayed on paperboard mounts, flip charts, chalkboards and flannel boards. The variety of material that may be included in this classification is infinite. For instance, in the area of charts, one might list progress charts, flow charts, inventory charts, schematic charts, dissection charts, organizational charts, genealogical charts, historical or time-sequence charts, striptease charts (where the information is revealed by the speaker one section at a time), and demographic charts.

The values of visual aids

Visual aids help the speaker to reduce his own feelings of tension.

They facilitate retention of information and images. Frequently a visual list of major points is an excellent memory aid, not only to the audience, but to the speaker, who can dispense with awkward cards, outlines, or manuscript while delivering his speech.

They attract the attention of the audience. People have greater interest in the realistic and concrete than in the abstract and symbolic.

They offer a way of simplifying complex material. Sometimes the subject is too large (the solar system, mountain ranges) or too small (atomic structure, bacteria) or to difficult to comprehend by words alone.

They increase the audience's interest in subjects in which there is limited personal experience.

They help the audience to understand relationships between concepts, facts, and objects. By the use of a direct visual, or by a visual analogy, parts may be related to the whole or vice versa.

Visual aid devices

The chalkboard

The most frequently used visual aid is the chalkboard, or blackboard, as it is commonly called. Chalkboards are everywhere and they are easily obtained. They may be built into the wall of the room or may be portable. The speaker may draw his own pictures, cartoons, maps, charts, and graphs at the time they are needed in front of the audience. He may use the board for unusual or technical words or the names of machine parts and operations. He may quickly erase material no longer needed. He may prepare in advance certain complicated drawings. He may use colored chalks for contrast and emphasis.

Effective use of the chalkboard demands attention to the following suggestions:

1. Plan your board work ahead of time. Try out your sketches or drawings before you are ready to use them.

2. Check your equipment in advance. Be sure the board, erasers, pointer, and templates are placed so that they are convenient to use. The board and chalk tray ought to be clean before you begin.

3. Keep the work on the board simple and legible. Any writing and lettering should be neat, orderly in appearance, and sufficiently large. A 3-inch character appears about one twenty-fifth as large to a person at the back of a room 26 feet in length as it does to the speaker at the board. Look at your drawings from the back of the room to be sure they are large enough to be clearly visible.

4. Try to talk about material on the board without turning too far away from your audience. If you are right-handed, stand to *your* right of the board as you face it. You will be facing more toward the audience that way and will not be hiding the board as much when you are sketching and writing.

5. If it takes more than a few seconds to make your sketch, it is advisable to put it on the board before you make your speech. It takes a good deal of skill to use the board for sketching and writing while you are trying to convey ideas verbally. Be sure that any words you do speak are not muffled by your efforts at marking on the board. Don't say much while facing the board.

6. Use a pointer when indicating important features rather than a chalk-covered finger that might smudge part of your material. The pointer allows you to stand clear of the board while speaking.

7. Be accurate in your spelling and your use of abbreviations.

8. Be consistent. For instance, put all "don'ts" in one column; all "dos" in another.

The flip chart

The flip chart is a pad of inexpensive paper (usually 30 by 40 inches) mounted on an easel or on the wall of the room. It may be used in the same fashion as the chalkboard except that crayons are used instead of chalk. It is less convenient for erasing material. However, it has the advantage of eliminating chalk dust, and the colors are brighter and more easily distinguished. Since the pages are flipped easily, drawings may be prepared in advance. Some suggestions for use of the flip chart are:

1. Flip the sheet after using the material so that the visual impact does not continue after the immediate need is over.
2. Remember that the flip chart is usually smaller than the chalkboard. Don't try to put too much material on one page.
3. A striptease effect may be used. Certain material may be drawn or written on the pages and covered by sheets of paper attached to the pages by adhesive tape. As a certain point is made, the speaker may strip off the covering sheets, revealing his visual emphases.
4. Don't flip the sheets too rapidly, particularly when the material is complex.
5. Ink and crayon marks are more visible than pencil, which will not show in certain lighting.
6. Be sure to check the order of the pages ahead of time.

The flannel board and magnetic board

Two popular devices for displaying visual material are the flannel (felt) board and the magnetic board. In the former, a large board (usually 3 by 5 feet or larger) permanently set up in front of the room, or portable to be used with an easel, is faced with flannel or felt. Cards similarly faced with felt or flannel will cling when they are slapped on the board. The magnetic board is similar except that the surface is metallic and the slap cards have small magnets attached to the underside. The cards may have important words or phrases lettered upon them. They may be graphs, charts, or cartoons. Used together they may portray a significant shape. One should be certain to prepare this material carefully. Putting the cards in order before presentation will help the speaker find the specific material at the express moment he needs it for emphasis or clarification. As with visual aids, when the material is no longer needed for specific purposes of information, it should be removed so that attention is not drawn needlessly to it.

Charts and graphs

Charts and graphs are vital for the technical data which an engineer or technician must present to various groups. Before preparing such material, be certain that the visual material is helpful or necessary. Remember your speech purpose. Keep that speech purpose constantly in mind when considering the types of visual aids you will use. If the aid helps to explain, relieves monotony, adds another sensory impression to your explanation or appeal, it will have value. Be sure to adapt the material to your audience. The aid must truly add to the impact of your speech; it must be adapted to the range of experience of your listeners. It should be impressive, neat, and original. Much of the material that must be presented to an audience is in the form of statistics. Graphic aids will help a speaker clarify sizes, positions, and quantitative relationships.

1. Table of organization chart. This system of connecting squares and rectangles shows the hierarchical structure or the division of work in a given organization (Figure 1).

2. The flow chart is designed to show relations of the parts to the finished whole or to the direction of movement (Figure 2).

3. Diagrammatic or schematic charts. These charts, by means of simple line drawings, reduce complex machinery, processes, and sequences to their essential elements (Figure 3).

4. Cutaway charts. Objects normally concealed are displayed by this type of chart. Frequently a portion of the interior in relation to the exterior may be shown.

5. Bar graphs, simple or multiple (see Figure 4).

6. Line graphs. These are, perhaps, the most frequently used graphs in technical presentation. A line graph may be single or multiple. Use may be made of the horizontal and vertical axes. Black and white lines of different kinds (unbroken, broken, dotted, etc.) can be used to contrast various concepts. Colors show these contrasting ideas more vividly (see Figure 5).

7. Divided circle graphs. These graphs, usually termed "pie

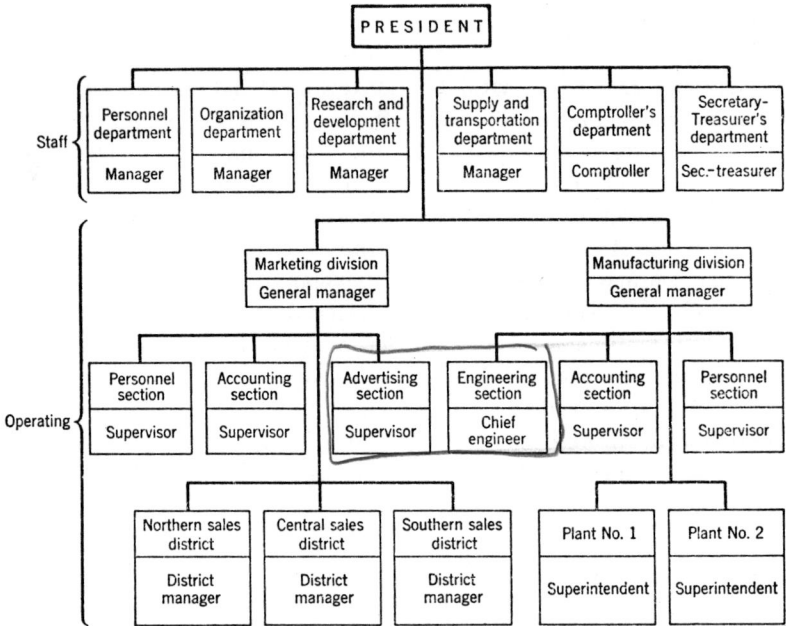

fig. 1

fig. 1. *Table of organization chart. This frequently used system of connecting squares and rectangles shows the hierarchical structure or the division of work in a given organization.*

fig. 2. *The flow chart. Flow chart showing the processing of raw alumina.*

fig. 3. *Diagrammatic or schematic charts. Schematic drawing of an automobile ignition system.*

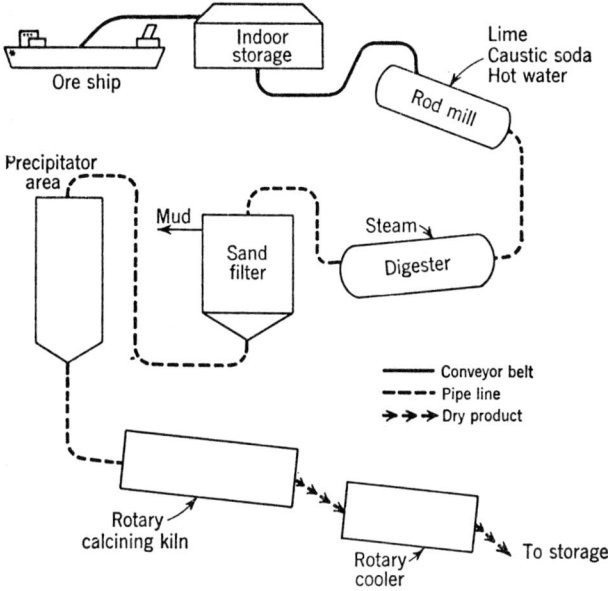

fig. 2

Ore ship

Indoor storage

Lime
Caustic soda
Hot water

Rod mill

Precipitator area

Mud

Sand filter

Steam

Digester

——— Conveyor belt
– – – Pipe line
→ → → Dry product

Rotary calcining kiln

Rotary cooler

To storage

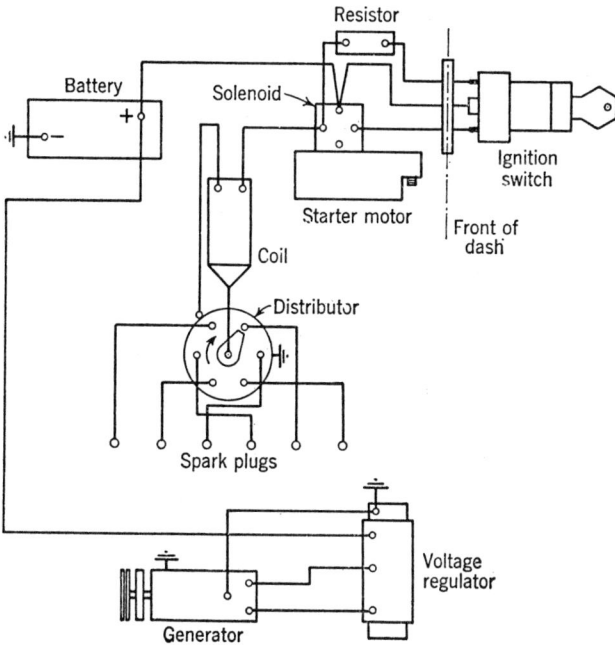

fig. 3

Resistor

Battery

Solenoid

Ignition switch

Starter motor

Front of dash

Coil

Distributor

Spark plugs

Voltage regulator

Generator

fig. 4

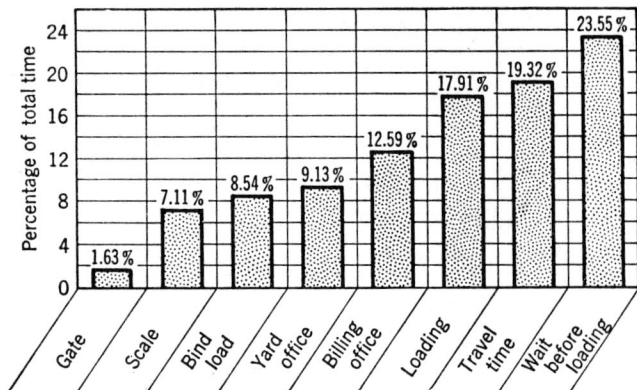

fig. 5

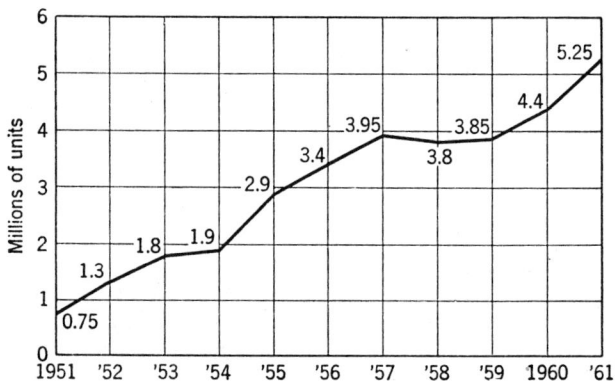

fig. 6

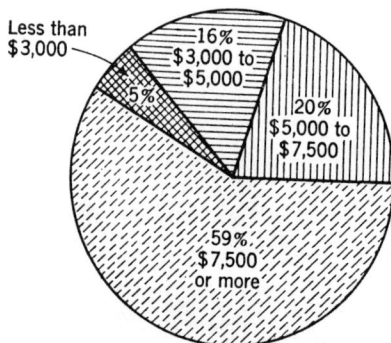

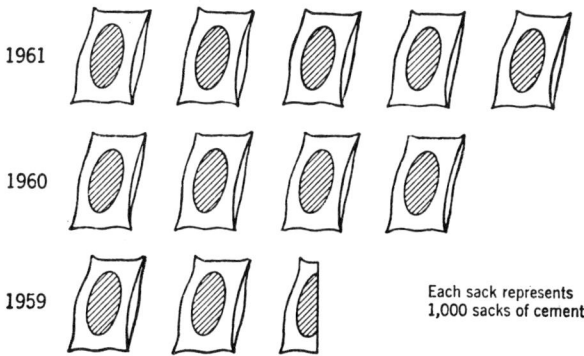

fig. 7

1961

1960

1959

Each sack represents
1,000 sacks of cement

fig. 4.   *Bar graph. Simple bar graph showing average
in-plant time for commercial truck loading.*

fig. 5.   *Line graph. Simple line graph showing
production for the past eight years.*

fig. 6.   *Divided circle graph. Divided circle graph
showing earnings of engineers in 1960.*

fig. 7.   *Pictograph. Pictograph showing amount of
cement used in plant during 1959, 1960,
and 1961.*

graphs," are used to show the relation of the parts to the whole (see Figure 6).

8. Pictographs. Pictographs are increasingly popular since they allow some use of originality and humor in portraying comparisons and relationships (see Figure 7).

Maps

Maps are used to show distance relationships, geographic subdivisions, historical changes, and isobars of various types. They should be simple, mounted well, and highly visible to the audience. If they are small, they may be projected before the audience. Use of color, bold lines, letters, shading, and even distortion may help to emphasize points of interest on the map. Colored cutouts can be pinned to the map or held in place with magnetic backing to differentiate locations and to show direction of movement. Arrows, letters, or numbers for reference may be devised with colored ribbon or industrial tape.

Projection devices

In these times most speakers have easy access to devices for the projection of visual material. The great advantage of projection devices is that highly detailed material can be drawn in small scale and then enlarged by projecting it on a screen.

1. The slide projector. Everyone is familiar with projection machines that enlarge $3\frac{1}{4}$- by 4-inch, 2- by 2-inch, or 35-millimeter slides. Drawings, pictures, graphs, or other material may be made up on these slides quite inexpensively. For example, many people make their own slides by photographing the material with the ordinary 35-millimeter camera that is so popular with tourists and amateur photographers.

Before using slides, the speaker should arrange them in proper order with clear thumb markers indicating the side to be turned up. He may operate the projector himself or he may use an assistant. The important thing is that the speaker practice with his assistant or by himself to assure the smooth articulation of the slides with the talk. We have all experienced the embarrassment of watching a lecturer whose slides are out of order.

When the speaker wishes to talk without displaying the picture, he may use a completely exposed film as a "blank." This will keep the screen dark and enable him to continue his talk without turning off the machine. If the speaker needs to be seen because his facial expressions and gestures are part of the presentation, the projector will have to be placed in a dark part of the room and the speaker in the light. Some projectors are so powerful that the image can be seen without darkening the room completely. If the speaker wants to be seen in between slide showings, he will have to arrange with an assistant to operate the general room lighting for him and darken or lighten the room at proper cue. Some rooms may be arranged so that the front of the room where the screen is located is darkened and the rest is sufficiently lighted to allow for note-taking. The speaker should examine the lighting setup in the room he will use, viewing it from these standpoints: (*a*) Does the speaker need to be seen? If so, does he need to be seen all the time or just between slide showings? (*b*) Will the audience be required or want to take notes?

2. Opaque projectors. The great advantage of these machines is that the material does not have to be changed into film or slides to be reflected on the screen. A speaker can make his drawing or chart on ordinary 8- by 11-inch paper and, by placing this paper in the machine, project it on the screen. The speaker may also use pictures, charts, maps, and graphs from books or magazines and project them on the screen without any previous modification.

3. Motion pictures. The great advantage of the motion picture is that the camera can be taken on location and a problem or process can be filmed as it is occurring. A process or problem such as drilling an oil well in Africa, building a bridge in California, assembling automobiles in Detroit, or working in an industrial plant or on a construction job can be recorded for later showing during a conference in the office or auditorium. Many films are available and can be rented or purchased.

Several companies have had their own "safety films" made by professional photographers and script writers to accompany talks made for the purpose of reducing accidents involving employees and equipment.

4. The filmstrip projector. A series of individual pictures appears in sequence on a strip of 5-millimeter film. The speaker talks about the picture and turns to the next frame, continuing the oral presentation. The pictures can usually be turned backwards if review or reference is needed. Dark frames can be interspersed if the speaker wishes to talk without the presence of distracting material. Many commercial filmstrips have sound accompaniment in the form of disk or tape recordings. When these are used, the speaker's task is minimal. To signal the operator that it is time to move to the next frame, a characteristic sound (usually a click or bell) is incorporated into the recorded material.

5. The overhead projector. This is a flexible device for visual communication. The projector casts an image over the speaker's head on a screen behind him. Since the image is projected over the shoulder of the communicator, he faces his audience at all times. He can provide excellent screen visibility without darkening the room or impairing ventilation. With his audience in full view, the speaker can observe reactions and adjust his program to meet the response of the viewers. He can set his own pace and extemporize as he wishes, commenting before, during, and after projection of a slide. He can alter the sequence of projectuals (visuals on transparent plastic) or return to a previously shown projectual without instructions or aid from an assistant.

The communicator may use the screen as a blackboard. He can draw or write with a grease pencil on projectuals or sheets of transparent plastic, without turning away from his audience. He does this by using the horizontally placed "stage" of the machine as a writing desk. He can write or draw with a pencil or stylus on a carbon-backed film, producing, on the screen behind him, a white image against a dark background.

Several sheets of film may be superimposed on the stage, permitting the use of many colors to identify the different elements of the projected image. The communicator can remove transparent projectuals one at a time to show fewer elements or build up several components into a composite image. For instance, it is possible to project the framework of a house in black, add the electrical system in blue, and the plumbing in red. Mechanical units can be effectively presented by adding components or by removing them. The transparent projectuals (usually about 8 by 10 inches) may be prepared by photographic reproduction or by using personal art skills. With a minimum of instruction and proper equipment, professional-looking projectuals can be produced. Opaque materials may also be prepared in this manner.

Models and mock-ups

If models or mock-ups are to be used, the speaker should be certain that he has rehearsed with them *recently*. All moving parts should be checked to avoid the embarrassment that occurs when a model does not behave according to specifications. Material of this sort should be large enough so that all the significant details are plainly visible to all members of the audience.

Photographs, drawings, charts, and cartoons

Materials of this sort should be securely mounted on stiff backing to prevent bending or curling when being displayed. The speaker should prepare a place to display the pictures at eye level and test the easels and stands to be sure they are strong enough to support the material without tipping or swaying. The speaker should investigate the lighting of the room to find a place where sufficient light is available for proper viewing. Commercial dulling spray can be used to dim out reflecting surfaces which might be distracting for the audience.

Preparing your own material

Visual presentation should possess: *unity* in that it shows one basic idea at a time, one central theme; *simplicity*, because the trivial, the unnecessary are eliminated, the lettering is simple and easy to read, the terms are not ambiguous, and the symbols and abbreviations are familiar to the viewers; *organization* in that it is arranged for rapid perception and comprehension; *visibility*, since every bit of information is easily seen by the most distant viewer.

For additional information on graphic material see:

1. Calvin F. Schmid, *Handbook of Graphic Presentation*, The Ronald Press Company, New York, 1954.
2. R. R. Lutz, *Graphic Presentation Simplified*, Funk & Wagnalls Company, New York, in association with Modern Industry Magazine, New York, 1949.
3. Mary Eleanor Spear, *Charting Statistics*, McGraw-Hill Book Company, Inc., New York, 1952.

Auditory aids for speakers

Purely auditory aids are rarely used to assist the technical man in putting over his ideas. Sound motion pictures and recordings accompanying filmstrips are sometimes of great assistance, but they are mainly used alone and not as concomitant parts of the speaker's material. In these electronic times, however, recording machines and tape recorders are comparatively inexpensive and easily obtained in portable form. In fact, one type of tape recorder can even be concealed on one's person and operated by battery. Conversation and various other sounds may be easily recorded and played back at strategic points in any oral presentation.

Sounds may be used to create a mood or atmosphere. For instance, if the talk is about an airport, a prerecording of planes landing or taking off might set the stage. Accurately timed, well-chosen sounds could add realism to a presentation. A safety talk might be punctuated by the *sound* of an accident. The recording device could be used to repeat some bit of material for educational value or even to present verbatim reports. It is not suggested that the speaker accompany any persuasive appeal by adding a musical hearts-and-flowers as background, but judicious use of well-chosen and rehearsed sound material *may* add vigor to the verbal symbols.

Recently a scientist was asked to talk to a lay audience on "progress in space research." He knew from past experience how bored a group can become when listening for a long period of time to technical data. He brightened his presentation by starting a tape recorder and asking the group to listen intently. What they heard were the beeps of the sputniks the Russians had put into orbit and the corresponding sounds that American space vehicles sent out. The audience was held in rapt attention.

Assignments and exercises

1. Give a four-minute talk explaining a process or procedure: "How to make . . ." or "How to do . . ." Use visual material to make your explanation vivid and clear to the audience.
2. Construct a talk which employs statistical material. Use charts and graphs to illustrate your ideas.
3. Use a chalkboard or flannel board to illustrate a piece of equipment or apparatus to the group. Make the drawings as you speak, building the ideas sequentially. Use colored chalk (or inks for flannel board demonstration) for contrast or clarity.
4. Give a talk in which you utilize one of the projection devices: slide machine, movie, overhead projector, etc. Make your own transparent or opaque slides.
5. Read a technical article or speech in your field. Make a report on this material (either spoken or written) showing how the content could have been improved by the use of visual material. Devise at least three visuals that could have been used to enhance the presentation.

7

FIRING ON ALL CYLINDERS OF THE BRAIN

The creative speaker

A case in point **Just imagine!**

George Lumper, electronics engineer, employed by Eagle Electronics, is about to address the board of trustees of the Maple Street Church. The board of trustees consists of fifteen people, men and women. Housewives, lawyers, real estate salesmen, bankers, doctors, and insurance men make up the audience.

George is trying to persuade the board to install a closed-circuit television system in the overflow room of the church to enable those not seated in the sanctuary to see and hear the minister. After some of the routine matters are taken care of, the chairman of the board calls on George. George begins as follows:

"Well, I've done quite a bit of research, and I've gone over several models. I went out to Brown Engineering and looked over their new industrial model, but I don't think it's what we want. Their 'sync' generators and 'av mixers' are too complicated. Of course, they are pretty darn good. (Some members of the audience are beginning to unstick their clothes from the chair seats and stare at the ceiling fan.)

"But, as I say, I've looked over the field pretty thoroughly here, locally, and I think I've come up with the best unit for our purposes, at least in my opinion. (He gives a self-deprecating laugh. A ghost of a smile comes to the minister's lips and then vanishes. The minister really wants this project to go through, and he can see it slowly dying.)

"Now, the Smith Model 103-B 2/3 interlaced picture with

XETMA 'sync' seems to be the best deal for us. It's got horizontal driving pulse and also vertical driving pulse, at least up to three dash six p-p, which is really about all we'll ever need. The spectral response in our 6198 vidicon tube is really very impressive, and when we equip the camera with the $f/1.5$ lens stop, we can handle about anything that comes our way. I believe one camera control unit will be enough for us. After all, we're not NBC. (He tries a little humor. Nobody laughs, not even the minister.)

"This control unit is mighty flexible as it is equipped with gain control, black level, electrical focus, beam, target, and on-off controls. X-scope elipse-form monitor and operator intercom come with the unit. Since we won't have to do much dollying around, I believe the B-999-6 tripod with friction head will serve nicely, and it's a bit cheaper than the professional model. Now, I can get the company to give the church a nice package deal which includes the 108-C television camera with three lenses; that $f/1.5$ I mentioned earlier, the $f/1.9$ and the $f/1.10$. We will also get the camera control, the video monitor, the wave-free monitor, the 'sync' generator, and, of course, full power supply equipment. The imput plugs are standardized, so that we can probably cue in somebody's old TV set as an extra monitor, if someone would like to donate one to the church."

When George finished, nearly everybody on the board was dozing. They really didn't understand much of what George was talking about, and consequently they lost interest. To them the speech was dull, uninteresting, and baffling. They felt this closed-circuit TV business was too complicated for the church to take on.

What was the matter with George? He certainly knew his subject. He went to a lot of trouble to prepare. He had all the facts. He spent a great deal of time getting his material together. What was lacking? *Imagination!* A dictionary defines the noun "imagination" as: "the act or power of forming mental images of objects not present to the senses."

This is what George Lumper failed to do—to form a mental image of the audience and of what a closed-circuit television unit would mean to them. He failed to look at the television equipment through the eyes of the audience. He did not ask this question of himself: "What is there about this equipment that will be exciting, significant, and interesting to the audience?"

In a way, George was self-centered. The symbol "*f*/1.5" conjures up an exciting picture for George. The symbol "6198 vidicon tube" makes George think of the wonder of the construction of this instrument. The whole world of electronics is very dramatic for him. The key words in this instance are *for him*. What about the members of the board: Minerva Minnowman, head of the religious education committee; Larry Bridges, head of the finance committee? Did the words that George used create exciting mental images for them? George might have imagined how wonderful this television unit could be for the older church members who are hard of hearing; how they could watch Reverend Miller's lips while a good loud sound projection was coming to them from the loudspeaker. Everybody would be "sitting in the first row." There would be no back seats.

Imagine how important and proud Ed Bogus, head of the planning board, would be when he could announce to the boys in the office and at the Lion's Club: "Our church has the first closed-circuit television unit in town. Brother, we're modern over at the Maple Street Church. You Methodists had better look out."

Imagine what a valuable experience it would be for the minister to be able to preach in front of a television camera. Then, when the finance committee finally decided to raise enough money to televise the Sunday sermons on one of the local stations, Reverend Miller would be an experienced television speaker.

Imagine what Minerva Minnowman, head of the religious education committee, could do for the children in the church's day nursery. On rainy days the kids could produce television puppet shows. Some of the kids could act as puppeteers, and the rest could watch the show on the monitor in the overflow room.

Imagine how attracted to the church the teen-age boys would be when they learned that they could serve as camera men for the Sunday sermons. Why, when you think (form mental images) about it, this closed-circuit television gadget could be the most exciting thing that has happened to the Maple Street Church in a long time. Wouldn't it be great? Just imagine. Yes, just imagine, and that's what George Lumper failed to do.

Forming mental images

An old cliché maintains that a picture is worth a thousand words. A series of mental pictures formed by the speaker as he thinks of how he can appeal to the minds of the listeners is as important as a thousand facts. Think of your audience and try to envision what will stimulate them, create the proper mental images for them, and make them realize the significance of your message. Then try to project your message and communicate your facts in light of what will sharpen their mental images, strengthen and vivify their impressions of what you are saying.

1. Consider everything you know or can find out about your audience. Are they parents? Are they experienced technicians or beginners in the field? Have they had some experience with your topic? Do they like sports? Are they white-collar men? Can they interpret statistics? Where do they eat lunch? Have they resisted new ideas in the past? Do they know each other very well? Look for some clue.
2. Think of ways to appeal to *this* audience.
3. Dream up the mental pictures that you want to arouse in the minds of your audience.
4. Try out the words that will re-create these images. Say them aloud.

You can accomplish these mental processes by having at your service a facile, ready, lively imagination.

Stimulating the imagination

Imagination is not a gift of the gods for the fortunate few. It is a capacity that can be improved, deepened, and enriched. "An analysis of almost all the psychological tests ever made points to the conclusion that creative talent is normally distributed—that *all* of us possess this talent to a lesser or greater degree—and that our creative efficacy varies more in ratio to our output of mental energy than in ratio to our inborn talent."[1]

As in the case of developing the muscles of the body, imagination can be strengthened by daily use and exercise. If you want to improve your imaginative ability, you will have to be as faithful in practice as the weight lifter who dutifully works out on schedule each day. Here are some types of imagination that you must cultivate before you can arouse them in the minds of other people.

Using sensory memory

Memory of sensory perception is the act of recalling vivid experiences that appealed strongly to one or more of the senses. We gain our knowledge of the world around us through our nervous systems. The senses of sight, hearing, smell, taste, feeling or touch, kinesthesia, etc., send sensations to the brain where these impressions are ordered for understanding.

When we were children the senses were sharp and acute. The world around us was new and exciting, and our senses were responding freely and vigorously. The sight of a field of waving green grass, the touch of the cool water of the old swimming hole, the taste of a peach off the neighbor's tree were intense, memorable sensory experiences.

As we grew older, parents and teachers began the process of teaching us sophistication. We learned that it was not proper to writhe on the floor in pain when we stumped our toes, particularly when "company" was present. We learned not to scream with delight when we tasted strawberry ice cream. In other words, we learned to inhibit our responses to sensory stimuli. When we reached our teens we began to be highly sophisticated, because we were supposed to act "real cool" and not appear excited or upset about anything, particularly in the presence of our peers. As we grew older we controlled our reactions more and more in order to impress girl friends, teachers, and employers. Consequently, the nervous system became insulated and most of the fresh, vivid reactions to the environment we experienced in childhood were dulled.

To expand the imagination we must reverse the process. The

[1] Alex F. Osborn, *Applied Imagination*, Charles Scribner's Sons, New York, 1957, p. 14.

insulation on our sensory "wires" must be cut away, and our senses must be opened to the world for fresher, more uninhibited responses to the flow of stimuli around us. Take a little time and try to re-capture and re-create in the imagination some strong sensory experiences. Begin with simple ones.

Try to remember eating a watermelon. How did it look—green, cool, large, with icy frost or drops of moisture on it? (Sense of sight.) Remember how heavy it was to lift and how cold and slippery it felt to the touch? (Sense of touch.) Can you hear the knife cutting into the rind or the dull splat as you dropped the melon on the ground to break it open? (Sense of hearing.) Can you recall the wonderful taste experience as you bit into the sharp angle of the slice—the sweet juice filling the mouth, the musky taste, and the coldness against your nose and lips? (Sense of taste and thermal sense.) Remember how you strained to get over the fence when you heard the farmer who owned the field coming angrily after you? (Muscle strain.)

Try to remember how a tin cup of steamy coffee tasted as you sat around a campfire in the chill of the twilight: that pungent, acrid coffee smell; the sharp aromatic taste; the warmth spreading through your midsection as you sipped it.

Try to remember your first plunge into the ocean surf: the cold, tingling feeling of the water on your body; the salty taste in your mouth; and the burning sensation in your nose and eyes; the bubbling, frying sound of the foamy white surface as you floated swiftly in on a breaker; the blue-green color of the ocean as the sun sparkled on the white-capped waves.

These experiences will take a different form for each individual. Reconstruct the sensory experience in detail, striving to bring back as sharply as possible to the nervous system the remembered sensations. Do not expect to get a strong sensory image the first time. The impressions will gain in strength and vividness as practice continues.

Using memory of observation

Being conscious of what the senses are picking up and sending to the mental processes enriches your memory of these sensations. A sharp, accurate memory depends on strong first impressions and an intense awareness of them. For example, as you walk down the street in your neighborhood, open your senses to the immediate environment. If you see a beautiful flower, pause to look at it, absorbing the colors intensely, noting the patterns of the petals and leaves. If you see an interesting cloud formation, take time to observe it acutely, perhaps visualizing forms that the clouds suggest to you. If it should begin to rain, take the opportunity to sense the wonderful, intermingled odor of the wet rain and dry earth. Suggestions for other exercises in observation are as follows:

1. Two people take the same route from one place to another. As they walk along they make it a point to observe the environment as fully as possible. When they arrive at their destination they compete with each other in trying to recount in detail what was observed enroute.

2. Try to recall the color of the walls, the height of the ceiling, or the pattern of the rug of your living quarters or the scene just outside your main window.

3. Try to bring back to memory a familiar process: starting a power mower; the steps and ingredients in making a banana split; the preparation and assembling of a special type of fishing gear; or the "stripping down" of a rifle.

Using memory of emotion

Emotional interpretations are an important part of imagination, for when mental images are formed there is usually an accompanying emotional reaction. If you remember the fresh, tingling coolness of a swim in the ocean, you may also remember a feeling of elation or happiness. If you recall the sensation of pain from the bite of a sand crab on the beach, you may also recollect a feeling of rage or fear.

It is essential that you imagine the point of view, and probable emotional responses of your audience. This enables you to arouse favorable and enthusiastic feelings when you present your ideas. In developing your power to imagine how the audience will feel toward your speech, you must develop a sensitivity to emotional reactions.

You may increase the sensitivity of the imagination by memory-of-emotion exercises in which you recall feelings you have had in reaction to particular experiences. The following are examples of such exercises:

1. Bring to mind a physical fight that stands out among your childhood adventures. Remember the fear you experienced when the bully told you to meet him after school. Recollect the apprehension you felt as you waited for the last school bell which would summon you to meet this formidable foe on the playground. Can you recall how your hands trembled and became sweaty, and how your stomach grew cold and knotted? Try to remember the horrible expression on the bully's face when you saw him approaching. Re-create in your imagination the cries of your schoolmates urging both of you on to battle; the pain when the bully bunged you one on the nose; the salty taste of blood and the feeling of horror at seeing your own blood flow freely; the hot rising up of righteous anger (after all, he started it!); the physical release of anger as you lashed out wildly with all your might; the dull pain as you cut your fist against his teeth; the sweet surge of victory as the bully turned and fled, bewailing his injuries; the wonderful warmth spreading through you as your friends congratulated you on your triumph on the field of honor.

2. Recall the fearful experience of seeing a burning house. The pungent smell of wood smoke; the crackling flames; the terrified cries as the victims try to save their valuables; the excitement of the arrival of the fire department, lights flashing and sirens screaming; all can be re-created in your memory and then in your spoken words.

Using the experiences of others

In addition to personal memories and impressions, the experiences of others are good stimulation for the imagination. In paintings, ballets, books, motion pictures, and plays men have recorded their reactions to human existence. These art forms represent the ultimate intensity in communication. They reflect a selective process wherein the artists, author, or director has molded the most meaningful moments of his life into an artistic expression.

Sometimes we feel that our lives are drab. We seem to have spent all of our time on the same dull street in the same tedious town. Faced with a problem demanding imagination, we are apt to say: "I can't think of anything new" or "I don't have any ideas." We seem to be completely devoid of inspiration or originality. Now is the time to call upon the experience of the artist to charge our "imaginative batteries."

We must be willing to break hundrum patterns. When the wellsprings of inspiration have reached a very low state, a strong stimulant is needed. It is necessary to venture off the beaten path, to step out of the rut of routine, to seek out a source that is new and different. If an individual is a realist, he should select a book or motion picture that is highly imaginative, unreal, or out of this world. The goal is not escape or relaxation as afforded by the westerns or whodunits. The aim is to gain mental and emotional stimulation that is available through intelligent, unique, artistic sources. The reconstructed experiences offered by motion pictures, art, the theater, literature, and music are there for the taking. Exposing yourself to these sources will add new dimension to mental life, regenerate original thinking, and stir the imagination.

Some productions of Walt Disney are excellent examples of the use of imagination to increase the impact and clarity of communication. When you watched "Fantasia," the imagination soared as the beautiful colors, symbolic shapes, and fantastic creatures whirled and danced to the accompaniment of a moving musical score. When it is necessary for Disney to get down to business and teach—to communicate information—he still retains his original, imaginative approach. The television show which Disney produced about atomic power is a case in point. The problem was to convey to an audience of wide diversity in age, background, and experience the basic theory of atomic fission. Using his imagination, Disney drew an analogy between atomic power and the old creature from fable, the bottled genie, who had infinite power when released from his confinement.

Cases in point   **"Factual information plus"**

In order to demonstrate chain reaction, Walt Disney filmed an interesting experiment. Scores of mousetraps were placed on a large table and "baited" with Ping-Pong balls. One Ping-Pong ball was then thrown at a baited mousetrap, which erupted with a loud snap, shooting its ball onto other traps which likewise exploded to send other celluloid missiles caroming into other traps, and so on. The chain reaction was portrayed in an interesting and fairly accurate manner. The Ping-Pong demonstration had action and sound effects and was analogous to the process that was being explained.

The producers of an educational television show, "Adventure," were faced with the problem of making the science of genetics understandable to their viewers. The staff assembled a troupe of ten ballet dancers. Wearing costumes that were symbolic of chromosomes and the physical characteristics that the chromosomes carry (blood type, eye, skin color, hair, etc.), dancers representing male sperm and female ova "twirled and twisted, grouped and regrouped while a lecturer recounted how the millions of combinations of parental chromosomes govern bodily characteristics of the offspring being formed."[2]

These ingenious educational television productions are examples of how the imagination can be used to make factual information interesting and appealing.

Education for imagination

Individuals who are being trained in highly technical disciplines may find that the aspects of learning which cultivate the imagination are being neglected. Mastering even a small portion of the ever-growing body of scientific knowledge requires concentrated study in ever-narrowing, specialized areas. The old maxim "learning more and more about less and less" is becoming a reality.

The isolation of scientific endeavor from the so-called humani-

[2] "Dancing Chromosomes," *Life Magazine*, p. 57, Nov. 8, 1954.

ties is a grave problem. When the wellsprings of creative thought are vitalized by broad intellectual experience, the task of drawing out new ideas to improve communication becomes easier. Students involved in technical education need to make a special effort (perhaps using extracurricular time) to include some literature, history, philosophy, and fine arts in their education. Schools, colleges, museums, libraries, etc., offer opportunities for adults to fill in these gaps in their education.

In the Disney production on atomic power and the television show about genetics, factual information was the basis of the message; but an important ingredient was added for the improvement of communication—imagination. Individuals who have long been in the rut of a completely factual environment may find entrance into the world of imagination rather painful. It is essential for the improvement of the imagination that the realist not be alarmed by a feeling of extreme insecurity as his feet leave the solid, dependable ground of facts. "Relax, let your senses whirl and your imagination soar into the world of illusion," is the best advice. Some people become highly disturbed when they view a play or read a book that is not true to life as *they* know it. Open your mind. Seek adventure in the world of the creative imagination.

The process is one of changing the glass through which the world is viewed—of exchanging the extensional lens of the microscope for the intensional lens of the artist's creative imagination. The extensional lens of the microscope reveals what is before it in an accurate, objective, nonemotional light. The intensional lens of the artist selects, fashions, emphasizes, and sometimes distorts in a vivid, emotional way.

When you view, for the first time, some examples of modern art a feeling of bewilderment or irritation may be your reaction. If you are accustomed to representational or realistic types of painting, you may be annoyed or disgusted at the paintings of the nonobjective schools. Gino Severini's "Dancer at the Bal Tabarin" is a case in point. At first glance, the painting looks like a portrait of a woman with several heads and legs. What is the artist trying to do? He is trying to express motion. In the early 1900s artists became influenced by current concepts of science. Theories concerning life as a dynamic process appealed to the imagination of the artist. Even a staid kitchen table became a dance of whirling electrons and protons. Seeing the universe in a condition of constant movement, the artist tried to depict motion in his work and to depart from the traditional style of portraying subjects in an arrested state. In "Dancer at the Bal Tabarin" Severini attempted to show the movements of the dancer.

The important lesson may be expressed as follows: Do not flee back into the safe world of facts when some imaginative work offends the senses by its distance from secure reality or its detachment from anything you have seen or heard before. A willingness to undergo feelings of insecurity and bewilderment is necessary in order to expand the horizons of the imagination. Most of the great engineers and scientists have had active, vivid imaginations. Without imagination and the ability to envision things that had never been, the great accomplishments of Einstein and De Forest would have been impossible.

Revolutionary theories in mathematics and physics and the application of such theories to advance man into the age of space travel and electronic marvels have come about by applying imaginative, creative thinking to the available facts. After all, if we review some of the adventures of Buck Rogers as depicted in the well-known comic strip of 1932, we would not be as amazed by the rocket ships, gravity belts, etc. as were the readers of that time.[3]

It is possible to combine the accurate, factual lens of the microscope with the colorful lens of the imagination. This combination is particularly necessary in the process of communication. Factual information is made more personally significant and impressive to the listener when it is illustrated, projected, and portrayed in an imaginative fashion that expands the experience, desires, and hopes of the listener. The person who is involved in scientific pursuits should learn to live dangerously and leave the factual world, occasionally, for journeys into the land of fancy. The development of a creative imagination is essential in the education of the scientist, for it is through the application of creative thinking to available facts that great advances in science are made.

[3] Philip Knowland and Richard Calkins, "Buck Rogers, 2049 A.D.," *The Dallas Morning News,* p. 11, Feb. 25, 1949.

Assignments and exercises

Exercises in imagination

1. Visit a modern art museum or get a book from the library about modern art. Bring reproductions of some of the pictures to class. Explain the meaning of the symbols in the pictures. Give a report of your personal reactions to modern art.

2. Study a science fiction story. Present a critical review of the story in which you point out where you believe the writer went too far into fancy and where he stayed within the bounds of reasonable future predictions.

3. Select some drawings or photographs of modern architectural structures. Present a critical review in which you point out bugs in the architect's design, that is, where you believe the design is faulty from a functional point of view.

4. Attend a production of a play. Present a critical report in which you describe the unbelievable or untrue elements in the plot, theme, or characterizations.

5. Bring one of your favorite musical recordings to class. Explain why you like this particular selection. Play parts of it to illustrate your points.

6. Read a short story by a contemporary author (Steinbeck, Hemingway, Saroyan, Faulkner, etc.). Give your reactions to the story along the following lines:

a. Is the story true to life?

b. Is there some valuable theme or message?

c. Is the plot interesting?

d. Are the characters well-drawn?

e. Would you recommend this author for enjoyable reading?

7. Read an early science fiction writer such as Jules Verne or H. G. Wells. Report on which of his imaginative ideas have become realities and which have not.

Applications of imagination

1. Make a report to the class about the exciting versatility of modern plastics; for example, how epoxy resins are employed

in aircraft construction, house building, and automobile manufacture. Use your imagination to present some original ideas
concerning the utilization of these modern plastics.

2. Present an idea for an improvement in the design and construction of an appliance that would make for better and
more economical operation.

3. Present your ideas on improving the college curriculum for
engineering students. Discuss courses, teaching methods, laboratory projects, and facilities.

4. Present your plan for a more functional design for one of the
buildings in the vicinity.

5. Explain and illustrate some of your predictions in future designs of automobiles or aircraft. Let your imagination have
full sway. Try to go deeply into the future.

6. Tell how you would vitalize one of the underdeveloped areas
of the world. Explain how irrigation projects, atomic power,
new developments in building construction, etc., could be employed to raise the standard of living.

7. Present your design for a new thrill ride for an amusement
park. Show how this device can be both exciting and safe.

8. Present your plans for improving safety in automobile travel.
Discuss your ideas for highway design and devices for control
and direction of traffic.

9. Explain a complicated scientific process in an imaginative or
pictorial fashion.

8

EXPLORATION AND EXCAVATION

Research for oral communication

Case in point *Bored, bothered, and bewildered!*

Something had to be done about it! Lost-time injuries at the
Vasco Valve Company were definitely on the increase. Already
this year, in June, the number of injuries that required medical
attention was as high as last year's total! Walter McGhee sat at
his work-filled desk feeling absolutely miserable. He had been
quite vociferous at the monthly meeting of department heads.
"We'll have to make it clear to all departments," he had said,
"that this curve must turn downward in coming months. This
situation is intolerable!" So, *he* had been scheduled to talk to all
the engineering supervisors to inform them on the problem, to
encourage them to spread the gospel of safety among their various groups, and to show them how they could implement the new
program, "Safety—Your Personal Commitment."

Walter had a copy of a general talk on safety that he had
picked up in the personnel department. "I'll read this thing to
them," he thought. As he read it over, however, his heart sank.
The piece was written in a stilted, pedantic, generalized style.
"I'd like to catch the stupid PR man that wrote this mess of
clichés," grumbled Walter. "But what can I do? I've got to make
this darn talk tomorrow. I'll just have to read it to them. Ugh!"

Walter did read it to his assembled supervisory engineers and,
as he had predicted, they were bored and unsure of their responsibilities in the matter. What was the matter with Walter? He
had not prepared. He had not recalled, from his twenty years in
the plant, examples to make the talk interesting and applicable

to his audience. He had not talked to some of the supervisors to ferret out specific incidents. He had not gone to the scenes of accidents to see the situation firsthand. He did not winnow available statistics for impact figures that might have startled the engineers. He did not use anecdotes that were applicable to the current situation.

A new book on safety problems had just been published. In two current technical magazines the entire safety problem was discussed by experts in the field. These were available in the plant library, and more material was to be found in the nearby university library. He did not go to the plant library to discover how his company compared with others in accident rates, what procedures were being followed to promote safety, and what success resulted from changed techniques. With a little research Walter would have found a number of suggestions and solutions, but Walter was unaware of their existence. His failure to arouse and inform his group may have cost more lives and resulted in more accidents, added costs, and delays for his company.

Research source number 1: you

Any time you speak to a group, weigh the importance of the information you are going to expound. If you speak for ten minutes to an audience of twenty, multiply 21 by 10. Two hundred and ten minutes of time spent! How much is this time worth? Add the energy and money involved in assembling the audience, organizing the meeting, etc. Your audience has a right to expect that you make *total preparation*.

The first source for this preparation is yourself. We have already outlined the idea of individual brainstorming. This may be the best beginning for organizing your thoughts. Before you go to the books and periodicals, examine your own ideas. Too many speakers feel that the first step is into the library. Take that step eventually, but first research yourself. Personal experimentation and experience are excellent materials. It is strange how loath people are to tell about the truly exciting events that have punctuated their own lives. As Vachel Lindsay has said: "Every soul is a circus."

A case in point **"I was there!"**

In 1947, George Schell, a member of an adult class in professional speaking, insisted that he had nothing unusual in his own experience to speak about, "at least, to this group." In a later assignment one of the students reported on the "Story of Hiroshima," by John Hersey, which had just been published in *The New Yorker*. George took exception to some of the material. After all, *he* had been a prisoner of war of the Japanese and had seen Hiroshima not long after the explosion. "Gee, why didn't you tell us about that when you were supposed to tell about an exciting experience?" asked one of his fellow students.

Let us assume that you now have a list of notes assembled after a rigorous, personal inventory of your own ideas. Set these aside for some time; then reread them. Can you assemble them in some organized fashion, keeping your purposes and audience in mind? Are some deletions or additions necessary? Is your point of view wrong?

Research source number 2: observation

Now, add to your outlined material any other personal kind of research you can develop. For instance, should you make a trip or see something else? Check your memory with actual observation, if possible. If you are talking about airport construction, refresh your memory by heading out to the International Airport 15 miles away. It will take a little time, but wouldn't your thoughts be revitalized? Mightn't you gain new insights from another firsthand look?

Research source number 3: the interview

Can you get any information by interviewing someone? The telephone is right there at your side—or not too far away. It is amazing what can be accomplished by a few calls. Do you want to report on the sort of equipment being used to photograph technical drawings? Call up a few of the departments of photography and reproduction in your area or a few of the equipment dealers. A personal interview will bring you inspiration you never dreamed about. See the right man and be sure to take careful notes about what you hear. If you intend to quote an interviewee, be sure to get his permission. Read back to him what you thought he said.

When you have obtained all your firsthand information, talk over your speech with someone. You don't have to find a prospective member of the audience. The very act of talking through your ideas shows the strengths and weaknesses in the structure and content of your speech. If you thrill or bore *one* person, the effect may be magnified when your audience is larger. As you tell your ideas, words will pop up. Write them down.

Research source number 4: the library

The next step is library research, gathering ideas from other people. You will have to discriminate and limit your reading because of the exigencies of time. You will want to read more carefully when your purpose is to think through the subject and skim when looking for particular items or statistics. Unless you have an extraordinary private library, the public, school, and company technical libraries will be your major research centers.

Using the library

1. Get acquainted with the library and the librarians. Most librarians like to help researchers. Checking out books and collecting overdue fines are not their sole duties. Librarians are highly trained individuals who enjoy ferreting out information. To them, a search for unusual material is a treasure hunt whose reward is a load of books, pamphlets, and periodicals for your benefit.

a. Don't be afraid to approach a reference librarian; that's what he is there for.

b. Don't expect the reference librarian to answer your research questions for you. His function is primarily to lead you to likely sources.

c. Be specific in your questions and requests. Write down your subject of inquiry to show the reference librarian.

d. Don't be afraid to come back if you don't find what you want in the first source the librarian recommends. If you miss the first time around, he will know of other sources for you to investigate.[4]

2. Know the floor plan of the library. Where is the card catalog? Where are the reference books? Locate general and technical periodicals, and newspapers. What material is available on microfilm? How do you work the microfilm reader? Can you borrow material from other libraries? Is there a depository for government publications and pamphlets? Are there special uncataloged materials? Are there charts, maps, pictures, slides, films, records that may be borrowed? Does your library use the open-stack system so that you can browse? If it has closed stacks you will be more dependent on the card catalogs.

The card catalog

Become familiar with the card catalog. You will find books classified by author, title, or subject. The card will tell you the size of the book, the number of pages, the age of the book, and its copyright date. (You will want to use the most recent sources; science is advancing rapidly.) A number of editions may be an indication that the material is popular and in high repute. You may find an outline of chapters or subdivisions listed on the card. The author entry usually gives the fullest information, including special notes. Typical library index cards look like this:

[4] Robert W. Murphey, *How and Where to Look It Up,* McGraw-Hill Book Company, Inc., New York, 1958, p. 32.

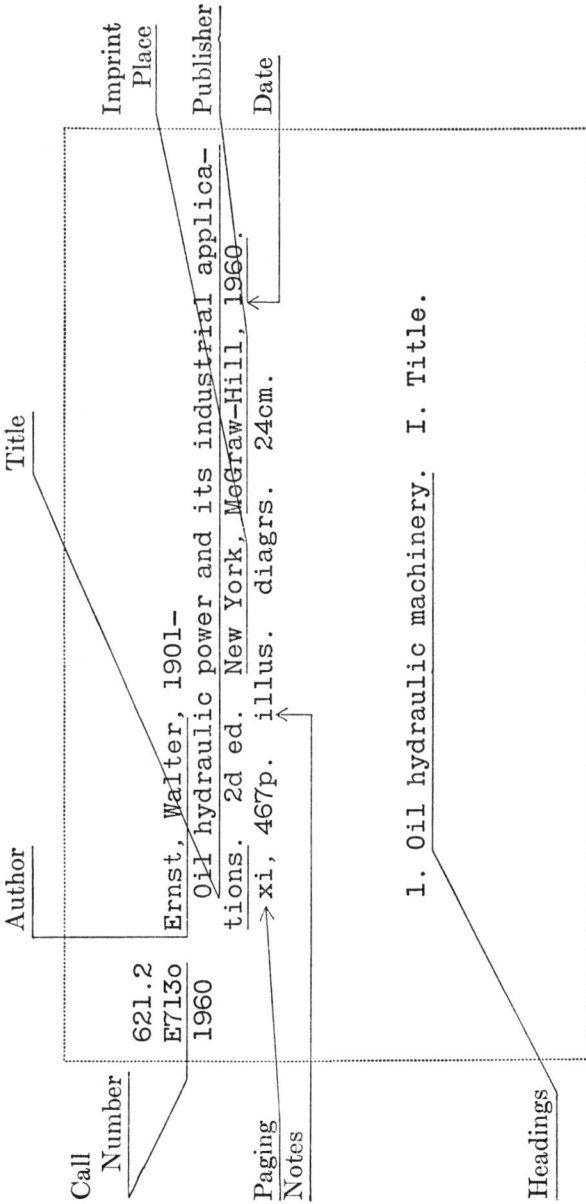

Call
Number

Author

Title

Imprint
Place

Publisher

Date

Paging
Notes

Headings

621.2
E713o
1960

Ernst, Walter, 1901–
Oil hydraulic power and its industrial applications. 2d ed. New York, McGraw-Hill, 1960.
xi, 467p. illus. diagrs. 24cm.

1. Oil hydraulic machinery. I. Title.

Author Entry

Call
Number

621.2
E713o
1960

Author

OIL HYDRAULIC MACHINERY

Title

Ernst, Walter, 1901–
  Oil hydraulic power and its industrial applica—
tions. 2d ed. New York, McGraw–Hill, 1960.
  xi, 467p. illus. diagrs. 24cm.

  1. Oil hydraulic machinery. I. Title.

Title Entry

Call
Number

Author

Subject

Title

Oil hydraulic power

621.2
E713o
1960

Ernst, Walter, 1901–
  Oil hydraulic power and its industrial applications. 2d ed. New York, McGraw–Hill, 1960.
  xi, 467p. illus. diagrs. 24cm.

1. Oil hydraulic machinery. I. Title.

Subject Entries

The reference room

Visit the reference room. The reference room of a library is a fascinating, valuable source of material. It contains general indexes and guides to periodical literature, encyclopedias, dictionaries, fact books, atlases, and references applying to special fields.

1. How to use reference books. The major sources for information concerning the reference room itself and its contents are:

Ulrich's Periodical Directory, edited by Eileen C. Graves. This is a classified guide to a selected list of current periodicals, foreign and domestic. Included are subscription prices of foreign periodicals in American currency, an alphabetical listing of the outstanding indexing services, a selected list of current newspapers, United States and foreign, and a classified list of periodicals.

How and Where to Look It Up, by Richard W. Murphey, is an excellent compendium of major reference books (with a special section on science and applied science), and gives excellent information on how to use the reference room.

Guide to Reference Books, by Constance Winchell, is kept up to date by supplements. It is complete in scope.

Sources of Engineering Information, by Blanche H. Dalton, is old but sometimes of value.

2. Indexes to periodical literature. Just as the card catalogs help you to locate books, the many indexes help you to find periodical material and digests of important articles. There are, as you will note, indexes and digests of foreign translations, too. The periodicals covered in an index are listed in the front of the volume. Librarians usually mark the ones available in their library. Some valuable indexes are:

Readers' Guide to Periodical Literature (1900–   ). This is a series of cumulative and supplemental catalogs. It lists the articles from approximately 130 popular periodicals from 1900 to the present time and brings material up to date in yearly and monthly compilations. Entries are made by author and subject.

Applied Science and Technology Index (formerly part of *The Industrial Arts Index*) indexes about 200 periodicals in pure and applied science.

Business Periodicals Index (formerly part of *The Industrial Arts Index*) indexes periodicals in the business field.

Engineering Index
Agricultural Index
Education Index
Index Medicus
The New York Times Index
Index to Vital Speeches
Technical Translations

A sample entry from *Applied Science and Technology Index* is shown below:

Boilers, MARINE
      oil firing
water wash of bunker C retards boiler slag on Atlantic tanker, W. A. Walls and W. S. Proctor, il. Marine Eng/Log 65:56–7+ Ja. '60

Explanation: An illustrated article on the subject of boilers, marine-oil firing, entitled "Water Wash of Bunker C retards boiler slag on Atlantic tanker," by W. A. Walls and W. S. Proctor, will be found in volume 65 of *Marine Engineering/Log,* pages 56–57 (continued on later pages of the same issue), the January, 1960, issue.

3. Abstracts or digests. To obtain a variety of information rapidly, abstracts or digests are valuable. Following is a partial list of abstracting services:

Abstracts of World Medicine
Biological Abstracts
Chemical Abstracts
Electronics Express
English Abstracts of Selected Articles from the Soviet Bloc and Mainland China
Geophysical Abstracts
International Aerospace Abstracts

Mathematical Reviews
Nuclear Science Abstracts
Science Abstracts—Section A—Physics Section B—Electrical
  Engineering
Solid State Abstracts
Technical Journals (U.S. Department of Commerce, Office of
  Technical Services)

4. Dictionaries. Do you want the exact word? Are you doubtful
about meanings? The dictionaries listed below may be of assistance:

Chambers Technical Dictionary (Tweney and Hughes)
A Dictionary of American English on Historical Principles
Funk and Wagnalls New Standard Dictionary
Engineering Terminology (Brown and Runner)
Oxford English Dictionary
Scientific and Technical Abbreviations, Signs and Symbols (Zim-
  merman and Lavine)
*Elsevier's Dictionary of Nuclear Science and Technology in Six
  Languages*
Condensed Chemical Dictionary
Webster's New International Dictionary, 3d ed., 1961

Other word books useful for synonyms or more precise vocabu-
lary include:
Roget's Thesaurus
Webster's Dictionary of Synonyms
American Thesaurus of Slang (Berry and Van den Bark)

5. Other useful specialized reference books. Among the many
books of tables are included:

Index of Mathematical Tables (Fletcher and others) may be used
  to locate a book of tables.
Chambers Six-figure Mathematical Tables (L. J. Comrie)
International Critical Tables (National Research Council)

Mathematical Handbook for Scientists and Engineers (Korn and Korn)

Certain handbooks are depositories of specialized information:
Handbook of Chemistry and Physics
Nuclear Engineering Handbook (Etherington)
Materials Handbook (Brady)
Civil Engineering Handbook (Urquhart)
Mechanical Engineers' Handbook (Marks, ed.; Baumeister, rev. ed.)
Air Pollution Handbook (Magill, Holden, Ackley)
Machinery's Handbook for Machine Shop and Drafting Room (Industrial Press)
Metals Handbook (American Society for Metals)
Minerals Yearbook
Electronic Engineer's Reference Book (Hughes)

For general factual materials you may use an encyclopedia:
The Encyclopedia Americana
The Encyclopaedia Britannica
Collier's Encyclopedia

Many specialized encyclopedias have been published such as:
Van Nostrand's Scientific Encyclopedia
Engineering Encyclopedia (Jones)
McGraw-Hill Encyclopedia of Science and Technology
Encyclopedia of Chemical Technology (Kirk and Othmar)

Usage books may be helpful if you are doubtful about your grammar:
Writer's Guide and Index to English (Perrin)
A Dictionary of Modern English Usage (Fowler)
A Dictionary of Modern American Usage (Horwill)

For information about people:
Dictionary of American Biography
Webster's Biographical Dictionary
Who Was When (De Ford)

Who's Who in America
Who's Who in Engineering
American Men of Science

For handy reference to facts and statistics of almost any kind:
The Statesman's Yearbook
The American Yearbook
The Statistical Abstract of the United States
Facts on File (World News Digest with Index)
The World Almanac
A Book about a Thousand Things (Stimpson)

For quotations:
Bartlett's Familiar Quotations
Cyclopedia of Practical Quotations (Hoyt)
Home Book of Quotations (Stevenson)
A New Dictionary of Quotations (Mencken)

The following is an annotated bibliography of sources for quotations which is especially useful in connection with Chapter 13.

Bartlett, John: *Familiar Quotations,* Little, Brown and Company, Boston, 1948. Contains index of authors and subjects.

Benham, Gurney W.: *Putnam's Complete Book of Quotations,* G. P. Putnam's Sons, New York, 1926. Contains quotations from the Bible and the Book of Common Prayer, as well as quotations from American, British, Greek, Latin, French, German, Spanish, and Dutch authors.

Droke, Maxwell: *Quote,* Droke House, Indianapolis, Indiana. A weekly publication that contains current quotations from speeches of business, religious, educational, and governmental leaders.

Fuller, Edmund: *Thesaurus of Epigrams,* Garden City Books, New York, 1948. Contains collection of clever and pungent sayings listed by subject. Also contains toasts for all occasions.

Shankle, George E.: *American Mottoes and Slogans,* the H. W. Wilson Company, New York, 1941. Contains alphabetical list of mottoes and slogans with their authors and the historical context in which the slogan was used.

Stevenson, Burton: *The Home Book of Bible Quotations,* Harper & Row, Publishers, Incorporated, New York, 1949. Bible verses listed by topic. For example, under "work" a biblical verse, "Thou renderest to every man according to his work," is listed.

Van Buren, Maud: *Quotations for Special Occasions,* The H. W. Wilson Company, New York, 1938. Index of quotations listed by special days and holidays, such as Washington's birthday, Christmas, Armistice Day.

Vital Speeches, City News Publishing Co., New York, 1960. This monthly magazine contains current speeches by prominent scientists, engineers, businessmen, educators, industrialists, and government officials.

Woods, Ralph L.: *The Businessman's Book of Quotations,* McGraw-Hill Book Company, Inc., New York, 1951. Aimed especially for speeches concerning business, industry, civic work. Contains subject index.

A concordance indexes material of a single author (or the Bible) by subject:

The Exhaustive Concordance of the Bible (Strong)
The Complete Concordance of Shakespeare (Clarke)
A Concordance to the Poems of Robert Browning (Broughton)
A Concordance to the Poems of Ralph Waldo Emerson (Hubbell)

For historical facts:
Dictionary of Dates (Keller)
Encyclopedia of World History (Langer)

For summaries of current controversial questions:
Congressional Digest
Reference Shelf Series

For pamphlets:
The Vertical File Service Catalogue

For government publications:
Catalogue of Public Documents
Monthly Catalogue of the United States Public Documents
U.S. Government Research Reports

For newspaper materials:
The New York Times Index

For microfilms:
Union List Abstracts of Microfilms
Dissertation Abstracts

For oddities:
Famous First Facts (Kane)

Brief Facts (Tavenner)
Things Not Generally Known (Wells)
Brewer's Dictionary of Phrase and Fable

A typical library research problem

If you should go to the library to gather information for a talk on the "Peaceful Uses of Atomic Energy" and you have no references to start you off, your procedure would be something like this:

1. Look in the card catalog. Check under such topics as Atomic Bomb, Atomic Energy, Atomic Energy—Economic Aspects, or other titles that occur to you if you have no author's name. Under Atomic Bomb, you may choose W. B. Kaempffert's little book, *The Many Uses of the Atom*, published in 1956. Fill cut call slips and get the books at the desk or, if the library has open stacks, find the books yourself. One book may lead to another.

2. Now, go to the reference room for magazine articles. Look first in the *Readers' Guide*. Work backwards for several years, checking possible headings such as Atomic Age, Atomic Power, Atomic Bombs, etc. You may choose, under Atomic Power Industry, the following reference: "Atom and the Workingman. J. Lear. il Sat R 40:62–3 My 4 '57" (which translated means "Atom and the Workingman," by J. Lear, illustrated, in the *Saturday Review*, volume 40, pages 62–63, the issue of May 4, 1957). Look in the front of the *Readers' Guide* to see whether "Sat R" is checked, indicating that this library has this magazine. Copy the reference and fill out a card at the periodical desk. Indicate title, volume, and date. The magazine will be brought to you for use in the room. Look through the other indexes for other articles.

3. Check the encyclopedias, yearbooks, and dictionaries easily found in the reference room.

4. Ask the reference librarian what other helpful sources of information are available in the room. Help yourself all you can. If you run into any difficulty, talk it over with the librarians. They will be glad to help you.

Hints on reading

1. Don't depend on one source alone. If your speech offers nothing but a condensation of a magazine article or a technical journal digest, the listeners could spend their time more profitably reading the original source. You must expect to read four or five times as much as you can possibly use in your oral presentation. Then you can select discriminatingly from a large accumulation of data. Of course, much will depend upon your personal experience with the subject matter.

2. Read from general to specific. It saves time to get as many general ideas as possible and then fill in the specifics. First, you may read encyclopedias and general reference books that trace broad outlines of the problem on which you are working. These larger overviews may help you formulate the organization of your material. They may also furnish you with additional sources to assist in your research.

3. Learn to scan. Thumb through as many books as possible when searching for information. Sometimes a quick glance at the table of contents will give you a bird's-eye view of the material covered by the author. As Bacon wrote: "Some books are to be tasted, others to be swallowed, and some few to be chewed and digested." Look through the preface to the book. Check the summaries of the chapters, if the book has them. Topic sentences are sometimes valuable signposts. Other special signals in the book will help you analyze its general information, style, and significance to your particular subject, such as heavy type, words or phrases in italics, and special graphs or charts.

4. Read with discrimination. Choose the most appropriate books for your purpose and begin to read. List the specific questions you want answered and read for answers.

5. Take notes while you are reading. Keep a complete bibliographical reference on every book or article you survey, listing

title, author, publisher, date, page number, and library reference number. The material may not seem usable while you are reading, but you may want to go back to the reference later and read it again. Notes are most conveniently taken and filed on cards. Use either the 4 by 6 or 5 by 8 inch size. Notes are valuable for:

a. Verbatim material. These notes will be used for quotations. Use quotation marks and indicate full bibliographical data on your card. You may want to look up the material again, or your talk may be published and require footnotes.

b. Paraphrased material. This will be helpful in the body of your talk. Be sure to cite your sources here, too, so proper credit can be given.

c. Summaries. You may want to make a generalization of some specific material for a review later.

d. Ideas. Sometimes, when you are reading a book, a reaction of your own suddenly bursts through. Write it down *at that time.* Cite your reference in this case, too, for purposes of comparison or agreement. Use some symbol to differentiate your own thoughts from the source material.

Checklist for a library research project

1. Books? Use the card catalog.

2. Magazines? Use the periodical indexes in the reference room.

3. Reference books? Use special bibliographies, dictionaries, and handbooks. Consult the special card catalog in the reference room.

4. Government documents? Use the monthly catalog of United States government publications.

5. Pamphlets? Use the vertical file and Public Affairs Information Service.

6. Microfilm? Microcards? Ask the librarians in the reference room.

7. Maps? Use the atlases or special map library.

8. The librarians? Ask if in doubt.

Assignments and exercises

1. Examine issues of several of the following news magazines: *Time, Newsweek, U.S. News & World Report, The Pathfinder, The Nation, The New Republic.* What similarities and differences do you find in format, organization, philosophy, and selection of news? Discuss your report with the class.

2. Do the same assignment as above, using various newspapers such as *The Christian Science Monitor, The New York Times,* your local newspaper, and a paper from a nearby city.

3. Report on the technical magazines in your particular field of interest. How many periodicals are actually published? Which ones are taken by your library? How far back do they go? Where are they indexed? Are they bound or microfilmed? Report on your reactions to selected issues.

4. Use suggested research methods to prepare a talk on a topic such as one of the following: Crystallography, phrenology, cochlea, electronic microscopes, cortisone, Gresham's law, graphology.

5. Do a special study on one of the "men of science." Make a talk about five minutes in length on his contributions to the world. Use at least four references.

9
THE TWENTIETH-CENTURY CRACKER BARREL

Conversation, interview, conference

Cases in point **"His best friend wouldn't tell him!"**

David Cunningham, a young engineer, has just joined the Canyon Electric Service Company. At coffee breaks the younger engineers gather together and swap pleasantries. Although several of the men have tried to bring him into the conversation, Dave seems to have little to say. He answers in monosyllables and seems to be completely baffled by the conversations, which range from football to politics. The others think he's an oddball or stuck-up. They hope they won't be called on to work or travel with him. After all, you can't be talking shop all the time. David doesn't feel so good about the situation either. His superior has sensed the strained feelings and wonders if David is really as intelligent as his college record would indicate.

"Organ recital"

Before working hours, the men in the drafting room usually gather at the desk nearest the door. They talk about fishing, their children, the day's news, etc. Whenever Ron Norman approaches, the men look at each other meaningfully. They know in advance what his opening remark will be. It usually runs something like, "Boy, do I feel rotten today!" Without any encouragement, Ron will launch into a clinical description of his current medical symptoms. It is amazing how the group scatters when his lugubrious words depress the tone of the discussion. He wonders why he was passed over for promotion. He ought to be in a supervisory position by this time.

Conversation

Conversation links people together in social life or in business life. Usually, conversation consists of pleasantries, remarks about controversial or uncontroversial subjects, and ideas of mutual interest. Through conversation one can achieve rapport with another person or with a group. One definition of the word *conversation:* "oral and, usually, informal or friendly interchange of views, sentiments, etc." The prefix *con* means *together, with*. Most of us have little difficulty in conversing with people we like and trust. Conversation implies give and take, listening as well as talking. Sometimes our strongest opinions about an individual are formed during or after a conversation with him. Future relationships with an individual are frequently based on a single contact during a single informal conversation.

Although conversation is rarely taught formally, it has great importance in determining your destinies in business and social life. You can improve your abilities in this important type of oral communication. First, make an inventory of your own conversation habits.

Conversation inventory

1. Do I have trouble starting a conversation? Picking a topic?
2. Can I help others to start a conversation?
3. Do I fail to keep conversation moving smoothly?
4. Am I dogmatic or condescending?
5. Do I cause embarrassment by talking about some tabooed subject?
6. Am I able to adjust to the attitudes of those in the conversation? To changes in attitude?
7. Do I talk only about myself, my family, or my own narrow interests?
8. Do I insist on describing complete plots of TV programs, books, or movies?
9. Do I turn every conversation into an argument?

10. Am I self-conscious about grammar, voice, articulation, or pronunciation?

11. Am I able to listen when it's the other fellow's turn to speak?

12. Am I sensitive to the other person's time limitations? Do I know when and how to end a conversation?

13. Do I have certain annoying mannerisms?

14. Do I show a sense of humor during conversations?

15. Can I bring others into the conversation?

16. Am I so specialized in my training, my reading, and my thinking that I am unable to enter into topics that others find interesting?

Improving conversational skills

When you have checked your own conversation habits and skills, you will be ready to do something about improvement or change. A famous conversationalist was asked how he had attained his ability. Was it inherited? Was it the result of intense reading or knowledge of human nature? "No," he replied, "Just long practice. I belonged to a large family. We had great conversations at mealtimes. But one rule was imposed. The conversation always had to be of general interest to the entire group at the table. When I was a little boy of seven or eight, with a burning desire to talk, it really taxed my ingenuity to have to make my own ideas and activities of *general interest* to all my family and the frequent guests."

A chess player's opening gambit sometimes sets up his later victory. Don't be afraid to prepare an opening gambit. What are the other fellow's interests? How do they dovetail with yours? What are some of the major news stories of the day (excluding the weather)? Don't enter a conversation just to get something off your chest or to show your brilliance. Maybe you have just read a new biography, but, unless your partner is a historian, it won't stimulate much of a conversation if you open with the obvious: "By the way, has anyone heard the latest scoop on Marie Antoinette?"

Are you well informed about any topic you introduce? If your first choice evokes no interest, be ready to introduce a new topic. Have more than one subject that you can talk about. Don't be known as "that baseball fanatic," or "that guy who always gives the government hell." Maybe the other person has something he is eager to discuss. Try to give him his opportunity. A thought-provoking question may start the conversation—something better than the cliché, "What's new?" Ask yourself, "What are *their* interests? What happened lately of particular interest to him or the members of *his* family?"

Flexibility is a necessity for trees that withstand strong winds; it is just as necessary for the conversationalist. Flexibility means adjusting yourself to others as they contribute comments and information. While keeping the conversation moving, be courteous, ask frequent questions, express agreement when you honestly agree. If the conversation lags, try another tack, but allow others the same opportunity to change the topic if they find a new subject more interesting and valuable. Don't fear occasional silences. Sometimes the thoughts that are being generated need a little organization before they are expressed.

Queen Victoria made known her disapproval of certain questionable topics by announcing regally, "We are not amused." Not everyone is so direct in his expression. Be alert to the attitudes of others and how their attitudes are changing. Perhaps you can be facetious about religion or politics, on occasion, but you may suddenly feel a chill that indicates you are treading on sensitive toes. Tabooed subjects vary in different groups. Many people dislike smutty stories; some are squeamish about medical symptoms. Practically no one enjoys hearing the entire plot of the movie you saw or the details of the TV comedy at which you laughed so uproariously last night. After all, can *you* improve on Bob Hope or Marshall Dillon?

Some people will say anything to get into a conversation. They rely on a "startle technique," spreading gossip, betraying secrets, saying anything to indicate they possess important information and are worth talking to. A person will not be trusted with confidential material if he is unable to keep important information to himself. It is embarrassing to hear someone make admissions about his family or his personal affairs that would be better kept private.

The "ring-tailed roarer" has gone out of fashion. Underplay, rather than overplay some claims about your abilities. Don't allow yourself to be trapped into exaggerating in order to impress people. If you want to air a prejudice, do so, but admit it is a prejudice and allow the others in the conversation the luxury of their own prejudices. Disagree when it is necessary, but don't do it disagreeably. Don't argue about every point that is raised. *Do* resist the temptation to top every story that is told.

What about your voice, language, and oral demeanor? Speak up! Don't be a mumbler. If you have something to say, let others hear it. Don't overuse pet phrases or words, such as: "Now, looky here"; "I declare"; "Doggone it"; "And here's the payoff." Too much slang or profanity may destroy your effectiveness, as may the urge to make a joke of everything. Resist tossing out the facile wisecrack that diminishes the importance of the other person's ideas.

Precision of grammar or pronunciation is commendable, but don't let worrying about whether you are using the proper locution stop your flow of conversation. Never dam the flow of language by calling attention to a minor grammatical blunder or flaw in pronunciation. Superior attitudes of this type will only mark you as a condescending pedant. People rarely appreciate unsolicited lessons in grammar, articulation, or pronunciation.

Have you ever wanted to choke someone who continually drummed on the table or desk with his finger tips while you were trying to express your innermost thoughts? Bodily mannerisms will handicap your conversational efforts. Do you scratch your face? Pick at or bite your fingernails? Protrude your tongue? Wrinkle your nose? Jingle coins or keys in your pocket? For a check on such mannerisms or annoying habits you may have to ask an outside observer to advise you. If you ask a friend (or your spouse) to observe and report about such habits, don't argue; just accept the report and do something about eliminating what might be considered objectionable to others.

Look at people when you talk to them and try to call them by name. People tend to feel more friendly toward you if you say their names aloud.

A long shaggy-dog story will fall flat if the other fellow has two minutes to catch a train. Recognize the importance of time to others. Don't grasp another's lapel (even figuratively) to detain him in a conversation in which *you* are tremendously interested. Prepare an opening that starts the conversation flaming and a conclusion that extinguishes the blaze of words. Remember the credo of the old-time vaudeville stars: "Always leave 'em laughing." At least, don't leave 'em yawning.

Interviews

Technically trained individuals participate in numerous interview situations. These interviews are conversations that are more formal and purposeful than the ones we have been discussing earlier in this chapter. They may be held across a desk or standing over a blue print. They may be for the purpose of giving and receiving information or policy, making or receiving assignments, establishing attitudes, buying or selling materials or ideas, planning work, settling disputes, training or indoctrinating, giving and receiving reprimands, making reports, etc. The important types include the job interview, the sales interview, the counseling interview, and the planning interview.

The job interview

Oral communication is always more successful if it is carefully prepared in advance. The job interview is no exception. As an applicant you should know as much as possible about the company to which you are applying, the particular position you hope to fill, and the man who will interview you. You should anticipate the types of questions that will be asked. Sometimes the interviewer purposely lapses into silence to allow the prospective employee to expound his ideas. Will you be able to talk sensibly about important and significant material if you have this opportunity? Sometimes the interviewer has a series of questions to ask. Are you able to answer, fluently, questions concerning your education, your experience, your ideas about the job for which you are applying? Can you discuss your ambitions and your reasons for applying to this particular company? Can you display your education without being unduly snobbish about it? Can you demonstrate your social ability; your knowledge about the affairs of the nation and the world? Can you express opinions without sounding dogmatic?

Inform yourself before the interview. When you make your survey of the company to which you are applying, list carefully certain questions you would like answered about the general corporate structure, the organizational scheme, the insurance program, the retirement plan, promotion possibilities, or opportunities for further on-the-job training. You are expected to ask questions as well as answer them. Obviously, these questions will not come at the beginning of the interview and should not be asked in such a way that they indicate a selfish interest in your own affairs. It is appropriate to ask specific questions about the type of work you are expected to do, the working conditions, and the man who is to be your supervisor. You may even inquire about the men who are at present the top executives of the company. Ask from knowledge, not from ignorance. Learn as much as possible beforehand.

Plan your conduct during the interview. Appear in conservative clothing. A coat and tie indicate respect for the interview situation. Don't dump your hat or overcoat on the interviewer's desk. Come to the interview alone unless you have been requested to bring your wife (or husband). Identify yourself immediately and be ready to follow the cues of the interviewer. If he extends his hand, shake it, but don't try to crush his fingers. Nor should you offer a wet-fish type of handshake. Look at him earnestly. If he waves you to a chair or asks you to sit down, do so firmly. Otherwise, remain standing. Assume an alert position and wait expectantly for his opening remarks.

If the interviewer wishes to engage in small talk before getting down to business, join him. (Use some of the suggestions listed in the section on conversation.) If he wants to begin the serious discussion at once, follow his lead by avoiding digressions. Be attentive to the interviewer. Do not smoke unless he suggests it. Even then, it might be wise to avoid the temptation. You will have to search for an ash tray. You may be handicapped in your gestures with a cigarette in your hand. Smoking may be a distracting mannerism in your case. Don't stare at any mail or papers on the desk. Keep your eyes attuned to him, but don't try to outstare him. Just look pleasant, relaxed and show him you are a good listener by occasional nods and indications of comprehension.

When you answer his questions, be as honest and sincere as you can. Make clear that you have something to offer his company. Don't be too eager, overanxious, or desperate. Don't try to get by with a hard-luck story. Don't gossip about other interviewers or make invidious remarks about other companies. Watch out for those mannerisms of speech and gesture. Try to appear unhurried and calm.

Exit gracefully. Be alert for a cue from the interviewer indicating when your time is up. Then, thank him; find out what further steps need to be taken, such as, filling out blanks, leaving address and telephone number; find out when or how you will be notified about the results of your interview; and leave promptly, firmly, and proudly.

The sales interview

(This will be discussed in Chapter 11.)

The counseling interview

Many business or governmental organizations use the counseling interview to build morale or to check up on interpersonal relations within a department. The interview can be diagnostic, too. It can help to discover how individuals in a group can work together more smoothly. It can pinpoint potential problem areas (just as in preventive medicine) before they become hopelessly infected. It can make an employee feel he is being appreciated for the good work he is doing.

Preparation of the counseling interviewer. As a counsellor you should be consistent in scheduling, selecting the place for the interview, keeping records of the interview, and handling the various individuals. If you buy a cup of coffee for one interviewee, you must do the same for all the others. Put your man at ease. Explain carefully the purposes of the interview and let him see what material you are noting in your record book. (You may write total appraisals later, as soon after the interview as possible.) Many people feel that these appraisals should be discussed later with the man you are interviewing.

Make an outline so that you can cover all the points you think necessary. As a counsellor, you are seeking answers to certain questions so listen, listen, listen. Ask questions that are open-ended so that they cannot be answered by a simple "yes" or "no." In other words, use questions of "How?" and "Why?" and "What do you think about . . . ?" rather than "Do you think that . . . ?" or "Can you . . . ?"

Before you undertake a counseling interview, you may want to check yourself against Professor Wiksell's questionnaire.[1]

[1] Wesley Wiksell, *Do They Understand You?*, The Macmillan Company, New York, 1960, pp. 158–159.

What is your man-to-man conference profile?

	Yes	Not sure	No
Do you do everything possible to make it easy for your men to talk to you?			
Do you make it a practice to see every one of your men for a planned talk at least every six months?			
Do you make it clear to each one that you have conferences with every man so that it becomes a natural procedure?			
Do you hold your interviews in private to avoid embarrassing the employee?			
Do you check the employee's folder to study his past record carefully?			
Do you find out what has been done in other departments with problems similar to the employee's?			
Are you careful not to judge and evaluate things you should not judge?			
Do you say "no" firmly and pleasantly when it is warranted?			
Do you encourage criticism without being offensive?			
Do you encourage suggestions?			
Do you tell the employee exactly where he stands?			
Do you encourage him to tell you exactly where you stand?			
Do you make the necessary follow-ups?			
Do you speak softly, in a pleasant manner?			

Preparation of the counseling interviewee. You may find yourself being interviewed by a company counsellor or your own supervisor. If so, you have certain responsibilities as an interviewee. You should be prepared in advance, bringing pertinent data to the interview regarding your job responsibilities. Refresh yourself concerning how your job or your department fits in with the chain of command. Be prepared to give appraisals about your department and the men with whom you work. Be ready to discuss frankly your own weak points and strengths. Try to give clear, concise information. Don't digress. Help the counsellor determine when it's time to conclude.

The planning interview

A case in point *"Plan ahead"*

The chief engineer of the design department of the Southwestern Electronics Company has called in his new assistant, Bill Garroway. He reminds Bill about an idea that has come to them from the production department. Bill and the chief engineer have been in frequent discussion about this project—a new triple-head pressure sealer to speed up production on certain components. This time the chief engineer seems to be more specific. He insists that Bill take notes on the views they are exchanging. Finally he announces, "Bill, that's what they're calling for in production and we'll have to build one. And Bill, it's all yours! I'm due in Washington the fifth of the month. I'm leaving tomorrow morning. Don't know when I can get back. You can use anybody you want on this job. You'll have to take over."

He has left Bill in a slight case of shock. Bill hadn't been clear when the interview started that this was to be his first big job on his own. He feels lucky that he did take fairly careful notes. He has the opportunity to ask questions and clear up any doubts about procedure, personnel, scheduling, materials, etc., before the chief leaves. If he is wise, he will use this last opportunity to obtain specific data before he plunges into the assigned task. (*Case continued later in chapter.*)

The planning interview may be face-to-face or by telephone. A supervisor may be assigning duties or giving instructions to a subordinate, or men of equal responsibility on the organizational chart may be attacking a mutual problem. In the planning interview the participants usually seek to give or receive information of mutual value or to lay out a course of action. The interview should be prepared for as fully as possible in advance, including the possibilities of unpredictable developments, questions, and objections that may arise. As with all interviews, the person responsible for calling the interview should set the tone from the beginning with a direct statement of the object or purpose. Use an outline to be certain that all ideas of importance are covered. This is especially important for telephoned assignments. A copy of the outline may be sent in advance.

The two-person planning interview is often too casual to be effective. It's just as difficult to make yourself clear and to remember what has been decided when there are two people as when there are fifty. Each man in the planning interview should utilize every available device for explaining, clarifying, and verifying conclusions. State major points clearly, using language that is easily understood. Keep the supporting material pertinent, in immediate juxtaposition to the ideas they support. Have paper and pencils handy for note taking and allow time for complete notes. If material of mathematical or spatial nature is involved, use a blackboard or a large, blank flip chart, graphs, maps and other visual material.

Sometimes participants illustrate by scribbling or drawing on a flat desk pad. Grease pencils, or crayons, should be ready for marking on this "talking paper." Allow plenty of time for questions, suggestions, and the usual "feedback." Compare and exchange notes to verify all points made. You may prefer that all notes be taken in duplicate and the carbons exchanged. Comparisons and changes may then be noted on the copies. These amended copies may be kept for future reference and files.

The conference

A conference is a meeting in which a group of people having common interests and problems exchange their points of view, relate individual experiences, and pool their ideas. The purpose of a conference may be one or more of the following: to arrive at some definite conclusions; to solve a problem; to adopt new ideas; to modify old ideas.

A case in point (Continued)   **"Confer and confuse"**

Bill Garroway must call a conference to initiate work on the new pressure sealer. He knows from past experience about the wasted time, the wrangling, and the procrastination at these interminable conferences. What was it someone said the other day? "This company ought to have been called the Southwestern Electronics and Conference Company. We're supposed to make electrical components, but all we do all day is hold conferences."

Let's see, who does he need for this project? Someone should be there from the design services department, the model shop, and the tool-control group. Ought to have a couple of fellows from production, too. Who else? Is there someone he is forgetting? No, guess not. There is a vague doubt in his mind.

Let's see. Should he call them, write a memo, or see them in person to brief them about the project? Calling them will take less time. He reaches for the phone. In a few minutes he has them all called. Suddenly it comes to him. Electrical engineering! That was the one he forgot! Of course . . . Jake Freedly. Where's that directory? Extension 482 . . . There . . . someone's answered. It's a new secretary. Better leave a message. "Tell Jake that Bill called. Tell him we've got a new project on that triple-head sealer job. We're having a conference tomorrow at ten in Mr. Wilson's office."

It's tomorrow already. Lucky we've got Mr. Wilson's suite for this deal. Couple of guys are here already. Enough chairs? "Hi, Arch! Hi! I'm Bill Garroway." Funny, this guy doesn't introduce himself. They're all here at last . . . except Jake from electrical engineering. Can't wait all day. "Let's begin, fellows."

About an hour has gone by. Lucky we found that old flip chart someone left around. There was no blackboard here. The fellows didn't seem to have many ideas. They let him carry the ball, all right. But he had put over the idea of sticking to schedule. Or had he? Funny . . . Jake Freedly hadn't shown up. Well, maybe we can figure out the electrical part without him. Maybe I'd better call and find out what happened to Jake. That number was 482.

"Hey, this is Bill Garroway. Was it you I talked to about Jake Freedly attending a conference? He never showed. What? Jake has left the company? He's opening up an outfit of his own? Why the . . . I mean, you should have told me. Who is in charge of electrical engineering now? I'll come down and talk to him."

Two weeks have passed and Bill has been pushing the "triple-head pressure-sealer job" with all his energy and knowledge. The schedule he has worked out and presented to the conference group is almost checked out. Of course, the electrical component had to be made by an outside contractor. Bill never did quite get full cooperation from electrical engineering. They hadn't had a representative at that first conference. Somehow, they never seemed to see the whole picture. He'd tried to fill them in with personal talks and had followed with written memos and specifications, but it didn't seem to work out.

Finally, the electrical component they had ordered arrived. What a shock! It was supposed to have been *one* unit built in triangular shape to fit the slot designed for it. Here, they've sent him *two* rectangular sections. All the components are there . . . but the shape of the housing! There goes the schedule all shot to pieces. The whole works are held up while we either make a new housing or redesign the entire rig.

The entire project hinged on that first conference. Let's take stock of that first conference. Much of today's business is accomplished by conference. The teamwork idea is stressed by many executives in government and business. Bill Garroway may have been an excellent engineer, but the success of his project depended on the cooperation and labor of many people. Obviously, he blundered in failing to contact the proper person in the electrical engineering department. He didn't establish enthusiasm and a sense of shared responsibility in that first meeting. His agenda or plan was not clearly thought through before the meeting. His meeting place was poorly equipped. Few or no records were made of the meeting.

We do not know anything about the progress of the conference itself, but we suspect he rather muddled through the time allotted. Bill had little confidence in the conference method, even though he knew he had to use its procedures to accomplish his assigned job. This chapter will continue with the general methods and skills of conference procedure. Anyone who is involved in conferences (and who isn't these days) should be able to check his own behavior against the ideas listed.

What are the values of a conference?

1. Several minds at work on a problem may be better than one mind working alone.
2. Many problems need to be seen from the points of view of all concerned, not simply from the point of view of one person.
3. Thinking together helps a group to work together. Cooperation of action results from cooperation in planning and deciding.
4. Persons who have a sense of participation in planning work and solving problems accept solutions more readily. They enthusiastically support the proposals. Conferences build within each individual a sense of responsibility for the whole program.
5. Conferences build morale. Being present when important matters are under consideration, each person feels recognized and significant.
6. When properly conducted, conferences build and maintain high levels of productivity.
7. Certain antagonisms, sometimes caused by more direct methods, may be avoided in conference procedure as members share responsibility for decisions.
8. Members of a conference may learn informally about ideas and feelings held by their colleagues.

What are the duties of the conference leader?

In the case previously cited, Bill Garroway was the most important factor in the conference he called. It was his responsibility to act as conference leader. Most conferences held today are directed by a leader or chairman. This leader frequently issues the call for a conference. He knows the purpose or purposes of the meeting. He decides who will make up the group, unless the participants are previously specified. (If the members of a particular department meet at certain times to discuss mutual problems, the personnel of the conference is automatically determined.)

The leader has certain duties to perform before, during, and after the conference.

1. Before the meeting:

a. The conference leader must know the exact purpose or purposes of the meeting.

b. He should know the group with whom he is going to work. What is its past history? Does the group know the elements of conference procedure? Have these people worked together before? He should make an individual analysis of each member participating in the conference.

c. He should notify the participants well in advance with precise data as to time and place and arrange for acknowledgments to be sent to him.

d. He should think out his work in advance of the meeting.

e. He should make arrangements for an adequate meeting place.

f. He should have on hand all the reference and working materials needed for a successful meeting.

g. He should arrange for the members to know the reasons for the meeting. He may confer with some of the participants prior to the actual time of the meeting, thus allowing them to help plan the meeting.

h. He should have in writing a complete agenda and a tentative timetable of the probable progress of the conference.

i. He should arrange for a secretary to keep accurate notes of procedures and decisions. These notes should include decisions reached on the schedule, future plans and conferences, and the roster of members present. Seeing in writing what has been accomplished encourages the members of the group and gives them a sense of achievement. If no professional secretarial assistance is available, the chairman or someone designated will take notes and write and distribute a report of the meeting to the other members.

2. Beginning the meeting:

a. The leader should plan a brief opening talk describing the situation and creating the mood of the conference.

b. He should state the topic clearly, succinctly.

c. He may cite case histories or anecdotes to illustrate the topic and to arouse or heighten the interest of the group.

d. He should define technical terms that may carry different meanings to various members of the group.

e. He should indicate what is out of bounds in the present conference.

f. He may break up the entire problem into smaller areas for easier handling.

3. During the meeting:

a. The leader should stimulate discussion, get everyone to take part.

b. He should act as a leader rather than a teacher or lecturer. Although the conference leader does present the problem, his purpose is not to "tell 'em" but to get an exchange of opinion and ideas. The purpose of most conferences is to make everyone feel he is working with the group toward a common goal.

c. The leader should offer other ways of looking at the issue and let the members disagree if they so desire. He should discourage argument, however. When people argue, *what they say* tends to be less important than *how they feel*. To contradict a person is to invite a restatement of what he said, sometimes with more emotionally charged vigor. Let the members of the conference convince themselves, if possible.

d. He should guide the discussion, keep it on the track. Thus, he may spotlight valuable contributions and handle digressions with tact.

e. He should make summaries as frequently as necessary to convince the group that they are getting someplace. These summaries, representing the thinking of the group, should be indicated visually on a large blackboard or paper chart. All members can then follow the progress of the conference.

f. The leader should learn to be a good listener. (See Chapter 15.) He may have more data, and experience, but the members of the group must feel important, too. A leader may be inclined to talk a lot because he wants to make an impression. Wanting to convince the group is a constant temptation.

g. He should schedule and manage the time so that all major ideas have sufficient coverage.

h. He should encourage the group to talk and do independent thinking. If members of the group do a lot of talking, they become involved personally in the problem. Let them discuss, fumble, recover, find their way. Let them discover the answers for themselves. Then they will have insight into and responsibility for the common problem. This method may be better than having the leader supply formal verbal statements about questions and problems that the rest of the group has not thought through.

A conference leader may find himself falling into the trap of thinking for the group, particularly if he is extremely concerned about the problem and knows a lot about it. It will be hard for him to maintain his objectivity. To accomplish his purpose he needs to be calm and unhurried. It takes time for individuals—and especially a group—to catch up with an idea that is novel and has many implications to be explored. A leader may find himself talking too much. He may be commenting after each contribution from a member. And his comments are likely to be judgments on the value and importance of each contribution. Or he may find that he is throwing out leading questions so that he will be sure to get the *right* answers and avoid wasting time on nonessential ideas.[2]

i. He should close the meeting on time. It is better to schedule another meeting than to insist on further discussion when the

[2] George V. Moser, "Avoiding Pitfalls in Conference Leading," *The Conference Board Management Record,* vol. 20, no. 11, p. 375, November, 1958.

members are fatigued or are fretting to keep other appointments.

4. After the meeting:

a. The leader should be responsible for preparing a report, copies of which should be sent to the members of the group for their approval and comment.

b. It is his responsibility to see that the meeting room is put in order and all notes are collected. He should remember to erase the blackboard and remove all charts, diagrams, and material used in the conference. This may prevent false or premature information from being circulated by other users of the conference room.

c. He should arrange for further conferences, if necessary.

What are the duties of the conference member?

The success of a conference rests not only upon the conference leader but upon the conference members as well. Conference members are called together because they, as a group, possess the knowledge and experience necessary to discuss and to help solve problems. They should assist the leader in compiling information, presenting new ideas, and crystallizing old ideas that can be applied to the problem under consideration. Each member will benefit from the information and suggestions contributed by other members of the group. Those who attend the conference will have a common purpose and will hold in common certain experiences and ideas related to the problem under consideration.

1. Before the meeting the participants in a conference should:

a. Reply to the conference leader indicating acceptance and restate the time, date, and meeting place.

b. Prepare as fully as possible for the problem to be discussed.

c. Bring pertinent data or material that bears on the problem.

d. Arrive on time and assist the leader in making introductions and getting acquainted with the other participants.

2. During the meeting the participant should:

a. Give the group the benefit of his experience.

b. Be impersonal toward the problem and toward the views of other members of the group.

c. Subdue any desire to show off or make a speech.

d. Keep his prejudices from becoming evident.

e. Be alert and give undivided attention to the discussion.

f. Be patient when results are slow in developing.

g. Appreciate the other fellow's point of view.

h. Avoid the temptation to argue.

i. Talk only about the problem under discussion.

j. Assist the leader in getting the results recorded.

k. Be for or against *what* rather than *who* is talking.

l. Listen to what others say and look at the person who is talking.

m. Be mannerly but take part in the discussion.

n. Be brief and definite.

o. Be a good sport and go along with what the group as a whole decides is the best procedure.

3. After the meeting the participant should:

a. Avoid gossip or spreading false rumors about the conference. He should say what he has to say in the course of the conference, not afterward in the cloakroom.

b. Start the duties decided on at the conference.

What are some useful conference devices and aids?

Visual aids such as charts, illustrations, and blackboards may be used to focus attention and to draw in all the members of the group. A chart upon which the leader lists points of agreement may be especially helpful in serving as a record from which the leader can prepare minutes for later distribution. Visual aids (See Chapter 6.) may be used to open the discussion in an interesting manner, to direct thinking upon the problem, to drive home a point, or to summarize the discussion.

A pertinent case study offered orally by the leader or a designated conferee may be an interesting way to open a conference. These cases may be written in advance and distributed well before the meeting so that the conferees may have time to ponder possible ideas and solutions. Overhead projectors offer a novel method of presenting case studies in striptease fashion. First the leader exposes the beginning of a certain case. Then he asks the members of the group to tell what they would have done in a similar situation. After some discussion, he reveals the actual progress of the case by removing another of the masking strips. The leader can even reveal excerpts of dialogue bit by bit, allowing the members of the group to interpolate their ideas about what should have been said.

Anecdotes, stories, and varied types of "for instances" break monotony or tension. Although a conference is organized primarily to expedite action, and you should be wary about wasting valuable time in triviality or bull session, its progress should not be allowed to become dull and purely routine. Anecdotes, etc., may also be used to illustrate a point or gain attention. Sometimes a carefully placed story may clarify a situation or help the leader break away from a ticklish or delicate subject.

Questions asked gracefully and strategically are important devices for leader and conferee. Questions from the leader will induce feedback from his listeners. He can find out whether members of the group are moving along with him at the same pace and in the same direction. Questions from the group may indicate interest and understanding on the part of individuals and of the whole group. A question may be used to open the entire discussion. Questions may be used as transitions to move the discussion ahead to another point. They may expand, amplify, or explain a member's contribution. They may help to introduce a point which is being overlooked. Questions may help to encourage persons who are hesitant. They may bring out helpful data, opinions, or experiences from members. Questions may help in discipline, cooperation, and team play. They may serve to summarize and give unity to divergent ideas.

In general, the more successful leaders avoid a "direct" question, that is, calling on a specific member by name, unless they have a very definite reason to do so (to bring out a particular viewpoint that one specific individual is ready to talk about, to interrupt two members who are carrying on a discussion of their own, to call an inattentive member back into touch with group thinking, to give a shy member an opportunity to say what is on his mind, to break up a long-winded monologue, to stimulate argument where the leader knows a member has views opposed to those just expressed).

Experience shows that the direct question has real value as a tool in conference leading but that it can be easily overdone.[3]

Questions, judiciously used, should strive for consensus, a unanimous feeling concerning an idea. The leader may announce general agreement on a certain topic before proceeding. If there are no objections, he may assume consensus and thus keep certain participants from going on record as being opposed. Sometimes the very fact that a man is on record forces him to stand by his beliefs no matter how his actual feelings may alter during a period of time. It is not necessary for every disputed idea to be resolved by vote of the majority. In fact, the leader should be chary about submitting ideas for voting. This would emphasize division and force participants to go on record, perhaps prematurely.

Working with various types of individuals

The leader of a conference frequently feels that members of his group share the attitude expressed by: "Tell us! We'll listen, only leave us alone. Don't ask us to do anything or to risk anything. We certainly aren't going to do anything to expose our uncertainty, confusion, and insecurity in the presence of this crowd. We're not going to be made fools of or be ridiculed or shown up. We'll play it safe. Anything you say is O.K. We can take it or leave it. Only we hope you'll make it interesting, enjoyable . . . and short!"

The leader usually feels his greatest responsibility is to arouse enthusiasm and interest in the project or idea under discussion. The less authoritarian his attitude, the more he makes the members of the group feel the conference is a shared responsibility, the more likely are the members to respond with eagerness and sincerity. How would you handle some of the following problem cases?

1. *The conference member who talks too much.* A conference sometimes becomes a dialogue between the leader and an overtalkative member who may have important things to say but should not be allowed to monopolize the discussion. Develop a technique that will bring the rest of the group into the discussion.

[3] *Ibid.*, p. 376.

a. "What do the rest of you think about the point just raised by . . . ?"

b. "That was a good point Jim raised." (Write it on the blackboard or chart.) "How about somebody else suggesting one?"

c. "Bob's been carrying the ball all afternoon. How about a suggestion or idea from someone else?"

2. *The member who knows all the correct answers.* The leader will occasionally be confronted with a member who through experience, intelligence, or superior job position knows most of the answers and does not hesitate to be the first to answer the leader's questions. Usually this individual does not realize that he is causing others to hold back. It is often possible to make him understand he is dominating the thinking too much by:

a. Tactfully addressing questions to the other side of the room: "Did you want to speak, Jerry?"

b. Asking questions of other individuals: "That's a great idea, Smith; let's hold on to it for awhile and see what Robinson thinks about this matter."

3. *The member who wants to dominate the group.* The conference group will either tend to sit back and give this man the floor or proceed to discourage him by pointing out weaknesses in his arguments. The leader should discourage either procedure by such statements as:

a. "Now, that's one man's viewpoint. How do the rest of you feel about this point Sam has just raised?"

b. "We want to get everyone's idea on this subject. Who holds another opinion?"

4. *The man who takes a long time to express himself.* A few people ramble on and require a great deal of wordage to express their ideas. It is well to use considerable tact in curbing them. Often the leader can catch the gist of their idea and help them frame it. These individuals often repeat themselves in their ramblings. The leader may bring their thoughts to focus by such remarks as:

a. "Now just a minute, Al. I want to be sure to get all of these points down. (Writing on the board) The first point you made was. . . . Now what's your second point?"

b.   "Let me try to boil your idea down, Al. I want to be sure to get all of these points down. As I got, it, you think. . . . "

5.   *The member who is timid or lacks self-confidence.* Such a member may be new to the conference group, recently promoted to his job, or unfamiliar with conference procedures. The leader can help him get on an equal footing with the rest of the group. Sometimes members of the group fail to talk because they have difficulty in expressing themselves. An individual may feel he has nothing to offer the group. This man may be capable and experienced and able to give many commonsense ideas to the conference if he is persuaded to talk. The leader may help such individuals by remarks such as these:

a.   "Tom, you're new to the group here. I would like to get your slant on this problem."

b.   "Alex, you're probably closer to the operations than most of us. What is your reaction to this problem?"

c.   (By way of encouragement, after a tentative offering) "Now that is a good point. It gives us a different slant on the problem we've been discussing."

6.   *The man who is disinterested.* The conference group may include individuals who are disinterested because they do not recognize the benefits to be derived from active participation in the conference. Sometimes a person is so wrapped up in personal problems that he does not enter into the discussion. Subtle flattery may be of assistance in such cases, such as:

a.   "Art says little, but when he speaks, his ideas are worth listening to. What do you think about this idea, Art?"

b.   "I know we'll want to get Sam's slant on this proposition."

c.   "You'll remember how Bill solved our previous problem. How do you think we can handle this one, Bill?"

7.   *The member who is antagonistic.* The leader may discover a member who definitely has no use for conferences and thinks they are a waste of time. He may wreck the conference if his views spread to the other members. Show him the value of this particular meeting at this particular time with such remarks as:

a.   "This particular conference was called for the specific purpose of. . . . It's the only way we can get the combined brains of this group to bear on the problem expediently."

b. "George, you know why this conference was called. Do you know any way we can solve this problem more efficiently?"

c. "It's a pleasure to work with fellows like Martin who want to get the job done efficiently and dislike wasting valuable time. That's what we're aiming for in this conference."

8. *The man who brings up touchy subjects.* The leader has an excellent opportunity to gain the respect of the group by the manner in which he handles delicate or touchy subjects not pertinent to the problem at hand. These deviations may deal with friction between departments or persons, blunders on the part of individual members, company policies or practices outside the province of the conference group, company politics, etc. Forestall such situations from arising and handle them tactfully when they do evolve. Some helpful techniques might be:

a. To ignore certain wisecracks.

b. To inform the group that the subject is outside the scope of this conference.

c. To defer the point to a later date when more information may be forthcoming by saying, "I think we'll have to leave this point for the executive committee to decide."

d. To point out the exigencies of time, indicating that this particular idea is cutting into the schedule previously prepared. ("We have only thirty minutes left on our schedule.")

e. To indicate that the procedures of the group are being recorded by the secretary. ("Elton, do you want that last remark on the record?") (See Appendix E for the rating sheet, Evaluation of a Conference or Discussion.)

Assignments and exercises

1. Write up the procedure of a conference you have observed or in which you have participated. Use the rating sheet (Appendix E) to evaluate the conference. In your comments, indicate the purpose of the conference; the general conduct of the leader and the participants, etc.

2. Prepare an agenda for a conference you might be expected to conduct.

3. Divide the class into several conference groups. Each group will meet and choose a problem that needs a solution. (It may be a campus problem, a technical problem, or a situation that requires role playing on the part of the participants.) Choose one of each group as leader. It will be his responsibility to decide when the conference is to be held. He will notify the members of the group, arrange for necessary equipment, supply the agenda, and hold the conference within the set time limits. Observers from the class will criticize the conference. (Use rating sheet.)

4. Divide the class into two-man teams. One member of the team will take the role of job applicant. The other will take the role of personnel supervisor. Each team will conduct a job interview. The class will observe and discuss the effectiveness of the interview.

5. Divide the class into two-man teams. One member of the team will take the role of employee, the other the role of department head. The employee will have questions in the area of his work, his general demeanor in the company, and his personal relations with his employer, his supervisors, and his colleagues. Each team will conduct a counseling interview. The Man-to-Man Conference Profile in this chapter may be used to point up criticism.

6. Form conversational groups of two or more. Each group will begin a conversation. Allow a few minutes for warm-up. Then the instructor will ask all groups but one to remain silent. The spotlighted group will continue for five minutes. Other members of the class will criticize their performance as measured by criteria set up in this chapter.

10

WHO, WHAT, WHERE, WHEN, AND HOW

Informing the listener

A case in point   **"What's in it for me?"**

John Masters, the plant manager of an Ohio company, overheard one of his foremen say to an employee, "You've got to report to the infirmary. When a man gets hurt he goes to the doctor. It's company policy." After the employee had left, shaking his head uncomprehendingly, Masters walked over to the foreman.

"What's company policy?" Masters inquired.

"Oh, the guy got his finger caught beneath some tubing. Tore his nail halfway off. He didn't want to go to the infirmary. Said it wasn't serious. I told him it was policy, that he had to go. I guess he didn't like it much."

"Do you know *why* it is policy to send an injured employee to the infirmary?" Masters asked.

"Sure," said the foreman. "Want to make sure an employee gets proper medical attention when he's hurt. That fellow works with grease—he could get an infection that would lay him up for a few days. He'd lose money and we'd lose his services. We don't want anything like that to happen if we can prevent it."

"Well, for goodness' sakes, why didn't you tell the man that? Why didn't you explain that you wanted him to go to the infirmary for his own protection instead of saying it was a matter of policy? I think you're just lazy. It's easier to say something is a matter of policy than to give an explanation. You're supposed to represent the company and explain its policies. You certainly muffed the ball that time."[1]

[1] James Menzies Black, "How to Win with Words," *American Management Association*, p. 18, June, 1958.

152

Alexander Pope said, "The proper study of mankind is man." The proper approach to making information clear to a listener is to begin with *him* in mind. How does a listener understand? What are his methods of comprehending, of grasping meaning? An examination of the ways people understand should be the starting point for planning communication whose purpose is to inform and to instruct.

Motivate your listener

A person must be motivated before he will learn. "Motive is not related to learning merely as a facilitating or inhibiting accidental circumstance. It is not something that may be present or absent; it is an absolutely indispensable something, a *sine qua non* of learning. Motive is indispensable to learning because it represents the antecedent, dynamic background out of which emerge both original behavior and its modification."[2]

If you want somebody to receive and to understand information, you have to make clear to him why this information is important to him. For example, an orientation talk about company policy to new employees should be approached along the lines of *why* this information is vital and essential to the new employee. What will strike his interest immediately? Information about his salary? His working conditions? His insurance benefits? Probably so. Whatever the subject, it should be approached from the standpoint of why it is beneficial for the listener to understand the information.

"All living beings show in their life processes a directiveness or trend toward a goal or end of their activity. In other words, they are always seeking or working toward some goal which is the natural issue of their behavior. It is inconceivable that a living being would react to anything unless that thing stood in a very intimate relation with, or had a vital meaning for, its trends of activity and the goals toward which its activity is directed."[3]

The above concept has a specific implication for the communicator who wishes to instruct. *Relate the goals of the communication*

[2] W. D. Commins, *Principles of Educational Psychology,* The Ronald Press Company, New York, 1937, p. 315.

[3] *Ibid.,* p. 19.

to the personal goals of the listener. For example, if the problem is to get the listener to understand the mechanism of a digital computer, the communicator should emphasize how the new device will help the listener perform his work more easily and efficiently. When the listener feels that the information is essential in helping him move toward his own goals, then he is willing to open his mind to instruction.

Use an integrating pattern

Psychologists tell us that human beings understand a problem by seeing in it some integrating pattern that logically relates the parts to each other and to the whole. "Learning is a process of perceiving of relationships, and learning takes place only when a structure, pattern, or organization is perceived which relates the parts to the whole and to each other."[4]

"To integrate" in this sense means to unite ideas so that they form a complete whole. In order to unite ideas, you must have a plan or a vehicle for doing so. When a human being sees a lot of separate elements, he doesn't understand them. He cannot understand until he arrives at some scheme of relating them and forming a complete whole. As long as he sees only separate elements, he cannot comprehend the meaning of the whole. A stranger in New York City is lost until he studies a map. Once he realizes that avenues run north and south, and streets run east and west, he has a system for orienting himself. When the neophyte first looks at the inside of a television set he sees only a mass of wires, tubes, and gadgets. This conglomeration of metal and wires has no meaning for him. He can, however, learn the function of this mass of gadgets if a schematic drawing is presented to him which shows the relationship and purpose of these items and how they work together to form the whole of a television receiver.

The communicator must find a scheme for tying his ideas together. The fact that the communicator knows the information thoroughly is only the first step in communication. The next step is to find some basic key which will act as a relating instrument for the thought processes of the listener. For example, in explaining impedance

[4] James Stephens, *Educational Psychology,* Holt, Rinehart and Winston Inc New York, 1951, p. 25.

ratings of wires, the key idea of "storing up" or "accumulating" would serve as the integrating idea. In explaining a transformer, the capacity to "convert" or "change" could be used as the basic idea of instruction.

Select and emphasize the main points

After a pattern has been established, you must highlight the major features so they stand apart from the details. Then, each main point can be seen in relation to its subordinate supporting material. This makes the pattern more meaningful. There are many ways to accomplish this purpose. Use all of them or those which seem most beneficial for the occasion.

Preview the major points

The communicator can begin by presenting the main points of instruction, orally or visually. "The basic movements involved in manipulating a television camera in studio production are (1) dollying, (2) panning, (3) tilting, and (4) trucking. I shall begin by discussing dollying."

Repeat the central theme

The central idea may be highlighted by repeating it as each new point is brought up. This helps to focus the listener's mind on the main point of the talk, and serves to emphasize the relationship of each new point to the central idea. For example:

I. Industry can serve the community (central idea)
    A. *Industry can serve the community* by asking its employees to enter into civic betterment projects.
        1. PTA
        2. Scouting
        3. United chest drives
    B. *Industry can serve the community* by maintaining a clean, attractive plant that enhances the appearance of the city.
        1. Attractive as well as functional architecture in the buildings

  2. Well-kept grounds and landscaping at the plant
  3. Smoke control and general neatness in grounds and buildings

Summarize frequently

The summary is a good device for keeping the main ideas separate and distinct. The listener must know when the communicator is through discussing one step and is passing on to explain the next. The summary acts as a boundary line between main ideas, serves to highlight and round them off, and keeps the subordinate material which supports and explains *main idea number* 1 separate from *main idea number* 2. For example:

I.
  A. Lubricating the G-2 Motor
    1. Cleaning air filter
    2. Draining and replacing crankcase oil
    3. Oiling movable parts

  (Summary: If you will remember that the lubrication procedures for the G-2 Motor involve three steps: cleaning the air filter, draining and replacing crankcase oil, and oiling all movable parts, we can finish with lubrication and can pass on to the next step in the care and maintenance of the G-2 Motor.)

Highlight the main points with questions

A significant idea can be emphasized if the speaker will stop and ask for questions about it from the audience. The questions will serve to concentrate attention on the point and get the audience to think more thoroughly about it. Sometimes these questions are rhetorical; that is, the speaker asks them only to emphasize the obvious answer.

Use evaluating statements

A speaker may state that a factor is important if he supports this assertion with reasons. This simple method is often overlooked by instructors, who take it for granted that the listeners will realize the essentiality of a point without being told. Example: "If you gain nothing else from this discussion concerning common minerals, I would like you to remember this one vital statement: More salt is used in manufacture of chemicals than any other material and the average American uses about six pounds a year to season his food."

Example: "If I stress editorializing at the local community level it is because this is where broadcasters are finding the greatest need and it is here they are building the great new tradition."[5]

Vary the delivery

The communicator can make the important ideas prominent by his delivery. By talking more slowly, by pausing before and after key words, by increasing the volume on important sentences, by repeating significant thoughts, and by reinforcing his vocal line with gestures, the speaker can make important words and sentences stand out for the listener.

Classify the material

Man is constantly bombarded by stimuli. Sights, smells, and noises are flashed to his brain. He would be unable to synthesize a picture of the world outside his body unless he could separate these various messages into different classes of objects, happenings, and concepts. A system of classification is essential for any kind of progress. "Biological science made little progress until it was realized that animals must be grouped according to their fundamental similarities in structure and then arranged into a workable system of *classification*."[6]

The next step after classification is to use terms or class names to stand for categories. For example, a communication about how

[5] Newton N. Minow, Chairman, Federal Communications Commission, address before the National Association of Broadcasters, Public Affairs Editorializing Conference, Shoreham Hotel, Washington, D.C., Mar. 1, 1962.

[6] Ralph Buchsbaum, *Animals without Backbones,* The University of Chicago Press, Chicago, Copyright 1948 by the University of Chicago, p. 32.

to operate a machine might be classified into three categories: (1) controls, (2) fueling, and (3) maintenance. These main categories may be broken down into further classifications.

1. Controls
a. Starting
b. Quality control
c. Speed control
d. Stopping
2. Fueling
a. Gas
b. Oil
c. Water
3. Maintenance
a. Lubrication
b. Cleaning
c. Parts replacement

When the various aspects of running the machine are divided into categories, each aspect can be taken up and explained in detail; then related to the operation as a whole.

Talks of instruction and indoctrination are often difficult to make; but, by using the principle of classification, the process of passing on information becomes easier. Look at the subject from the standpoint of dividing it up into functions, phases, purposes, locations, or methods. Give names or labels to these parts. Explain the makeup of each category. Show how all these categories relate to each other, and how each takes its place in the context of the whole.

Appeal to many senses

The ability of the human being to receive sensations from more than one source is called "multiple sensory perception." A person may gain knowledge about an object by looking at it, listening to it, touching it, smelling it, and tasting it. Since the human being receives his messages by means of his senses, the speaker should use as many of these avenues to the brain as possible when sending his messages. The more related sensations that are available for reception by the listener's nervous system, the more avenues to understanding are opened to the listener. The communicator can supplement his spoken words with working models, mock-ups, motion pictures, slide projectors, and other audio-visual devices that are available to him. (For suggestions concerning the use of such materials, see Chapter 6.)

Assignments and exercises

1. Assume the role of personnel manager. Prepare a speech of indoctrination to a group of new employees. Discuss some of the following topics: insurance benefits, wages, hours, and vacation policies. Illustrate the principles of motivation and integration in your organizing process.

2. Prepare a talk in which you explain how to operate a machine. Emphasize the principle of classification.

3. Pretend that you are a supervisor explaining a job responsibility to a new man. Use a job that you have held and with which you are familiar. Employ the principles of differentiation and multiple sensory perception to assist you in preparing this talk.

4. Explain the operation of the student governing body (student senate, student council, etc.). Highlight the main points with rhetorical questions that you believe might be uppermost in the listeners' minds.

5. Select three new developments in your field of technical specialization. Discover a basic key to understanding for explaining each. Select one of the three to explain to the group.

11

CONTROL BOARD FOR INFLUENCE

Persuasion and selling

A case in point **A big step outside the lab**

When Ben Wiley joined Conveyer Belt, Incorporated, he thought his job would be strictly technical. For a few months he worked in the various departments of the plant learning the manufacturing methods, the quality-control procedures, studying problems of design from blueprints to models to actual fabrication. Then his superior called him in with a shocking proposal. "How about joining the sales staff for awhile, Ben? We believe that one of the engineering personnel ought to accompany our salesmen. Technical problems come up that they are not always able to cope with. As a matter of fact, how would you like to go out and do a selling job for us? You know the product well. You know, or can learn, the applications for which the machinery is designed. You ought to be able to persuade some of our customers that CB is the best brand for all their needs."

Now, Ben has become a salesman! He knows exactly how the "flighting" of his conveyer is formed. He has metallurgical knowledge about the stresses and flexibility of his conveyer. He knows how the troughs are fabricated, and even how the various kinds of driving apparatus, couplers, bearings, or shafting should be installed. But selling! That's another story. Or is it?

As Bernard Lester puts it: "Engineering skill has been associated largely with design and production. Planning a design and then completing its fabrication or construction are steps that have human appeal. The results are clear to the eye, and the accomplishment has drama. Yet the whole procedure of production depends upon orders from customers or a waiting market. Unless the fruits of design and production are put to work—*are sold*—our whole economy is baseless. Orders must be created. Though you cannot see an order being made, the process is nonetheless real. Nor is it less subject to careful systematic planning and execution."[1]

The engineer who goes into the selling field uses his technical skill. But he must combine it with a knowledge of economics and the principles of persuasion and salesmanship. "His work combines the skill of an engineer and that of a business man. Beyond this come an understanding of people and their reactions, and an ability to demonstrate, persuade, and convince."[2]

It is assumed that the technical person has gained, or will learn, the skills necessary for the successful performance of his job. Knowledge of the business economy, contracts, written correspondence, etc. are important for the technician-salesman. They are beyond the scope of this book. We will, however, explore the field of persuasion and the rapport with others which plays, perhaps, the most important role in salesmanship.

Persuasion defined

Persuasion may be defined as the art of influencing others to believe or act as desired by the speaker. From the time of Aristotle to the present day, book after book has been written dealing with the techniques necessary to make others "believe or act" as you may desire them to believe or act.

The persuader's personality

From an ethical standpoint, the person who wishes to influence actions and beliefs should have faith in his own views and ideas. Part of persuasion is the firm conviction that what you have to sell is worth buying. However, strong convictions alone do not always persuade. Sometimes the personality of the speaker is inextricably bound up with the selling or persuading process.

[1] Reprinted with permission from Bernard Lester, *Sales Engineering*, John Wiley & Sons, Inc., New York, 1950, p. 3.

[2] *Ibid.*, p. 4.

Be a gentleman

The day of the hard sell has passed. The flashily dressed salesman who tricked his way into the purchaser's office, blustered or out-talked his victim into buying something for which he had no use, and had a fund of dirty stories and bribes as a major selling device, is gone. The modern-day sales representative is expected to follow George Washington's advice: "A gentleman does not dress or talk loudly. He does not flatly contradict the person with whom he is conversing. He does not present his opinions as being better than the opinions of another. He does not argue. He does not push in where he is not wanted."

Max Stansbury, writing in *Supervisory Management*, describes a good way to fail: "In voicing your opinions you must be very decided and positive in your views. You are required to take it as a personal affront if anyone suggests views contrary to yours. In that case, you can disagree, good and loud, perhaps making a few reflections on the other man's intelligence or motives. This is a particularly handy approach to use on people you have just met. Right away they can mark you down as a man they want nothing further to do with, and you are therefore well along on the Corduroy road to failure, unencumbered by any new friends."[3]

Be positive and self-confident

A gentlemanly attitude is desirable, but the persuader or salesman must have a confident and forward-looking viewpoint. He should be honestly optimistic about his product and ideas and how they can benefit the people he is trying to persuade. "Confidence is the foundation of successful selling," says J. C. Aspley.[4] Dress, appearance, posture, mien should all echo an atmosphere of courage, bold-ness, and daring. After all, you have a real desire to serve. The prospect or the listener wants to benefit from your counsel. This does not mean that you should cultivate an air of superiority. It

[3] Max Stansbury, "The Man Most Likely . . . ," *Supervisory Management,* and the American Management Association, vol. 2, no. 2, January, 1957.

[4] J. C. Aspley, *A Short Course in Salesmanship,* Dartnell Corporation, Chicago, 1961, p. 17.

does mean that with your friendly, helpful attitude goes an air of ability—and a straightforward manner of thinking and talking.

The use of logic

Some groups or individuals may be persuaded by logical thinking alone. The following types of logic may be used to prove the quality of the plan or the product and thereby clinch the sale.

1. *Inductive reasoning.* When we proceed from a series of instances or pieces of evidence to a conclusion or generalization, the process is called *inductive* reasoning or argument. Although you may never be able to examine all of the instances that may occur, a sufficient number may be drawn upon to indicate that the conclusion you draw is valid for its circumstances. Thus, if you are selling a type of rock bit for drilling oil wells, you can point out that this rock bit has been used successfully in all parts of the world. If you have enough instances showing the practical use of the bit to represent an acceptable sampling, then the customer will determine by induction that the rock bit should be usable for his drilling problems.

2. *Deductive reasoning.* When we proceed from the general rule to a particular case, we are developing the type of argument called *deductive* reasoning. The pattern of the sylogism has been used for centuries for deductive argument. In this method, you usually state a broad and general rule, a generalization applicable to particular cases (major premise). Then a statement is made to bring the particular case being investigated into the scope of the general rule (minor premise). A conclusion is then made which contains an inference made from the premise. For example, you might say:

Major premise: "It has been proved that industrial plants operating in climate areas where the temperature reaches 90° for seventy days a year, need air conditioning for optimum efficiency and productivity on the part of the employees.

Minor premise: "A check of the United States government weather map shows that your industrial plant is located in such a climate area.

Conclusion: "You need to air-condition your plant."

3. *Analogy.* When you make the assertion "because two things or circumstances are known to resemble each other in certain observed respects they will also resemble each other in other unobserved respects," you are reasoning by *analogy.* The reasoning may move from specific item to specific item or from general concept to general concept. Naturally, the validity of the conclusion will depend on whether or not the resemblances outweigh the differences.

One of the favorite aeronautical jokes tells about the engineers who examined the bumblebee. By analogy with their observances about wingspread, weight, lifting power, etc., they concluded that the bumblebee could not fly. But the bee, not knowing anything about aeronautical engineering, kept flying just the same. In this farfetched case, the differences in the comparison must be presumed to have been far greater than the resemblances. However, an oft-quoted statement indicates that "Man is primarily analogical rather than logical!" The parables of Jesus, basically analogies, have had tremendous persuasive force for nearly two thousand years. An example of the use of analogy follows: (*a*) Our Model-B taxicab, especially designed for long-distance carrying, has been operating efficiently and profitably in Los Angeles, a city which is spread out over a large area; (*b*) You are about to operate a cab franchise in Houston, Texas, a city which is also spread out over a large area; (*c*) Therefore, you need our Model-B taxicab.

4. *Causal reasoning.* Suppose that you are proposing a particular course of action to a prospect. You might reason from cause to effect, from effect to cause, or from effect to effect, depending upon the order in which arguments are presented. If the first event is invariably antecedent to the second, and is indispensable to that result, we can make a good case for causal relationships.

A persuader, or salesman, can maintain, "These planes have

not had any serious accidents since we installed this new safety device." This implies that a long history of safety was *caused* by the installation of the device (effect-to-cause reasoning). He could add, "Since we have had this long safety record, revenues of this airline have substantially increased" (effect-to-effect reasoning). A stronger case for asserting a causal relationship could be suggested if the persuader could say, "Before B Corporation installed our Model X Safety Guards on their equipment they had an accident rate of 11 per cent. After twelve months of using our Safety Guards, the accident rate has dropped to 5 per cent" (cause-to-effect reasoning).

The use of evidence

You use evidence to convince an audience that your ideas are sound. Usually, evidence is divided into two major areas: evidence of fact; and evidence of opinion.

Facts. Factual information is information that can be verified by a reliable source or process. Information found in trustworthy encyclopedias, technical journals, almanacs, and textbooks is considered factual. It is important, however, that the speaker evaluate and tabulate the source of his factual information. Results of scientific experiments which have been approved by experts in the field may also be considered as factual. The persuader should consider recency when selecting his facts. In technical areas time marches on rapidly and data may become outdated as new discoveries are made. Be sure to get the latest information.

Opinion. Beliefs, opinions, or statements of judgment are impressive evidence if they have been expressed by a great number of laymen or a recognized expert. Sometimes the opinions of a few selected experts have more persuasive value than those of many unselected laymen. This is especially true in technical matters. When you use authoritative opinion as evidence, be certain that the authorities or experts pass the tests of competence, lack of prejudice, and of consistency. For example, a mining company, in presenting an argument showing the purity of its quality of sand, lists a supporting statement from an impartial chemical firm of great repute in the specialized field.

The use of psychologic

Man seems to be set in motion by biological and biosocial forces. Biological drives include hunger, thirst, fatigue, visceral tensions, various reactions to pain, cold, heat, and the desire for self-preservation. The greatest drive is that of self-preservation, although the others will prompt action. The strong sex drive, which may be part of the drive for preservation of the race, is known to be highly compulsive during the fertile years. Any appeal which will satisfy these drives will have persuasive power.

A second driving force is more biosocial. Such *motives,* as we will call them, are based upon our relationship with our social environment as well as our physical environment. These motives have been learned by each individual in relationship to his own society. It does not matter that these motives are forced upon us by others, or have been adopted in our efforts to conform to the mores or laws of the group. They form powerful influences in modifying our behavior. Leo Reisman's *The Lonely Crowd* and *The Organization Man* by William H. Whyte, Jr., point out the desire for conformity on the part of the citizens in the United States and the power of the motives for conformity in guiding behavior. A persuader or salesman uses his knowledge of such motives in order to influence others to believe or act as he desires. He frequently is so subtle in method that the listener (purchaser) does not realize that his motives are being exploited. A list of motives that impel Americans has been analyzed by many psychologists and experts in marketing. Maslow has divided them into groups: (1) need for safety; (2) need for belongingness and love; (3) need for importance, respect, self-esteem, independence; (4) need for information; (5) need for understanding; (6) need for beauty; (7) need for self-actualization.[5]

Milton Dickens offers a basic list of motives common to our society: to make money, to be healthy, to avoid danger, to be attractive to the other sex, to get married, to beget and rear children, to care for one's parents, to have friends and companions, to enjoy physical comforts, to gain social approval, to conform to

[5] A. H. Maslow, "Higher Needs and Personality," *Dialectica,* vol. 5, pp. 257–264, 1951.

customs and traditions, to have personal freedom, to maintain self-respect, to have a clear conscience and peace of mind, to satisfy curiosity, to have adventures, to compete successfully against other people, to help other people, to have a worthwhile religion, to achieve ideals, to achieve financial security.[6]

Barriers to persuasiveness

Obstructions are sometimes raised between the salesman and his prospect because of the experiences of the prospect with unscrupulous, self-seeking individuals. J. C. Mangan, authority on salesmanship, lists these barriers and ways in which they may be dissolved.

Suspicion. Most people suspect that you have an ulterior purpose, that your motives are shady and untrustworthy. As long as this suspicion remains in their minds, your progress at persuading can't advance a single inch. Dissolve suspicion by laying all your cards on the table; by showing all the facts; by honestly admitting your selfish advantage; by showing the unfavorable side of the thing and answering the objections before they are raised by the other man.

Inertia. The universal sin of all mankind is laziness. People simply will not move, will not budge, even to do themselves a favor. They make up their minds but their bodies refuse to function in order to furnish the final action. So they stay put. They stick to habit. Dissolve inertia *with your own spirit.* Spirit is contagious, spirit is full of life force, spirit can instantly turn a weak vegetable into a dynamic human being. Turn on the spirit. Vibrate! Become intense!

Fear. You're afraid, I'm afraid, everybody's afraid. The two principal fears are the fear of being killed and the fear of being ridiculed. The life-preservation instinct causes people to hold on to their money when they might otherwise invest it in you, your cause, or your product. The instinct to avoid the scars of ridicule prevents them from accepting your request to participate in public events, to appear in the spotlight, to take the initiative. Dissolve fear by showing a little consideration. You can't reason anybody

[6] Milton Dickens, *Speech: Dynamic Communication,* Harcourt, Brace & World, Inc., New York, 1954, pp. 52–53.

out of fear, but you can show them sympathy and thus make the fear a little less important.

Pride. How many of your associates and acquaintances are too hard to handle? Are they too proud, too stubborn to buy from you, to receive a well-meant suggestion, to join with you in your objective? These are the people who "can't be sold anything." Dissolve pride by glorifying it. Build up that proud, stubborn individual! Go to extra length to show your respect and honor. He may then consent to be persuaded!

Incompetency. Some people are apparently not worth persuading because they haven't the money to buy, even if they wanted to. They haven't the force, the standing, or the authority to contribute tangible help to you. Seems like you oughtn't fool with them at all! Dissolve incompetency by giving it *importance.* If the man hasn't the money, sell him anyhow. If he's sold well enough, he may raise the money among his relatives or friends. If he hasn't any standing or authority, treat him with the utmost attention and respect. Act toward him as if he were a man of great importance. The good will you create in him may be quickly forwarded to the person who really has the authority.

Jealousy. Few people who started on the same basis as others can bear to see themselves outdistanced by those others. In persuasion you may have to play one person against the others, for envy and jealousy have a driving force of millions of horsepower. Everybody secretly wants to "keep up with the Joneses." (A firm may be more easily persuaded to buy new equipment if it is informed that its competitor has purchased up-to-date machinery.)[7]

Formula for salesmanship

Many volumes have been written on the art of salesmanship. They seem to parallel the rules set down for all successful communication. The first step is to obtain the prospect's attention. Is anybody listening? If you achieve attention, you may go on to the second step of arousing desire for your commodity, services, or ideas. Then comes the final step of closing the sale and securing the agreement to purchase and make the necessary payments.

[7] James Mangan, *The Knack of Selling Yourself,* reprinted with the permission of the publishers, The Dartnell Corporation, Chicago, 1951, pp. 52–53.

The sales interview

The "pre-approach." Before a sale can be made, a salesman must obtain an interview. The "pre-approach" is very important. When an appointment is secured by letter, telephone, telegram, or other means, the salesman will want to know how many people are to hear his presentation, what sort of room will be used, what visual aids will be supplied or needed, and the exact time he should appear in order to arrange his equipment or samples. He will have to ascertain the ability of his prospects to make decisions about the purchase of his product or services. He will want to know as much as possible about the amount of technical knowledge his audience possesses.

The approach. The next part of the interview is usually called the approach. The seller introduces himself and his colleagues or assistants, if he has any. He tries to create a favorable impression. Then he goes through the steps of securing attention, creating interest, conviction, and desire. It is imperative to have a time scheme. If the buying audience is educated to the need for the idea or product, the salesman can save time by using the *direct* approach. He goes straight to the heart of the matter, explaining benefits and the necessity for immediate action. If the customer is unaware of the product or idea, the persuader may use the *educational* approach. That is, the salesman takes some time at the beginning to educate the customer concerning the need for the product and the history, background, use, and development of the product.

The heart of the talk (sales interview). H. A. Overstreet is quoted as saying, "Selling, to be a great art, must involve a genuine interest in the other person's need."[8] You must talk in terms of your prospect's interests. You must answer his silent (or sometimes vocal) question: "What will it do for me?" The crux of the sales talk lies in relating the logic, evidence, and psychological motivations directly to the customer's real needs.

The close. The salesman must learn to sense the rhythm of the sales interview. He should be sensitively aware of the customer's reactions so that he will not talk past the psychological moment when the buyer has already made up his mind to go along with

---

[8] H. A. Overstreet as quoted in Percy H. Whiting, *The Five Great Rules of Selling*, McGraw-Hill Book Company, Inc., New York, 1957, p. 69.

the salesman. We have heard the oft-quoted story about Mark Twain, who is said to have been listening to a powerful, persuasive preacher. The topic was the need for funds to help missionary work in darkest Africa. Twain was supposed to have been so convinced that he determined to give all the money he had in his pocket to the cause. But the preacher kept on talking and Mark decided that a few dollars would serve the purpose and his conscience just as well. The preacher kept on talking and the famous humorist is supposed to have declared: "Finally, when they did pass the plate, I swiped ten cents out of it." The speaker in this case had obviously not developed a sensitivity to the psychological moment when his prospects were ready to give the maximum response to his appeal.

A well-prepared presentation will contain the seeds of a carefully prepared conclusion which may be a summary or even a dramatized example or analogy. Then the persuader asks for the definite approval of his sales talk. Since he is feeling the pulse of his prospect at all times, he might try for approval at various times during the presentation. This is known as the "trial close." If the purchaser is willing to buy, it is unnecessary to continue talking after the sale is made. The salesman should finish his presentation courteously and efficiently, leaving the door open for future interviews and presentations.

The sales engineer

In recent years this comparatively new profession has become important on the industrial scene. "For the man qualified both technically and saleswise, perhaps no profession offers more challenging activity. The application of sales aptitude to technical problems, and the complementary application of technical aptitude to sales problems, call for the best of both kinds of aptitudes."[9]

The sales and engineering representative, or the sales engineer, acts as liaison man in the development, manufacture, or application of products. He and his firm usually act as a contracting agent on behalf of one or several producing groups. He may deal with purchasing people, or directly with company engineers, or with combinations of business and technical personnel. The sales engi-

[9] Lee O. Thayer and George E. Harris, *Sales and Engineering Representation*, McGraw-Hill Book Company, Inc., New York, 1958, p. 16.

neer tries to solve technical problems by persuading his listeners to adapt his ideas on efficiency and economy. Instead of buying weight, size, close tolerance, automatic lubrication, and cast aluminum, the purchaser buys economical performance under all conditions of work, and the various supporting services the supplier can render. The sales engineer needs both technical knowledge and verbal skill to present his ideas clearly, persuasively, and effectively so that the purchaser will not only understand and be convinced, but will also be stimulated to action. Close liaison between technical skill and economic productive skill by means of competent communication will determine the extent to which our national resources are invested in space-age hardware and invincible armed preparedness.

Assignments and exercises

1. Choose an article or product to sell. Sell it to the members of your class, using the material of this chapter as an outline for a sales talk.

2. Establish a need for a product or service that you as a sales engineer might be called upon to present to a group of purchasers and technical men. Write up your method of obtaining an interview; outline the visual material you might need for your presentation. Indicate questions you might be asked and how you will answer them. Prepare a closing. Present this to the class for their criticisms and suggestions.

3. Present an idea for a change in university rules and regulations before the student council. Think about your audience. Consider the kinds of logic and evidence that will influence them to accept your proposal. Remember the appeal of the psychologic. Relate your proposal to human motives discussed in this chapter.

4. Select a controversial issue in national or international politics about which you have strong convictions. Use some of the methods discussed in this chapter to persuade the audience to accept your point of view.

5. Choose a persuasive article or speech or an editorial from a recent magazine or newspaper. Indicate the evidence used and/or the appeals to the basic motives listed in this chapter.

12 GAVEL AND GABBLE
Conducting a meeting

A case in point **"Madame Chairman! Madame Chairman!"**

The annual meeting of the State Industrial Nurse's Association is scheduled for February 7, 8, 9, at the largest and newest hotel in Capital City. Mary Eberhart, a competent young lady in charge of the clinic and medical facilities at Superior Industries, finds that she is becoming distracted and worried as the time approaches for the convention. For the first time in her busy young life she is faced with the prospect of standing before a group of her peers and *making a talk*. In fact, she is chairman of one of the sections of the annual meeting.

She has written to and obtained acceptance from the national executive secretary of the organization, who has agreed to be one of the participants on her program. Another of the panelists will be the director of industrial relations and personnel of her own firm. A doctor from Capital City, who is renowned as a humorist as well as an expert on industrial medicine, will be a third member of the group. The topic has been chosen, the format made up, the time limits set. Why is Mary so upset that she finds butterflies whisking their wings in her midsection a whole month before the scheduled time?

Mary wants to make a favorable impression at the meeting. If she handles her section well, she may be in line to be nominated for the presidency of the state association. As chairman of the meeting, she'll have to make introductions and handle questions from the floor—and she has never done these things before. She has seen programs wrecked by incompetent chairmen. Why did she ever allow herself to be talked into this horrible ordeal? And yet—there's the possibility of doing a good job and getting that nomination. That would mean added prestige for herself and her company.

Technically trained people and their colleagues in the business world are called upon to take part in meetings of all sorts. Organized groups hold conventions. These conventions are attended by members of a profession or an industry and associated auxiliary groups. When an individual rises to some prominence in his field, he is frequently more than just an onlooker at these conventions or professional meetings. He may be asked to introduce a speaker; he may be in charge of a meeting; he may act as master of ceremonies at a banquet; he may become president of the group. These speaking situations need skillful preparation to be successful.

Introducing the speaker

A good speaker may be handicapped by a poorly presented, cliché-burdened introduction. The following suggestions will help you prepare an introduction that will concentrate attention on the speaker and his subject.

Be brief. Two minutes should be the maximum time allowed for any introduction. If you can give the salient information in less time, so much the better.

Pave the way. Before the speaker begins, be sure to have all the physical apparatus arranged, the microphone turned on to the proper volume, the speaker's stand cleared, illumination provided for easy reading, visual-aid equipment tested, chairs turned toward the speaker and the seats in front occupied. The audience should be polarized for the speaker's first words.

Omit clichés. Avoid the overworked phrases such as: "It's an honor and privilege to present .."; "A man who needs no introduction . . ."; and "It gives me great pleasure. . . ."

Don't flatter. Don't be fulsome in your praise. Don't list so many honors and offices that the introduction sounds like a eulogy and forces the speaker to apologize for his introductory "obituary."

Don't direct audience response. Don't editorialize about the speaker or his talk with remarks such as: "He's a very humorous speaker, and you'll split your sides listening to him"; "He has a wonderful message for you . . . one I'm certain you will appreciate . . ."

Don't flub the name. Be sure to pronounce the speaker's name in the manner *he* prefers. Some introducers prefer to announce the speaker's name twice. If the name is difficult to catch, spell it out.

Don't mumble the title. Announce the title of the speech distinctly and enthusiastically. (Be sure to ascertain the title before you start preparing your introduction.)

Do individualize. Try to incorporate one interesting short anecdote concerning the speaker, a bit of information which makes the speaker unique.

Adjust to the audience, speaker, occasion. Emphasize why this particular speaker is presenting this particular subject before this particular audience on this particular occasion.

Be a springboard. Finish the introduction by emphasizing the speaker's name and/or the title of his speech. This can be accomplished without the usual clichés if you use more volume, vocal emphasis, a different pitch, or a significant pause before the final pronouncement. Then, anticipatory applause may burst forth from the audience, and the speaker can begin with his audience at a high level of interest.

Conducting a meeting

Technically trained individuals must sometimes organize and conduct an important meeting. It may be a meeting of a section of a professional organization, an interdepartmental group meeting, or a social or religious group meeting. The planning of the meeting and the dispatch with which it is run are the responsibilities of the person who is in charge.

The meeting place

The person in charge may delegate the task of making arrangements for the meeting place, but he is responsible to the group for the desirability of the room in which the session is being held. He should consider the following points:

1. *Appearance.* Your meeting room should be as attractive as your budget and labors can make it. It should be cleaned and arranged for your purposes by the time of your meeting. The chairs should be faced at the proper angles for listening or participating. Any impedimenta left over from previous meetings should be removed or disguised.

2. *Size, heating, ventilation, furniture, noise level.* Schedule your meeting in a room that will seat all participants comfortably. Do not hold a small meeting in one corner of a large room. Try to make the room look well filled. Be sure that the temperature is close to an optimum 70 degrees and keep it that way. Remember that a rise in temperature accompanies bodies in close proximity. Smoking raises problems of ventilation, and some people crave those cigarettes and cigars. You may have to call a recess in order to clear the air. Folding chairs are an occupational hazard with which you'll have to cope. If you must use the uncomfortable "funeral-parlor" type chair, call for a stretch now and then.

It is difficult to compete against noisy traffic sounds, cleaning machines, or a next-door meeting separated from you by a thin partition. Do something about the racket or expect failure. If the meeting is worth holding, it deserves maximum quiet. Be sure to turn off any music that may have been piped in by the ever-helpful management. Naturally, you will insist that your own members are respectfully quiet. Try to keep traffic at a minimum. Sometimes it is wiser to close the doors of your room and post an usher outside to seat late comers and to warn them to enter quietly.

3. *Stage setting.* Frequently an audience is polarized by a central focal point. The speaker's platform may be raised, and all the chairs turned to face it. At a banquet meeting, flowers and decorations may be used to make this area attractive. Don't allow these decorations to hinder the important business to follow. How often have you seen a small speaker trying to make his face seen over an imposing bouquet! Banners and displays may be used to advantage behind the speakers. But beware! Don't arrange a background featuring printed material which demands attentive reading just when you want attention focussed on important words from your speakers. A single, large, spotlighted symbol may be more effective than myriads of slogans, statistics, and charts. If displays and visual materials are to be used later in the meeting, try to keep them under cover until they are needed. Arrange the lighting so that the speaker is in the most importantly illuminated portion of the room. Arrange for his stand to have sufficient light so that he can read his notes.

4. *Service.* Have an engineer available in case the microphones, lighting, ventilation, etc., need adjusting. Know how to obtain janitorial services rapidly. Additional furniture, water, or glasses may be needed, objects may have to be moved, ash trays may need emptying.

If the meeting includes a meal, have the waiters serve it before you start to conduct business, during a break, or after the meeting is over. They may delay clearing away until after the group has adjourned. It is embarrassing to everyone if the manager orders his waiters to clear the tables while the meeting is still in progress. A procession of coffee servers and the smell of freshly brewed coffee hardly add to the attentiveness of the audience. Dessert and coffee should be served after the meeting or during a break. Be sure that you arrange the timing with the waiters.

The master of ceremonies

As master of ceremonies you are the host of the group, stimulating everyone to have a good time and to be at his best, making all concerned feel relaxed, friendly, and certain that the meeting is most worthwhile. Philosophers such as John Dewey and writers such as Dale Carnegie agree that the greatest satisfaction to all men and women is the opportunity to feel important. The MC should give this opportunity to as many of the group as he possibly can. Praise the speakers, the activators of various parts of the program, and members of the audience. As MC give full attention to the proceedings. Show the speakers that you are interested and concerned with what they are saying. It is only the poorly prepared MC who holds whispered conferences concerning the remainder of the program while a speaker is exhorting the audience.

Plan of procedure. The first step toward a successful meeting is a plan of procedure. Although an effective master of ceremonies must be highly flexible, he must have a carefully thought-out plan. This outline will cover every event of the meeting from the entrance of the spectators and participants to the publication of the proceedings. Make this outline in two columns so that you can list events on one side and the names of those responsible for carrying out the details on the other. A sample outline is shown on page 178.

Planning conferences with your chief aids should be begun early. Keep accurate accounts of these meetings and send reminders to those who have promised to fulfill certain duties. Use as many people as possible to help you hande the meeting, but be prepared to take over if someone shirks his duty. Who is to provide the decorations? When will they arrive? Who has charge of the menu? Have they provided for fish if the meeting is to be held on a Friday? When will the head-table occupants arrive? Who will provide place cards? Careful preparation will avoid *some* of those embarrassing slipups.

Timing the events. The success of the meeting may depend upon its timing. Make out a careful time schedule and keep it before you as the meeting runs on. If necessary, appoint a timekeeper. Some masters of ceremonies have a time clock that rings when it is time for the next event. The meeting should start on time and end when the members of the group expect it to end. All events should be carried to completion without confusion so that embarrassment is avoided. Let your participants know *in advance* that you intend to adhere to your time schedule. Warn long-winded speakers, introducers, or "makers of remarks." If they recognize that you are determined to stay within limits, they will respect your firmness. Allow some leeway for laughter and applause as well as comings and goings. A good way to keep your speakers in line is to appoint a timekeeper who will give an unobtrusive warning when the speaker gets dangerously near his scheduled termination point. One

Time	Event	Person responsible
5:45	Head-table guests will assemble in room D.	*Dave Rinehart* will greet them at the door and steer them to room D. *Chris Stein* will welcome them in room D and give instructions about going in to the banquet and where they are to sit. (Remain standing during invocation.) Inform Rev. Leslie.
6:00	Call meeting to order. Signal for head-table guests to march in.	*Chairman* *Jim Primrose* to *Chris Stein* who will lead guests to table in the order planned.
6:02	Signal for all guests to rise.	*Chairman*
6:05	Introduce Rev. Leslie. Invocation.	*Chairman* *Rev. Leslie*
6:07	Have members take seats. Present Calvin Baker, past president.	*Chairman*
6:08	Introduce guests at head table who will not take active part in program.	*Calvin Baker*
6:13	Present Jim Lundstrum who will introduce Mayor Lawrence.	*Chairman*
6:14	Introduce Mayor.	*Jim Lundstrum*
6:16	Welcome to the group.	*Mayor Lawrence*
6:21	Signal waiters to enter with food.	*Hal Burroughs*
6:24	Dinner	
7:00	Etc.	

method is to have someone next to the rostrum place a card, with a one- or two-minute warning on it, onto the speaker's stand. Another method is to raise a warning card from a place directly in front of the speaker or from the back of the room so that only he is aware of the passage of time.

Seating arrangements. The major participants and persons of eminence are seated at the head table or on the platform at most meetings. The spouses of the participants may be included if there is sufficient space. If the meeting is conducted with some formality, a gracious and imposing beginning may be made by the procession of honored guests to the head table. The honored guests should form a line outside the meeting room and march forward at the appropriate time. They should be told where their particular seats are and whether they should sit at once or wait for a signal from the MC. Guests should also be advised on how to acknowledge their introductions. If you wish the audience to hold the applause until the entire group has been introduced tell them so in advance. Those who are to speak should be seated close to the speakers' lectern and microphone.

Sharing the limelight. The master of ceremonies is in charge of the meeting, but he does not have to introduce everyone, make all the announcements, or receive all the attention. Delegate certain of the details so that more of the group will have that valuable sense of participation. The usual procedure is to call the meeting to order with an invocation, a creed, a collect, a pledge of allegiance, or a song. The introduction of the important personages is next. The introductions should be short and free from overwhelming praise. Guests of the members may be introduced from the floor by their respective hosts. In all cases, the master of ceremonies should indicate whether applause is appropriate by leading it himself or announcing that applause will be withheld until a stated time. It is not necessary to introduce individuals who will be presented later on in the program.

Announcements should be made clearly and to an attentive audience. Learn to wait for absolute silence before you proceed to make any of your remarks. The audience will adopt the exact amount of decorum you demand from them. If there are several short talks and one major address, be sure that more time and emphasis is on the important introduction.

Beginning and closing on time. We have already discussed the methods of beginning a program. The main purpose is to focus attention on the activities that will follow. Begin on time! A group soon learns whether the MC will begin on schedule, or whether it is advisable to arrive a half hour late. They will take their cues from your habits. Sometimes it is wise to establish a certain starting signal that can develop into a tradition.

Close the meeting with a note of finality. Be prepared with words of thanks to the speaker, the final song or a stroke of the gavel, and the words: "This session of 19— is officially closed." Don't allow the meeting to fizzle to a close with a few unimportant announcements. Make every effort to finish your meeting on time so that members will not start sneaking out. When you close, "close all over."

Parliamentary procedure for the presiding officer

The presiding officer is the key to the success of any meeting. If he is not a capable parliamentarian, he should have someone on hand who is. Slide-rule-style mechanisms for parliamentary procedure are available. They will tell at a glance the precedence of motions, the usual rules of debate, whether or not the motion is amendable, the type of vote required, etc. One of these is called "Pan-L-View Slide Rule on Parliamentary Procedure." It may be obtained from Edward J. Ryan, 708 Church Street, Evanston, Illinois, at a moderate cost. The chart of motions, classified according to purpose and precedence in Appendix F, may suffice.

Why use parliamentary procedure?

Parliamentary procedure should be used when the membership of a group is relatively large and when the purpose of the group is action. The formal procedures are beneficial when there is diversity of opinion and when action, such as voting, is necessary to decide on what the group will do. Some form of Robert's *Rules of Order* is customary when no other rules are laid down.

Majority versus minority. The code of rules known as parliamentary procedure provides for rule of the majority while protecting the rights of the minority. It is assumed that the will of the majority (even by one vote) should prevail until the group has changed its sentiment. *Efficiency* demands discussion of only one matter at a time. Rules are constructed to provide *fair play* in reaching decisions. While the articulate members may govern the minds and emotions of the hearers, each member has an equal right to be heard, equal *time* is allowed for discussing all sides of a question. The rules may be learned easily by anyone. Since they provide for fair decisions there is more chance for wholehearted approval of actions taken by the group. However, a vociferous minority should not use knowledge of the rules to hinder or block the action of the group.

The order of business

The usual order of business is listed below:

1. *The call to order.* The meeting should begin at the designated time. Usually a quorum is necessary in order to conduct business. The quorum should be defined in the rules of the organization. By common practice it is presumed to be a majority (one more than half) of the members of the group. Some groups may stipulate a lesser percentage. When the chairman calls the meeting to order, he should ascertain the presence of a quorum by count or roll call. The meeting continues promptly to the second phase, after attention is polarized, by: "A quorum being present, we will proceed to the order of business."

2. *The reading and approval of the minutes.* The secretary's minutes are a complete account of the previous meeting. After they are read and approved, they constitute a permanent record of the procedures of the group. Thus, after the chairman's announcement: "The secretary will please read the minutes," the group should listen intently to this important document. To save time, the minutes may be duplicated and passed out before the meeting begins.

The secretary's report begins with the time, date, and place of the meeting. The number present is usually indicated. The secretary should record carefully every motion, with its initiator and seconder, and the disposition of the motion. All other business, discussion, and action are listed verbatim or in summary form. The secretary's minutes should be free from personal bias or irrelevancies. The minutes should be typed or written legibly so that they can be referred to in the future. Provision should be made for binding and filing the minutes.

After the reading of the minutes, the president should ask: "Are there any corrections or additions to the minutes?" If there are no objections, any suggestions may be added by the secretary. If there are objections, the proposed changes must be stated and dealt with as motions (discussed later on in this chapter). Usually, no changes are suggested. In that case, the presiding officer states: "If there are no objections, the minutes stand approved as read."

3. *Committee reports.*   Reports from outstanding committees are appropriate right after the reading of the minutes. Regular committees such as the treasurer's committee or the membership committee have priority. Reports of special committees follow. If no action is required by the group, the chairman may say: "If there is no objection, the committee report will be filed as made." Thus the group accepts the report without acting on any of the ideas listed. If action is required, the committee chairman may make his recommendation in the form of a motion.

4. *Unfinished business.*   Any business from the previous meeting, deferred due to lack of time or information, is now on the agenda.

5. *New business.*   New business may be proposed by the chairman or by any member of the group. The president usually has new business on his agenda. It will save time and energy if the chairman is notified in advance. If a motion is typed out and presented to the chairman, he can pass it to the secretary for inclusion in the minutes. The chairman may announce, "We are now ready for new business. Mr. Jones has a motion he wishes to bring to your attention."

6. *Announcements.*   When all business has been concluded, the president calls for announcements. It is expedient to have them read by the president. Announcements should be presented in legible form to the presiding officer before the meeting. The president can read these along with the others he considers necessary.

7. *Adjournment.* Unless the organization has a rule indicating the time for adjournment, the meeting progresses until the business has been completed. If a member moves to adjourn the meeting, the chairman puts the motion to a vote. If it carries, he declares the meeting adjourned. If no motion is forthcoming, the chairman may suggest: "We are ready to entertain a motion for adjournment."

How to conduct an election

Usually the rules of a group state the method of nominating and electing officers. One method is by use of a nominating committee. Sometimes this committee is chosen by the presiding officer or an executive group. Sometimes the committee is elected by the members of the group. The advantages of using the committee method are: (1) deliberations concerning canidates' qualifications can be held in secrecy; (2) the availability of candidates can be ascertained in advance; (3) the committee can consider whether or not the candidates will be a representative group and will work together harmoniously. Usually the nominating committee is selected at one meeting and makes its report at the next session. The presiding officer, usually under the heading of new business, may call for a report in the following manner: "It is now time to proceed with the nomination and election of officers for the coming year. The chairman of the nominating committee is ready with his report."

The chairman of the committee presents the slate of officers. Nominations do not require seconding. The chairman then announces: "The nominating committee has nominated Henry Thomson for president. Are there any other nominations from the floor?" If there are no other nominations from the floor, the presiding officer calls for the vote and the nominee is declared elected. He then proceeds through the slate of officers in the same manner. If other nominations are offered from the floor, they are recorded by the secretary. After a reasonable time, the vote is taken. (If a motion is made to close nominations, a two-thirds majority is necessary to carry the motion.)

The vote may be by show of hands or by secret ballot. In a secret ballot the candidates are not deprived of their vote, and members are not embarrassed by making known their predilections publicly. Usually a majority is required for election, but some organizations may require only a plurality (the greatest number of votes when three or more candidates are in the running).

If the group does not use the nominating committee, the presiding officer announces, "Nominations are now open for the position of president for the ensuing year." He will accept such nominations as they are offered. As mentioned before, no seconds are required but they are not forbidden. The president may declare nominations closed if no new candidates are being offered. He should be careful not to close nominating proceedings too quickly. Steamroller tactics may have a harmful effect on the future deliberations of the group.

Speeches in behalf of a candidate are always in order. Some organizations prefer that the candidates leave the meeting room during these deliberations. It is wise to vote on the highest officer first and then go down the slate one at a time. Defeated candidates are then available for other offices. All officers who are regular members of the group have the same legal right to vote for candidates. The presiding officer should appoint tellers who will be responsible for counting the votes whether they be by show of hands or written and secret. The chairman will then announce the result of the ballot publicly.

How to handle motions

The motion is a proposal submitted to an assembly for its consideration. It is introduced by the words, "I move . . . ." It is then discussed and adopted or refused. There are rules governing the precedence of various kinds of motions. Some motions must be seconded; some are debatable; some require a simple majority for acceptance; others a two-thirds majority. The rules may seem complicated, but they are governed by determinable logic. (See Appendix F for Motions in Order of Precedence.)

It is assumed that discussion is in order only when a motion is before the house, that only one motion can be discussed at a time, and that discussion should be germane to the motion. If the group wishes to indulge in informal discussion without using rules of parliamentary procedure, it may *by motion* change itself into a committee of the whole. The group returns to its previous status to take up formally any business it has just discussed in committee.

Motions classified as to purpose and precedence. Motions are ranked according to priority so that fair and sensible action can result. One group of motions is called *privileged*. These are related to the welfare of all the members of the group. They have the highest precedence. The second group, in order of precedence, is called *incidental motions*. These deal with personal privileges and should be taken up in an order determined by the presiding officer. A third group, in order of precedence, is called *subsidiary motions*. These deal with disposal or modification of main motions. The *main motions*, even though they carry the weight of business in a meeting, hold the lowest rank in priority. This group has no particular order of precedence within itself.

A. *Privileged motions*
1. To fix the time of the next meeting. This motion has the highest precedence. After all, the group must decide when and where it will meet again (unless this is specified by its standing rules), or it will be disbanded permanently by adjournment.
2. To adjourn. This motion suspends the business of the group until its next meeting.
3. To recess. This motion provides time for an intermission of stated length.
4. Questions of privilege. These questions involve the welfare of the assembly and privileges such as freedom from disturbances, discomfort, and objectionable conduct of the chairman.
B. *Incidental motions*
1. Arising to a point of order. A member may rise to a point of order when he recognizes an infraction of the rules or regulations of the group, or when he believes that a member or officer has used improper language or actions.

2. Appeal from decision of the chair. When a member does not feel that the chairman has made a fair or proper decision he may appeal for a vote of the group on the presiding officer's ruling.

3. Parliamentary inquiry. This is a request made by a member to the chairman or parliamentarian on a point of parliamentary law.

4. Withdrawing a motion. A member may wish his motion withdrawn before voting has begun. Any objection to this is handled as a motion.

5. Suspending the rules. This applies to rules of order and allows a motion to be considered at a time contrary to its usual order. This does not apply to (or permit violations of) the constitution or bylaws of the organization.

6. Request for information. This permits a member to receive information concerning pending business. He may question a speaker, the chairman, or any member of the assembly.

7. Objection to consideration. This motion may be made when the subject is objectionable, irrelevant, or improper.

C. *Subsidiary motions*

1. Table a motion. The object here is to lay aside a motion when the group is at an impasse in order to attend to more urgent business. If a motion is not later taken from the table, it is automatically lost.

2. Previous questions. This brings the pending question up for immediate vote, closes debate, and prevents amendment.

3. Limit debate. The purpose here is to limit the time for debate in order to expedite business.

4. Postpone to a certain time. This motion delays action on a question but fixes a specific time at which it may face disposition.

5. Refer to a committee. This motion sends the question at hand to a committee, which will study it further and report to the body of the group.

6. Committee of the whole. The purpose here is to change the meeting into an informal committee. The chairman may appoint some other member to preside and enter into the discussion with as much vigor as any of the other members.

7. Amend. Amendments are proposals for changes in certain types of motions.
8. Postpone indefinitely. This motion is used to reject a particular question without putting it to a direct vote.
D. *Main motions*
1. General main motions. These are the most frequently used motions. Their purpose is to bring business before the group.
2. Special order of business. The object here is to set a certain hour and date for the consideration of a specific question.
3. Take from the table. This is a motion to reconsider a motion that has been tabled. Since the motion was originally laid on the table in order to transact some other business, it should not be reintroduced until this business has been transacted.
4. To reconsider. This places before the group a question which was previously voted upon. In modern parliamentary procedure, anyone can bring up a motion for reconsideration. The chairman should weigh carefully whether or not to rule "in order" repeated demands for reconsideration that may delay the business on the floor.
5. To rescind, annul, or repeal. The object here is to reverse an action already taken.
6. To renew. Although renewal is not considered a type of motion, it has the effect of bringing up again a defeated motion. Main motions which are lost may not be renewed at the same meeting at which they were voted on; but procedural motions, since they are not debatable and take little time, may be brought up for renewal if some new material has been brought out that may change the attitude of the assembly.

When and why to second, amend, or debate. For some motions, seconds are needed. The assembly does not want to spend time on any measure that does not have the approval of at least two members. However, individual rights are protected in questions of order and privilege because these motions do not have to be seconded.

Ordinarily motions are amendable; but if no purpose can be gained by amendments, they are out of order. For instance, if there is a motion to vote on a question, an amendment to that motion could only serve to change its intent.

Questions are debatable only when debate may furnish some knowledge or pertinent information. Consideration from the chair on a request for information is a member's right, no matter what debate may ensue. On a motion to vote, majority rule prevails but minority rights may be defended. A motion to limit debate requires a two-thirds majority so that a simple majority may not quash discussion and railroad business through too hurriedly. Most of the time a speaker may not be interrupted, but exceptions are made when personal privileges are being violated.

The main motion. The purpose of a main motion is to bring business before the group in a form in which it may be considered and voted upon. The motion should be clear, definite, and complete. It is usually presented to the assembly in the following manner: "Mr. Chairman!" After recognition by the chairman, the maker of the motion says: "I move that this group set up a scholarship fund of $1,000 from our funds. This sum will be allocated to a student to be chosen by our educational committee. The scholarship will be used for graduate work in electrical engineering at State University during the year 19— . . ." The motion requires a second to make certain that more than one person is interested in its consideration. It is debatable since it has presented a new subject for approval or disapproval of the group. A motion is not in order when someone else has the floor. A simple majority is necessary for a motion to pass. Although a motion may be reconsidered under certain circumstances, it may not be renewed at the same session. All types of subsidiary motions may be applied to it.

Amendments. After a main motion has been presented to the group and seconded, the chairman repeats it formally and it is open to discussion. Members may wish to suggest certain changes in the statement of the motion. An amendment may be in the form of an addition, elimination, substitution or division. To amend the motion above, a member would rise and, after being recognized, state: "Mr. Chairman, I move to amend the motion being considered by substituting $1,200 for $1,000."

The chairman proceeds to the discussion and then to the disposal of the amendment. If the amendment passes, it becomes an integral part of the motion and the whole motion with the change is discussed by the group. An amendment may itself be amended and any changes that are passed become integral parts of the amendment. But no further amendments to the amendment of the amendment are allowed. However, other amendments may be suggested to the original motion if the original amendment has been disposed of. An amendment which seems frivolous or which seems to destroy completely the sense of the original motion should be ruled out of order by the chair. An amendment should be relevant to the original motion.

Discussion on a motion. The presiding officer should allow free and full discussion of all motions that are debatable unless time limits are set. In general, a speaker for one side of the question should be followed by a speaker for the other. A member who has already spoken to the motion should be required to wait until other persons have spoken to the point unless certain specific questions need answering. The chairman should keep his own personality or power out of the discussion except to guarantee orderly procedure. If he wishes to speak to a certain motion, he may step down from the chair and ask someone else to conduct the meeting. At that time, he must be recognized by the temporary chairman, and observe the usual rules of decorum.

How to vote on a motion. After a motion has been moved, seconded, and stated to the assembly, it cannot be withdrawn but must be acted upon by the body. After full discussion is held, the group is ready for a vote. Sometimes, members seek to expedite by shouting, "Question!" This means they wish to conclude discussion and proceed directly to vote. If the chairman feels that no more discussion is forthcoming, he may take this suggestion and announce: "We are ready for the vote." But he should not be influenced unduly by the vociferousness of those who wish to close discussion. If any member is determined to close discussion, he may rise to move the closing of debate and the group progresses to a vote. A motion to close debate is not debatable, but it requires a two-thirds majority to carry. If the motion to limit debate does not get a two-thirds majority, the discussion is continued. Thus the wishes of slightly more than a third of the group can prevail. When a motion has been voted upon, the chairman should announce the decision. It then becomes part of the official records of the group.

Assignments and exercises

1. Select an important person in your field, a person who has made significant contributions in your line of work. Pretend that you are introducing this person at a meeting of a professional society or at a convention. Do some research on this person so that you know his achievements well. Make the speech of introduction.

2. Arrange for the group to meet for coffee in some room other than the classroom. Arrange the tables and chairs to resemble the typical banquet meeting. Assign a general topic such as "How Education for Engineering Can Be Improved." One student will act as master of ceremonies and ask others to give reports on the topic.

3. Ask the group to participate in a role-playing exercise. A group of businessmen want the city to construct a four-lane freeway through a beautiful section of the city, cutting down many old, beautiful trees and drying up a picturesque river. A group of citizens have banded together to stop the freeway project. Members of the group will act as businessmen, "Citizens for Civic Beauty," and members of the city council called together to consider the knotty problem. The chairman of the city council will use parliamentary procedure to conduct the meeting.

4. Conduct an election. Choose a vehicle for this exercise such as the school honorary or professional society, the trustees of a church board, the officers of a corporation, or the student self-governing board. Appoint a student to act as the chairman. Select several students to make speeches on behalf of candidates. A list of the officers and their responsibilities should be compiled and distributed to each member.

5. Organize a program for a company party, a civic-club luncheon, or a fraternity social event. Students will be divided into small groups and each group will be responsible for part of the program. Songs, dances, jokes, impersonations, skits, satires will be in order, as well as short inspirational or humorous talks. The program should be appropriate for the group. Appoint a student to act as master of ceremonies. He will introduce the acts and keep the crowd happy and attentive.

13 THE VOLTAGE BUILDS UP

Creating good will and building morale

A case in point **"Unaccustomed as I am . . ."**

When Jerry Richards returned to his desk on the fifteenth floor of the Union Utilities Building he found a stack of mail, messages, letters, memos, etc., awaiting him. He had been working out of town for the past four days consulting with other engineers on a big air-conditioning job for a new building being constructed in Longstown. Jerry is an expert in cooling and refrigeration for Union Utilities. Today, one of his memos is from the vice-president in charge of public relations. It is an invitation to attend a meeting in the vice-president's office on an aspect of public relations in which he, Jerry Richards, may be able to assist.

When Jerry arrives at the meeting, he discovers that the top brass of UU has decided to establish a speaker's bureau comprised of certain key personnel in the company. The public relations department will furnish kits of information dealing with company plans, ideas, hopes, and aspirations. The kits will include the plans for a new atomic plant which has been under consideration for the past two years.

The president of the company is anxious that the public be informed about Union Utilities. He believes it would benefit the company if the general public received a good image of the company. For this reason, President Grey has hopes that some of the key employees of Union Utilities will develop interesting speeches to carry to the various publics with which the company is dealing. Jerry and some of his colleagues are expected to or-

191

ganize acceptable speeches. Groups that need speakers for lunch-
eons and various meetings will be able to call on this new Union
Utilities speaker's bureau.

Goodwill speeches

How does the public regard our company? This question is being
asked more and more by those in charge of public relations of
large corporations. To ensure a positive answer to this question,
many companies are sending their employees out to answer the
calls of service clubs, PTA's, dad's clubs, church groups, and other
organizations that need speakers to fill their program schedules.
The nation's 4,500 Rotary Clubs alone consume almost a quarter
of a million speeches each year. Some companies run full-time
booking bureaus to line up speaking dates for employees. One book-
let sent out by the United States Steel Company's South Works
calls itself "A Manual for Program Chairmen." Its foreword, after
indicating that the top-notch speakers listed within are *free,* goes
on to explain: "We of United States Steel want you to know us
better and we want to become acquainted with you. And so these
ambassadors, all top men in their respective fields, have offered
themselves as emissaries." Another brochure states: "These well-
qualified speakers will travel within a radius of thirty miles to
speak before civic, fraternal, service, school, and church groups, or
women's clubs and other organizations."

Whether business executives want to explain their business, put
over ideas for new legislation, project plans for better industry
cooperation, or just make friends for their companies, they may
find that speech making is a unique and valuable channel of communication. As the president of one electronics corporation says:
"It's the best way to plant an idea and make people think and talk
about it." Leaders of industry feel they must do a better job of explaining their beliefs and goals. Clarance Randall, onetime chairman of Inland Steel Company, has said: "Society today demands
from management a restatement of the purposes of free enterprise.
Our creed is being distorted by our enemies, and we are not talking
back. Sometimes I ask myself guiltily whether we are capable of
talking back." Other companies feel similarly about the need for
explaining their contribution to the economy of a community.

The fact that a man is technically trained rarely excuses him from the obligation to speak before the numerous audiences that demand speeches for their meetings. These speeches are frequently called goodwill speeches. Their primary purpose is to establish good public relations. In a way, the speaker does a subtle job of advertising. He not only publicizes his company and the general line of endeavor in which it is engaged, but he also publicizes himself. The effective goodwill speaker marks himself as a man worthy of promotion, a person who can do more for the company than merely accomplish his technical duties efficiently. His possibilities for advancement in the executive field are enhanced. As *Newsweek* remarks: "There is no lack of demand for the services of any United States business man who can rise to the ring of spoon on glass with a 'few remarks' to inform, entertain, exhort, or anesthetize an audience generally made up of other businessmen."[1]

Limitations of the speech for goodwill

If the one and only purpose is to create goodwill, you may select almost any subject that does not arouse controversy. One of the previously mentioned United States Steel Company brochures lists speeches on the prevention of accidents, the problem of air pollution, living with automation, and secrets of success in the modern business world. Use a subject about which you can be genuinely enthusiastic. Your own experiences, hobbies, or ideas can form the background into which you weave the pattern of goodwill for your company. In a speech encouraging community cooperation, one man may emphasize rose growing; another the launching of the newest satellite; a third may talk on the development of the "little leagues." You should clear your subject with your own public relations department. You are a representative of your company whenever you appear before the public. If you wish to discuss the "profit system," make certain that your views are not contrary to stated or implied philosophies of the management of your own organization. If you hint that your company has important plans for new construction, be certain that you are not violating secrets or presenting ideas that might lead to false rumors.

[1] By permission from *Newsweek,* p. 94, Nov. 23, 1959.

Avoid excessively controversial topics when speaking as a representative of your company. Whatever your own religious, political, or social views, be careful not to antagonize elements of the audience unnecessarily. A speech dealing with education should not imply destructive criticism of the current school administrators if you mean it to be a goodwill speech. Be subtle in your praise of your company or profession. Everyone realizes that you are proud of your company or profession. However, your speech is not a twenty-minute TV commercial. Use the indirect method of allowing the audience to form its conclusions about the worth and integrity of the group in which you have such a vested interest. The "image" of Amalgamated Aluminum should emerge from logical or psychological conclusions developed in the minds of the individuals of your audience. Your duty is to suggest the patterns of thought that may result from your talk. "The goodwill speaker must be more than a jolly good fellow. He must be an optimist with his sleeves rolled up, a dreamer with perspiration on his brow, an evangelist who goes out of his way to spread good feeling."[2]

Suggested subject areas

Recent developments in industry. Scientific and technically oriented industries are changing so rapidly that most audiences welcome being brought up to date. A waterworks engineer might discuss the interesting potentials of processing sea water to make fresh water. An electronics engineer might predict future developments in long-distance telephoning.

An eminent member of the profession. The life story of an outstanding person in the speaker's work or profession often makes an interesting and inspiring speech.

Contributions to the community. Point up the general and specific contributions the speaker's industry makes to the economic welfare of the nation or the local community.

The informative speech. Speeches such as "How to Get the Most out of Your Air Conditioner," "Better Power Boat Maintenance," "How to Get Along with Your Employees," "Accident

[2] John M. Martin, *Business and Professional Speaking*, Harper & Row, Publishers, Incorporated, New York, 1956, p. 121.

Prevention in the Home," "How to Achieve Good Public Relations," contain helpful information and are appropriate topics for a good-will speech.

The speech of entertainment. Audiences love to be entertained and some businessmen have endeared themselves and their companies to the community by their abilities to make an audience laugh and forget its troubles.

The title

Choose a catchy, provocative title for your talk. The following are titles of talks concerning the desire and need for freedom in the United States. Which of them would intrigue you and compel your attention?

"A Handful of Sand"
"How Many Candles on the Cake?"
"Freedom Is Important for America"
"Don't Let the Crack Get Any Wider"
"There Is Always a Better Way—It's Up to You"
"How Can We Meet the Russian Challenge?"
"Whither Are We Heading?"
"Whistling Won't Do It"
"The Nose of the Camel"
"Your Responsibilities and Your Liabilities"

Building morale: the speech of inspiration

A case in point **Gloom and doom**

Gerald Sommers was in a tight spot. If he could pass the buck, he certainly would do it. He couldn't pass it to someone higher up. He had tried that and it hadn't worked. The vice-president simply passed it back to Sommers. He couldn't, with conscience, pass it to someone lower down. The men really needed to hear from someone of supervisory rank. Morale among the men was at a new low. The company had lost a government contract, and rumors of the worst sort were flying. The grapevine was buzzing with dire predictions; none factual. Someone in management had to communicate with the men to restore their confidence and to mitigate the bad effects of the rumors.

The president had called a conference and the outcome had been as follows: Gerald Sommers, chief production engineer, was selected to make a talk to all the men in the electrical and mechanical divisions. The president described the speech as a "pep" talk; the vice-president called it a "morale builder"; and the personnel director referred to it as a "heart-to-heart" talk.

Sommers was selected for several reasons. He had worked himself up from the ranks and had held many of the jobs that the men he would address were now holding. He was a graduate engineer. As chief of production engineering he was over many of the employees affected by the cancellation of the government contract. Everybody at the conference said Sommers was a "natural" for the assignment. Sommers felt that the word should be "sucker." The thought of walking into the plant Wednesday night and facing all those nervous, gloomy employees was almost more than he could stand. What on earth could he say to them?

Technical men are moving into the field of administration. One of the responsibilities that inevitably faces the administrator is that of inspiring and encouraging those who work with and for him. This situation not only arises on the job, but in community work as well. As a man gains stature in his profession, he is asked to assume more responsibility in civic work. At one time or another, people in charge of community betterment projects are faced with making a speech to revive the flagging spirits of their fellow-workers. In his profession and in his civic work, the technical man may be faced with the challenge of making the speech of inspiration.

The speech of inspiration is made for the purpose of restoring confidence and regenerating enthusiasm in order that the work of the individual or group may be carried forward with more efficiency and energy.

Ideas to stress in the speech to inspire

Naturally, each speech situation is different and the methods of meeting the problem of verbal inspiration will vary. The following methods may be modified and adapted to meet the specific problem.

Point to past successes. Refer to a successful experience that the listeners have had. When groups and individuals become depressed they have a tendency to remember only failures and to forget achievements. The "minus" is uppermost in their thinking; the "plus" is forgotten. As they descend the depression slide, they lose faith in themselves. After a while their entire lives appear to have been failures. As they talk morosely among themselves, they have an inclination to deepen the feeling of depression. A method of meeting this problem is to include in the speech to inspire a reference to times when the group has met this same problem or a similar one with success, showing, against the gloom of the present, a positive example from the past.

"Humanize" the competition. Make it clear that others no more capable than the listeners have met this problem with success. Knute Rockne, in one of his locker room pep talks, told his team that the much touted champions they were facing that day put their pants on the same way as any other men did, one leg at a time. By this homely example, Rockne made the point that his team was not facing a group of supermen. An automobile manufacturer once told his dealers that a rival firm had made a good sales record. Then he added, "If the X Motor Car Company can make a sales record with that product of theirs, I know that you men, who are *just as capable* as they are, can do better." It can be pointed out that the listeners should be able to solve their problem if people with no additional training or situational advantages have solved a similar one.

Point out advantages inherent in the situation. Turn your liabilities into assets. No one is so "bad off" that he does not have some talent or special ability that is particularly suited for meeting the problem at hand. The same may be said of a group. Perhaps the years of experience, the special training, the composite abilities of a group are peculiarly adapted to meet the problem. The group can be aroused and encouraged by the speaker's analysis of these potentialities.

Stimulate creative thinking. A feeling of gloom is generally dispelled once creative thinking begins and the group starts to use imagination to draw upon experience and training for thinking of a way out. Creative thinking can be stimulated by encouraging the listeners to make suggestions and present new ideas. When a group gets together in a brainstorming session to pool ideas and unite thoughts toward solving a problem, spirits are inevitably warmed by the creative process. The speech to inspire may well include an interval of audience participation wherein the group is asked for suggestions toward solving the problem.

Make specific suggestions for improving the situation. When the attitude of the listeners is one of dejection, high-sounding phrases about company loyalty, grit, and determination are not enough. "What can we do about it?" This is the question in the listeners' minds. It is difficult to revive flagging spirits unless some concrete plan of action is presented. Criticisms, compliments, and general suggestions should be followed by a concrete scheme for improving the situation. The approach in a speech of inspiration can be two-fold: (1) a general discussion to uplift spirits; (2) a clear, precisely formed plan of action that can be seized upon as a solution to the problem.

Use reward as motivation. The purposeful or goal-seeking aspect of human behavior can be utilized. A reward for renewed effort may be tangible and material. Rewards in the way of profit sharing, bonuses, and prizes have been used by sales managers and plant supervisors to increase the efforts of their personnel. Some companies have offered rewards that benefit the employee's family, such as household appliances for the wife or vacation trips for the whole family. These rewards have the advantage of placing the employee's family firmly behind him in his efforts to get ahead. The family accepts father's increased working hours with more understanding. Another tangible reward is that of the material symbol of achievement such as silver cups, medals, and blue ribbons. Gold stars are usable even among adults.

A case in point   **"Beyond the call of duty"**

The city of Grassmere was faced with a high accident record on the part of the truck drivers. The personnel chief thought of awarding an attractive plaque for a good driving record. The plaque was to be fastened prominently to the driver's truck. Meantime, the plaque was placed on display in the locker room. The personnel chief was able to include in his next pep talk an awards session in which a driver was presented with the plaque in front of all the others. The award added a great deal to the speech of inspiration. It served as a concrete example of achievement and spurred the other men on to win their safe-driving plaques. A swift improvement in the accident records was soon noted.

Intangible rewards are just as effective as the material ones. This point was made by a personnel director of forty years' experience who said: "Employees don't want money. What they want is somebody to recognize their efforts and to listen to their troubles." Employees can be encouraged to increase their efforts if the contributions they have already made are recognized and the importance of their future work is emphasized.

A case in point **"A shot in the arm"**

The president of a civic organization began his year in office with an inspirational talk to his volunteer staff. First he complimented them by emphasizing that their creative, energetic abilities had prompted him to ask them to be on his staff. He spent the rest of his speech emphasizing the significance of the project at hand. When he finished, the volunteer workers felt proud of their particular talents. They also felt that they were involved in an essential project that would bring prestige to themselves and to the community. They were ready to go to work.

Present the cold, hard facts. Sometimes it is necessary to confront the group with an unpleasant truth about the situation. If the group has a general underlying fear about conditions, but no specific knowledge of the problem, their morale may be lower than if they knew the facts. Fears and suspicions often turn out to be exaggerated and unwarranted when the actual dangers involved are known. You may want to present the situation in graphic terms. After the disagreeable facts are known and understood, a constructive effort can be made toward solving the problem.

Appeal to competitive behavior. Some people enjoy healthy, fair competition in which they are able to pit their abilities against others. The appeal to rivalry in sports is well known. It can also be used to inspire employees in industrial work. The employees must feel that they have an even chance. Then they may be stimulated by the speaker to compete with some other department or some other company. This appeal has been used to increase the output of production units and to spur research teams to compete for jobs and contracts. Before the speaker can use the competitive urge, however, he must make his group feel like a team, make them realize that they are a team. The trend toward more and more specialization in industrial work makes it difficult for some employees to remember that they are part of a large, precisely articulated team. Skilled technicians often work in small, relatively isolated groups. The inspirational speaker must make these employees realize their relationship to one another and help them to visualize the picture as a whole before he can weld them into a team to compete with some other company.

Tremendous growth in the size of the industrial plant is also a factor in the loss of group feelings. The individual is hardly conscious of the overall competitive business situation because he feels like a minute cog in a great machine. He doesn't realize that he is part of a team competing against other teams, because all he sees is his small job in a huge complex of industrial activity. An inspirational speech may explain the competitive nature of the American economy; the spirit and nature of free enterprise; the opportunity to use initiative, hard work, and creative thinking to compete against others in an open market. This can do much to make the employee see the importance of his effort in helping his company make progress and keep abreast of the competition.

Stress the interest of top management in the project. The distance from the individual worker to the managerial staff seems infinitely great. It is a long way from the drafting table on the first floor to the executive suite in the penthouse. The inspirational speaker should include in his talk a direct communication from management that expresses a knowledge of, and an interest in, the group's problems. A statement from the president concerning the significance of the project is good, but a brief appearance by the president is even better.

Developing the ideas in the speech to inspire

Inspirational speeches use the same techniques as other styles of oral communication. The conclusion or final sentence should be especially forceful, emphasizing your ideas unequivocally. Certain special devices discussed in the following pages will help vitalize your points. (See Chapter 8 for further assistance on research techniques.)

Quotations. Has somebody else said it more succinctly, emphatically, or colorfully? Quotations may be used in addition to the good, straight-from-the-shoulder prose developed in the personal style of the speaker. A vast storehouse of quotations may be found in poetry anthologies, books of quotations, magazines, newspapers, and house organs (company publications). They may be used to illustrate points and intensify themes. Pertinent thoughts of the great men in industry, politics, science, and letters will serve to lift the spirits and stir the imaginations of the listeners.

The simplest way to find something suitable is to investigate published collections of quotations. These books have helpful indexes in which a quotation is listed by its author, subject, or first line; under the special occasion for which it may be used; or under the title of the work from which it was taken. An annotated bibliography of quotation collections is to be found in Chapter 8.

A reading of the inspirational speeches made by men in business and industry reveals that these men rely to a great extent on quotations to strengthen and project their ideas. The following illustration was taken from an address by Benjamin F. Fairless, president of the American Iron and Steel Institute, speaking about the contribution America's skilled workers and technical men have made to industrial progress: "Andrew Carnegie once said, 'Let floods or fire destroy my plant from the face of the earth, but if I retain my organization I would be whole again in six months.' The final conviction I want to share is that you could take away all of America's plants and means of production. If all we had left were the people, the skilled workingmen and managers, we could, under our free system, once again lead the industrial world in a very short time."[3]

Humor. Laughter lightens gloom and strengthens the bond between the speaker and the audience. Sometimes, in an effort to drive home the urgent need for a more vigorous approach to the problem, the speaker will alienate his audience by too much ma-

[3] Benjamin F. Fairless, *Vital Speeches,* vol. 26, no. 9, pp. 270–272, Feb. 15, 1960.

terial of a stern, challenging nature. The speaker is no longer regarded as a leader but as a grim taskmaster. Something is needed to place the speaker back into the listener's circle. The feeling of "we" rather than "you men" must be restored. A humorous anecdote or good joke will help to relax the audience. Sharing a laugh adds warmth to the speech situation and keeps the listeners from being completely overcome by the seriousness of the problem.

The effectiveness of the humor depends on how closely it is related to the immediate problem at hand, the local environment, and the experiences of the listeners. The following joke was used in a vice-president's pep talk to the sales representatives of a large electronics company after he had been talking rather grimly about determination to get the job done: "A traveling salesman was marooned in a farmhouse during a flash flood. The water level was up to the windows. As he stood on the roof with the farmer's wife he noticed a strange sight. A straw hat came floating down with the current and, as it reached the end of the house, it turned around and floated up stream. Then it reversed itself and slowly floated back down. The salesman called this phenomenon to the attention of the farmer's wife. 'Oh, yes,' she said, 'That's Zeke, my husband. He told me this morning he was going to plow that north forty today, come hell or high water.' " The speaker then said to the audience, "That, gentlemen, is what I mean by determination."

Narration. Well-told episodes have a great appeal for most people. Plot and characterization always heighten attention. Stories which point up the need for renewed effort, which characterize actions of bravery, and which illustrate instances of creative thinking are inspiring to the audience. Inspirational narration can be used to depict an analogous situation showing how the problem was solved by determined effort and initiative; to paint a picture of the black future if the group does not accept the challenge; or to picture the bright potential if proper spirit is restored.

A case in point   **An ounce of ingenuity is worth a pound of money**

The leader of a research group faced a tough problem. The management had decided that the new machinery which the group desired would not be on the budget for the coming year. The new machinery was more up-to-date and easier to operate, and would have created more efficient working conditions. The leader had to maintain good morale while breaking this bad news to the men. To achieve this purpose he made an inspirational talk in which he told a story. He proceeded in the following manner:

"I am sorry, men, but I must tell you that budget item 4A has not been approved. I know that you sincerely thought this purchase necessary, and that now you probably feel that you are working under a severe handicap. Well, I am inclined to agree with you. You are working at a disadvantage but, in a way, I am glad. Now, before you throw something at me, let me tell you why. We haven't had a good idea come out of this department for a long time. Perhaps we've had it too easy. Maybe we've been sitting on our hands waiting for top management to solve all our problems with money. Sometimes the best ideas arise from a tough situation—a situation where people are called upon to fight against terrific odds without any outside help. They are forced to depend upon their own creative thinking and initiative.

"I read about an engineer who was sent to one of the under-developed countries in Asia. The country's economy depended upon the rice crop, and the rice crop was heavily dependent upon irrigation. The farmers were lifting water from one level to another by using skin pails and cloth sacks. This antiquated process was very slow, and sometimes the crop was damaged because enough water was not transported from the river to the fields at the proper season.

"The American engineer decided to help these farmers with their problem in spite of the fact that he had no budget. He was able to make a serviceable water pump using pistons from old jeep engines that had been left in the country after World War II. Then he met with another problem. There was not a length of hose or pipe in the country. He sat down and tried to think it out. One day he got an idea. He could use hollow bamboo stalks for pipes. Bamboo was plentiful and grew around every farm. Then another problem arose. What kind of machine could be used to power the pump? After discarding several ideas, he remembered that the chief mode of transportation in the country was the bicycle. Nearly every farmer had one. Why not use the pedal system of the bicycle to drive the pump? He borrowed a bicycle and soon modified the chain and pedal system to work the pump.

"He thought his troubles were over but they weren't. The farmers could not afford to give up their only means of transportation for long periods of time. Most of the farmers were too poor to own more than one bicycle. But the engineer refused to be stumped. He kept using his brain and finally came up with an answer. Perhaps you have already guessed his solution. He rigged up a treadmill which was adapted to fit the back wheel of the bicycle. In this way the bicycle could be clamped into a bamboo frame against the treadmill to run the water pump, and removed, by simply undoing a few clamps, anytime the farmer needed to pedal into the village for supplies.

"This engineer was working under severe handicaps. He had very little except his own initiative and brain power. (Pause) I'll bet this will be one of our best years in this department because we do realize that we have a handicap, and we'll set out to fight against it. I know you men are smart and creative. I'll gamble your abilities against a lost budget anytime. I'll bet you two to one we come up with more new ideas this year than we ever have before, simply because we *are* working under a handicap."

Statistics. Mathematical data may be used in the speech to inspire in the following ways:

1. To show a record of accomplishment. This speaker's purpose was to generate enthusiasm for the Federal Highway Program when he said, "Let's look at the record. Since July 1, 1956, nearly 94,000 miles of federal-aid projects have been advanced to contract. This total includes 85,000 miles of projects financed from ABC funds and 8,800 miles of projects on the Interstate System. . . . During this same period 89,000 miles have been completed, including 4,700 miles of basic construction on the Interstate System. Last December, at San Francisco, I reported to you that all of the work, including the pavement, had been completed on about 1,700 miles of new Interstate highways. As of now, with good construction weather still ahead of us, that figure has risen to 2,880 miles and the major portion of this mileage is already in use. This is a truly remarkable achievement."[4]

2. To show cause for alarm. ". . . We must ask ourselves the question—with all of this ferment and with all of the intriguing opportunities in engineering these days, why is the enrollment in engineering curricula continuing to decline? Freshman enrollment in engineering decreased 13 percent in 1958 as compared with 1957. Again, in 1959, a further decrease of 4 percent was recorded. Why?"[5]

3. To show possibilities for future accomplishments. The purpose of the following reference was to restore faith in the American economy: "This conference should not be completed without outlining briefly some of the new frontiers for America in the years ahead. The exciting potentials of a dynamic, growing American economy are almost unbelievable. A $750 billion gross national product is within our reach by 1975, if we grow at the rate of 3 per cent; and by 1968, if we can increase our growth rate to 5 per cent."[6]

Analogies. A comparison may be made between a situation where the proper spirit and effort were evident and the situation at hand. This analogy is from a speech intended to inspire engineering students to continue professional improvement after graduation from college: "A successful football coach spends hours and hours drilling his squad on the fundamentals of blocking, tackling, passing, kicking, etc. This is equivalent to what you are going through in engineering school—rudiments and fundamentals. Then the coach scrimmages his squads to drill them in the various plays until the particular signal called by the quarterback automatically induces the proper motion of each member of the team. This

[4] B. D. Tallany, "New Directions in the Highway Program," an address delivered before the 45th Annual Meeting of the American Association of State Highway Officials, Boston, Mass., Oct. 12, 1959.

[5] T. Keith Glennan, *Vital Speeches,* vol. 26, no. 8, pp. 236–239, Feb. 1, 1960.

[6] Richard M. Nixon, "Business Is the People," *Vital Speeches,* vol. 24, no. 23, p. 720, Sept. 15, 1958.

corresponds to the young cadet engineer in training—the first applications of his fundamental training. Then the coach has skull practice to plan the strategy for the coming game. This part of the analogy brings me to the next point I want to emphasize. The young engineer who closes his books on graduation, closes his mind and loses place in the progress toward excellence. Wherever you go after graduation you will find or you can make opportunities for continued pursuit of learning in your chosen specialty. Nearly everywhere there are evening graduate programs in engineering where you can continue your pursuit of excellence. Many companies and engineering offices offer inducements to their young men to carry forward their engineering training. This is the 'skull practice.' "[7]

Assignments and exercises

Goodwill speeches

1. Select a company you know something about. Prepare a goodwill speech to the Rotary Club in which you attempt to make a favorable impression for yourself and your company.

2. You are a member of the armed forces assigned to a missile base recently established near a small town. The people of the town are uneasy about the proximity of the base to the town. They have heard rumors of the dangers of missiles exploding by accident and the possibility of atomic warheads falling nearby during practice and training missions. You have been assigned by the commanding officer of the base to speak to a town meeting for the purpose of mitigating the fears of the townspeople and convincing them of the advantages of the base.

Speeches of inspiration

3. You are the president of the student council. The administration of the university has vetoed an important project or plan

[7] Joseph W. Barker, "The Professional Aspects of Engineering," an address delivered at Southern Methodist University, Dallas, Tex., Feb. 25, 1959, p. 6.

that the members of the council wanted to put into effect. The members of the council are angry and discouraged. Many of them have threatened to resign. Your job: Make a speech to this disgruntled group to unify the council and start them working on another project.

4. You are the chairman of the United Charity Fund Drive in your community. The drive has failed to collect the needed amount of funds. You have called a meeting of the block-worker leaders. Make a speech of inspiration in which you try to revive their energies and enthusiasms for renewed effort to collect more funds.

5. A large contract has just been cancelled at your company. Many people have been temporarily suspended from employment. The remaining employees are worried about the future. Low morale is beginning to slow down production on the work at hand. As vice-president, make a speech of inspiration to these employees for the purpose of reestablishing optimum efficiency.

6. You are the key speaker at the reunion banquet of your graduation class. The school is in need of contributions from ex-students to help meet current expenses and to increase the endowment fund. Make a speech of inspiration in which you try to stimulate the feelings of loyalty and gratitude toward your alma mater.

TRANSMITTER AND RECEIVER

Listening to others

A case in point   **The ears have it**

Mid-Tex Aircraft Corporation has received a letter from one of its prime contractors, Smith Air-Motive. The letter states that an inspection team will arrive in six weeks to evaluate compliance of manufacturing processes and methods with Smith Air-Motive's specifications. The senior vice-president calls in the manager of quality control at 11:45 A.M., just before the lunch hour. The manager of quality control is trying to get away early for lunch in order to buy some gardening tools for his wife. He rushes in to see the senior vice-president.

Senior Vice-president: Howdy, Al. I know you're probably wanting to get away for lunch, so I'll make this quick. An inspection team from Smith Air-Motive is coming here pretty soon to analyze our compliance with their manufacturing specifications. Check on everything we're doing for them, will you?

Manager of Quality Control: Righto, Bill, I'll get right on it. (As soon as I get back from lunch, he adds mentally.) He hurries out of the senior vice-president's office. He does not pause at his own office to write down what the senior vice-president has said. He has a hard time getting all his errands finished and, after munching a cold sandwich and drinking a cup of coffee, he rushes back to the office. When he arrives at his desk, he remembers that he was supposed to do something for the senior vice-president. He looks at his note pad, but it reveals nothing. He racks his brain.

Manager of Quality Control (To himself): Let's see, it was something about a progress report or . . . oh, now, I've got it. He wanted me to run a specifications check on Schmidt Aeronautics. (The manager of quality control is too embarrassed to call the senior vice-president back for confirmation of his thoughts.) Yes, that's it.

(The manager of quality control calls in the chief inspector.)

Manager of Quality Control: How are you doing, Fred?

Chief Inspector: I'm so busy today, I don't know who I am. That bomber stabilizer is giving us plenty of trouble . . .

Manager of Quality Control (Interrupting):   Don't cry on my shoulder, boy. We need a current status report on process specifications for Schmidt Aeronautics.

Chief Inspector: Schmidt Aeronautics. Okay, if I don't lose my mind over this stabilizer, I'll get somebody on it right away.

Manager of Quality Control: Thank you, Fred, I'm depending on you.

(The chief inspector hurries out. The manager of quality control dismisses the matter from his mind, and starts another project. About 4:00 P.M. he receives an irate telephone call from the chief inspector.)

Chief Inspector: What kind of a curve are you trying to throw me, Al? It's not enough that I'm going crazy trying to make an Air Force deadline for this bomber stabilizer, but you make me tie up my inspection foreman all afternoon chasing a dead lead.

Manager of Quality Control: What the dickens are you raving about, Fred?

Chief Inspector: We haven't had any contracts with Schmidt Aeronautics for over a year. Why did you make me spend all day checking on their process specifications? Are you . . . ?

Manager of Quality Control: But the senior vice-president said . . . . This wasn't my idea . . . . I . . . . You mean we don't do business with Schmidt Aeronautics anymore?

Chief Inspector: Listen, pal, you better check this deal out before you throw it to me like a hot potato. After fooling around all afternoon, the technical data supervisor gave me the word. We don't do business with Schmidt Aeronautics, so we couldn't want a process compliance check.

Manager of Quality Control: Oh, I'm sorry, Fred. I guess I'd better . . . .

Chief Inspector: Yes, I guess you'd better! (Hangs up.)

(The manager of quality control calls the senior vice-president's office. In order to save face, he talks to the secretary. She is able to give him the correct information.)

Secretary: It's Smith Air-Motive that we want the report on, Mr. Benson.

Manager of Quality Control: Oh, thank you, Miss Burnett.

(The manager of quality control hesitates to call the chief inspector again because of their last heated conversation, so he goes under the chief inspector's head, and telephones the assistant inspection foreman directly. There is a lot of noise in the assistant inspection foreman's office, and he has trouble hearing on the telephone.)

Manager of Quality Control: Hello, Paul, this is Al.

Assistant Inspection Foreman: Who?

Manager of Quality Control: This is Al Benson, quality control.

Assistant Inspection Foreman: Oh, yessir, Mr. Benson.

Manager of Quality Control: I want you to check on something for me. You don't need to bother Fred with it. I know he's busy with that bomber stabilizer.

Assistant Inspection Foreman: Yessir. Well, I'm busy on it, too.

Manager of Quality Control: You've got to get on this for me. It's a request from the senior vice-president. I want you to check our process specifications for Smith Air-Motive.

Assistant Inspection Foreman: Well, sir, we're pretty busy with this bomber, but I guess I can do it.

(Just as the assistant inspection foreman puts down the telephone, he gets a rush call from the chief inspector saying they would have to work all night on the bomber stabilizer. While the chief inspector is talking to him, the assistant inspection foreman hastily scribbles "process specifications" on his desk pad so that he won't forget the call from the manager of quality control. As the assistant inspection foreman returns from alerting his lead men concerning the overtime work, he sees the note

on the desk pad. He is in a fairly disturbed state of mind because
the lead men weren't too happy about the overtime assignment.
He looks at the note, is puzzled for a moment, and then seems
to remember. He telephones the group engineer at materials and
processes.)

Assistant Inspection Foreman: Hello, Tom, this is Paul
Atkins in quality control. I've got a hot one from the manager.

Group Engineer: What's your trouble, pardner?

Assistant Inspection Foreman (He looks at his desk pad.) We
need a status report on . . . uh . . . all process specifications.

Group Engineer: Wow! That's a large order, man! Do you
know how many companies we do business with?

(The assistant inspection foreman is a bit shaken by the
reaction. He pauses and glances in vain at "process specifications" written on the desk pad. He is really not sure of his
information, but he doesn't want to appear ignorant. Instead of
rechecking, he guesses.)

Assistant Inspection Foreman: Er . . . uh . . . yes. The manager wants this report on process specifications as soon as possible . . . uh . . . let's say in three days. Can you do it?

Group Engineer: Well, I guess so. It'll mean we'll have to
drop everything else and, as I said, put in a lot of overtime. I
think we can. I'll check with the technical data supervisor.

The group engineer takes his problem to the technical data
supervisor who suggests that a complete survey be made of all
copies of the process manuals in the plant. Immediately the
wheels are put into motion to call in all copies of every process
specification manual. A thorough check is made. All copies and
pages are accounted for. Since these manuals undergo a complete
check once every quarter and, since this routine check up was
due in about thirty days, it is upsetting to the supervisor of
technical data to spend so much time before the usual checking
date. Overtime and all-night sessions are necessary to meet the
three-day deadline. Estimated excess cost for labor is $1,500.

The Smith Air-Motive inspection team arrived six weeks later
and the senior vice-president called for the report of the com-

pany's compliance with Smith Air-Motive specifications. Instead of a report of compliance, he received a statement that all process manuals in the plant were up-to-date. A real flurry started then. Not only overtime, but all-night sessions were involved in checking all processes to see that they complied with the Smith Air-Motive specifications. The Smith Air-Motive inspection team was dismayed that the report was not ready upon their arrival. They reported this failure to their president. This endangered Mid-Tex's good customer relationship with Smith Air-Motive.

Fifteen hundred dollars in excess labor, diversion of employees from important projects, employee fatigue from overtime and all-night sessions, bad temper and disintegration of personnel morale, failure to meet the correct assignment, and probable loss of business—all caused by faulty communication—mostly in the area of *accurate listening.*

Problems of the listener

Numerous leaders of industry have emphasized the need for effective listening. "I am convinced by my own experience and of that of others," said Henry Ford, "that, if there is any one secret of success, it lies in the ability to get the other person's point of view and see things from his angle as well as from your own."[1]

This is what Dr. Albert Einstein had in mind when he gave the formula for success as $X + Y + Z =$ Success. He said that X represented hard work and Y represented play. When asked what Z represented, he said, "That is the ability to keep your mouth shut." We can presume that a person listens better with his mouth shut!

Adjusting to the speaker's rate

While it is true that a listener can absorb more than the 125 to 150 words per minute that a speaker usually offers to his audience, the ideal listener can keep his mind from wandering by using the following techniques:

[1] Wesley Wiksell, *Do They Understand You?,* The Macmillan Company New York, 1960, p. 87.

1. When the listener thinks ahead of the talker, he can try to guess what the material is leading to and what conclusions may be drawn from the words being spoken at the time.
2. The listener may evaluate the types of evidence the speaker has used to support his points. He may check the relevancy of the evidence and the validity of each example or set of statistics.
3. The listener may check for unspoken thoughts that are implied by the speaker's words.
4. The listener may review the portion of the talk completed up to the present point.
5. The listener may perceive a verbal clue, such as emphasis or repetition, that performs the function of underscoring major points or ideas.
6. The listener may watch for visual clues to help orient him to the relationship or progression of thoughts.

Faulty extrapolation

You must be careful not to come to conclusions too rapidly after the introduction of a single example. A mathematician knows the importance of adding as many points as possible before determining the value of a curve or line. In listening, wait for as much information as possible before you render final mental judgment. Sometimes speakers build their ideas by increasing the order of importance of the supporting material. Wait patiently for the facts and opinions to arrive before making mental evaluations and determinations.

Reading into the speaker's message what you *want* to hear is a common listening fault. We all know about differences in reports from listeners who have heard the same sermon or the same political speech. If a person wants to hear agreement with his own point of view, sometimes he will automatically "not hear," or unconsciously disregard, facts and opinions that differ from his own beliefs. Don't project your own ideas into the information coming from the speaker.

Physical barriers to listening

You ought to sit in the best possible position to hear what is said. Face the speaker. Encourage him with attentiveness. If you know that your hearing ability is low, get a hearing aid or sit up front, close to the speaker. Don't allow yourself to be distracted by external noise or outside influences. Don't let the appearance or style of delivery of the speaker weigh too heavily upon your reception. If necessary, do something about a physical situation that hinders your best listening. You may ask a speaker to speak more loudly or to stand in better light or away from a position in front of a window. Don't be afraid to ask for repetition if the speaker's voice is low or weak. Don't become a lip reader. Don't stare at extraneous visual material such as leftover material on the blackboard.

Emotional barriers to listening

There are many personal barriers to listening. Emotions such as joy or anger can be a hindrance. There may be reactions to the speaker's dress, personal appearance, or mannerisms such as gum chewing, smoking, or tics. Try to omit your own personal problems from your listening assignment. Eliminate all possible domestic worries and thoughts about your next engagement. It is better to be rested and physically fit in any listening situation. If this is impossible, try to separate your own feelings of fatigue and illness from the material that is being spoken to you.

Even if you don't like a speaker personally, adopt an impersonal reaction to his words and ideas. Don't let your prejudices about the speaker's politics, religion, racial origin, etc. stand in the way of your careful attention to his presentation. Don't allow yourself to be sidetracked by his pronunciation, vocal style, or grammar. Sometimes a single mispronunciation makes a member of the audience begin to worry about how "that word" should have been spoken, to the detriment of continued good listening.

Certain words set up powerful emotional reactions in the mind of the listeners. Although the speaker should bear the major responsibility if he chooses value-loaded language, don't let a few slips wreck your semantic judgment. Nichols and Stevens list a number of "loaded" words such as: hick, kike, landlord, Jew, evolution, red-neck, wool-hat, sissy, sharecropper, venereal disease, Red, Communist, dumb farmers, antivivisectionist, nigger, yokel, square, Democrat, Republican, etc.[2]

The speaker's language may have been poorly chosen, but you, as a listener, should overlook emotional impact and try to evaluate the entire sum and substance of the message that is being relayed to you. The words may be used innocently by the speaker without the powerful connotations that are formed in your mind. Word meanings are not universal.

Preevaluation of the speaker

The listener may have already made up his mind about the ideas being expressed or about the value of the speaker's thoughts or information. If you go into a meeting with the feeling that what the speaker is going to say will be worthless, you have set up a powerful barrier to your listening. This happens frequently in training sessions, briefing sessions, or even college classrooms. The listener, feeling that he is only wasting his time, has turned off any receptive devices that might enable him to receive information or ideas. If you must be present, you might as well listen.

To paraphrase the old saying, "Even if it was good, he wouldn't like it,": Sometimes bad previous circumstances leave their scars. "The last time I heard Jones, he hemmed and hawed, confusing the whole issue. I'll get all this later by calling his colleague, Richardson." And so you miss everything that is said; and it turns out later that Richardson is no help either.

Taking notes

In *Through the Looking Glass* the White King, recalling the horror of his ride through space in Alice's hand, says: "The horror of that moment, I shall never, *never* forget!" "You will, though," the Queen replies, "if you don't make a memorandum of it."

Some people can listen, absorb, and remember while doodling and

[2] Ralph G. Nichols and Leonard A. Stevens, *Are You Listening?* McGraw-Hill Book Company, Inc., New York, 1957, pp. 89–90.

without any apparent effort at note taking. This does not seem to be true for most people, however. Keeping careful notes seems to improve most listeners' attentiveness. Later review is possible if the note taking is done in a careful, logical, systematic manner. Sometimes a speaker will hand out outlines or summaries of what he expects to cover in his oral presentation. This may lead to poor listening habits. "After all," you reason, "it is all down here for me. I can review this later if I want to remember what has been said." It is better to save outlines or abstracts for distribution *after* the talk has been made and the questions and discussions have been completed. A few brief ideas concerning note taking follow:

Keep your notes clear and readable. A few scrawled, abbreviated pencil scratches may seem appropriate at the time, but they are useless when you try to review them a week later.

Be brief, but complete, in what you note. You hardly expect to make a verbatim report unless you are using shorthand or speed-writing, but be sure that your comments make sense. A remark

Principle	*Support*
The three major requirements in our formula for stopping injuries:	
Knowledge	Correct work is safe work. Sloppy work breeds injuries. Our safety manual is an outline of safe work methods.
Motivation	Webster: A motive is anything that prompts one to do something. Chart: 1 per cent "habitual offender" drivers had 15 per cent of accidents. Motivation and knowledge act as two blades of pair of scissors.
Plan of action	Plan of action acts as hand guiding the cutting of scissors. Meetings are held monthly. "Yellow flag program" has helped cut down injury rate in plant.

such as "parrot story" may not untangle the web of memory weeks later when you try to make use of the ideas you have noted.

Set down the topic or thesis sentence of major ideas. Under these major ideas you may indent and list the supports such as examples, statistics, and definitions.

Summarize. If there is a lull in the proceedings, try to write a summary of the material covered up to that point.

Some outliners like to use a two-column approach to the problem. In the left column, they list the principles advanced by the speaker; in the right-hand column, the various methods of support are indicated. A sample of this type of note taking is indicated on page 216.

Assignments and exercises

1. Read a page of highly technical material to the class. One half of the class will take notes; the other half will listen but will not take notes. Compose an objective test on the facts in your piece of material and test the two groups. Which group has remembered the facts better?

2. Listen to a piece on a tape recording or read aloud by the instructor. Take notes during the first half of the reading, but not during the last part. How do you fare when questions are asked concerning the material?

3. Give a talk on an abstract topic or something outside the usual experience of your auditors. Ask the group to write a summary of your talk when you have finished. Collect the summaries and read the ones you think really caught the ideas and flavor of your presentation.

4. Outline carefully a short talk which you intend to present to the class. The class will be expected to outline this talk as you present it. Collect their outlines. How do they compare with yours?

5. Have a taped talk presented to the group. Test the retention of the material a week after the group has listened to it.

15 JOHNNY CAN'T READ—ALOUD

Reading a paper

Research papers and technical reports frequently deal with precise measurements, complex formulas, and detailed statistics. Sometimes these are read at professional meetings or to interested lay groups. In special speech situations the material must be read from a prepared manuscript to avoid omissions, errors, discrepancies, or undue emotionalism. Reports meant only for the cold eye of the mind may become dull and boring when read aloud if they do not allow for "the seductions of the voice and the magic of the personality of the reader."

A case in point **Lost in a sea of words**

"Members of the American Society of Mechanical Engineers, and honored guests, it is with great enthusiasm that I introduce to you Mr. Carl Riley, Los Angeles Division, Morse-Swanson Laboratories. I will make this introduction short because I know you are all waiting with interest to hear Mr. Riley's remarks about one of our gravest problems, the pollution of the air by exhaust fumes from motor vehicles. Mr. Riley is chief of design at Morse-Swanson and he is highly qualified to speak upon the subject, 'The Control of Hydrocarbons in Motor Vehicular Exhaust Systems.' Mr. Carl Riley."

Riley arose. He mumbled an acknowledgment of the introduction. He began to read, his nose buried in the manuscript. Soon after he began, several people in the last rows of the banquet hall shifted and turned restlessly in their seats. Riley was not reading loudly enough. Many could not hear him. Some people began to wave their hands, but Riley could not see this. He stared fixedly at the manuscript, never glancing up. Finally, a bold chap on the last row yelled, "Louder!"

This startled Riley and he got the idea. He attempted to read louder, but his voice sounded strained, high, and squeaky. Somebody rushed to the public address system control panel and turned up the volume, which produced a loud, disconcerting feedback noise. The noise frightened Riley and his voice became higher and squeakier. After the public address system was adjusted, Riley could be heard by more people but some still shifted in their chairs, hands cupped to ears.

Riley felt he was in a bad situation and began to read very rapidly to get it over with as quickly as possible. Punctuation marks flowed past Riley's eyes like telegraph poles seen from a speeding express train. He hardly paused for periods; commas didn't break his pace at all. The steady, rolling, rapid pace made every word sound alike. Important words, unimportant words—all got the same vocal emphasis from Riley.

"During the combustion process, approximately 97 per cent of the hydrocarbons are reduced to carbon dioxide and water."

The way Riley read it, this sentence sounded like, "Duringthecombustionprocess, approximatelyninetysevenpercentofthehydrocarbonsarereducedtocarbondioxideandwater." Many members of the audience became hypnotized and soon dozed off.

Riley had not practiced reading the paper aloud. He had written it in pencil, and after being presented with a clean typewritten copy by his secretary, he had plunged directly into the speech situation. Because of this lack of familiarity with the paper, he became lost many times. He didn't seem to understand the relationship of the thoughts he was reading even though he had written them. Lack of close acquaintance with the words and sentences, made him leave some sentences hanging in the air for he wasn't sure when a sentence would end. Upward pitch at the end of sentences produced an odd inflection pattern which failed to communicate meaning.

As a matter of fact, Riley was lost in a sea of words. He wasn't really thinking as he read. He was merely clattering out the words rapidly and mechanically like a nervous teletype machine. He would have done better had he mimeographed his paper, passed it out to everyone in the audience, and then sat down. The meeting was a waste of valuable time. The audience, at first interested, became bored, discouraged, disgusted. Riley had forgotten the point of the whole affair, *communication!*

No one wants to make the mistakes Riley did, yet, at every professional convention, at every meeting of a technical society, there is at least one Riley. These unfortunate reading experiences need not happen. A person can learn to read aloud with enthusiasm, forcefulness, and clarity. The first step toward better reading of a research paper is to write it in a clear, simple, direct, *oral* style that is aimed at being read aloud, listened to, and understood.

Writing for the ear

There is a difference between a report meant for silent reading and a report meant to be read aloud. The silent reader can check back to a former line for a refresher reference. He can reread a sentence several times for clarity if the meaning isn't clear at first reading. The silent reader can stop to analyze complex sentence structure, puzzling out the thought until it becomes clear. A group listening to an oral reader cannot do these things. An oral report is not an "essay on legs."

When writing a report or paper for oral delivery, the writer must keep one basic idea constantly in mind: The purpose is to write a manuscript that must be heard and understood by *listeners* the first time. He must construct sentences that can be followed easily and comprehended by listeners.

Keep the purpose in mind

When you prepare a manuscript for reading, refresh yourself concerning the purpose of the paper. Write a complete sentence expressing the purpose of the talk and keep this purpose in the back of your mind while reading. In a well-written paper all the thoughts will relate directly to the central purpose. If you keep the purpose in mind while you are preparing the report, you will be more aware of the logic of the material when you are reading it. Lack of such awareness results in a mechanical style of reading wherein the reader simply covers the ground without projecting any of the ideas.

Write and read in thought groups

Analyze the meaning of a sentence by dividing it into thought groups. Thought groups are phrases that hang together because they express a single thought. By isolating these thought groups, the meaning of a complicated sentence becomes clear. The following sentence is fairly complicated: If we apply a square wave of a given frequency to the imput of an amplifier, and the amplifier is discriminating against frequencies high with respect to the frequency of the square wave, the imput form will look much as the one you see now on the screen; that is, the corners of the wave will be rounded where the gain of the high frequencies has dropped.

Division of this sentence into thought groups helps to make it clear: If we apply a square wave—of a given frequency—to the imput of an amplifier—and the amplifier is discriminating against frequencies—high with respect to frequency of the square wave— the imput form will look much as the one you see now on the screen—that is—the corners of the wave will be rounded—where the gain of the frequencies has dropped.

By dividing the sentence up in this manner, the oral reader is able to concentrate on expressing the one thought in each unit, and then go on to the next. The oral reader allows the listener to digest each thought unit surrounding it with the needed pauses. Dividing the sentence into thought units furthers the reader's understanding and the listener's comprehension.

Emphasize key words

After the sentence has been divided into thought groups, these thought groups should be examined to find the key words. These important words carry the main burden of sense in the thought unit. When you read aloud, you will want to add vocal stress to the key words so that they stand out. Example: We make the *best audio amplifiers* on the market—but they are also the *most ex-*

pensive on the market —and this *high price* has cost us *many sales*—even among customers who demand *quality.*

The reader can add stress to key words in the following ways: (1) say the key word louder than the other words in the thought unit; (2) pause before and after the word; (3) stretch the sound of the word, hold the word longer than the other words in the unit; (4) use a combination of any of these.

Be sure of word meanings

Know the exact meaning of all words you write into your manuscript. There is no excuse for vagueness. If in doubt, consult a dictionary. In the case of new, technical terms not listed in the dictionary, consult an expert in the field. Sometimes, words have broader or narrower meanings than the dictionary has listed. For the purposes of interpretation, word meaning may be divided into two categories: denotative meaning and connotative meaning. Denotative meaning is the practical definition of the word. For example, one denotative meaning of the noun "cross" is given as: "an upright supporting a horizontal beam." The connotative meaning is the suggestive or associational value of a word. For example, the suggestive values of the word "cross" might be "faith," "church," or "Christianity."

It is necessary that you recognize the accuracy of the word meaning as expressed by denotative meaning and the suggestive potential of the word as expressed by connotative meaning. *Example:* An error in the data for heat treatment and temperature tempering of this metal could cause serious injury or death to the technician. When reading this sentence, the reader should know the practical meaning of "heat treatment and temperature tempering." He should also be aware of the suggestive, emotional value of "serious injury or death."

Avoid verbal booby traps

Colorful phrases sometimes become tongue twisters when you try to read them aloud. It is better to sacrifice the apt phrase than to sound like Stuttering Sam when you try to say it to a group. If a complex juxtaposition of words is necessary, mark the manuscript as a warning that you are approaching that verbal booby trap. *Example:* The muffler that our design department plans to develop functions on the // catalytic–carbon dioxide–oxidation // principle.

Preparing the manuscript format

The manuscript should be typed and triple-spaced. Wide spaces between the lines help the reader to keep his place in the text and to find his place quickly and easily when his eyes leave the manuscript for purposes of establishing eye contact with the audience, answering questions, or manipulating visual aids. Typewriters with especially large type (primer type) should be used by readers who are nearsighted and have trouble reading when the manuscript is placed on a rostrum or table. It is disconcerting for the audience to watch a speaker who squints or crouches over the paper while reading.

The manuscript should be neat and clean with no mark-throughs or strikeovers. If a last minute word change or correction must be made, it should be printed in ink. All pages should be numbered in a consistent fashion. Sentences should be completed on each page so that the reader will not have to turn a page in the middle of a sentence.

Marking the manuscript

As a reader you may use some of the following format treatments in preparing your manuscript for oral reading:

Underlining may be used to indicate emphasis. *Example:* After an extensive investigation, it was concluded that excessive G loading was the cause of failure. *Example:* As future sanitary engineers, these problems are your problems.

Quotation marks remind the reader that the word or phrase is being used in a special sense. *Example:* These so-called "diplomats" were later found to be spies.

Cue indicators should be clearly marked in your manuscript if visual aids are being used with the paper. *Example:* The Akron tube is one of the most versatile pieces of equipment that we manufacture.

As shown in Figure 1, it can be used as a push-pull, balanced imput preamplifier in our broadcast-type products. The two halves of the tube, when connected in push-pull, will give more than twice the amplification of a single triode section. In addition, the push-pull connection will result in the cancellation of any noise or hum generated by the imput stage.

If connected as shown by the dashed lines in Figure 2, the dual triode becomes a stereo preamplifier.

Pronunciation marks. Difficult or unfamiliar words may be written out, using dictionary markings with which you are familiar. *Example:* The atomic tests were conducted at Eniwetok (ĕn-ĭ-wē′-tŏk). Or the reader may use his own form of spelling to indicate pronunciation. *Example:* In addition, the following services are covered to varying degrees: special diets, X-ray treatments, physical therapy, pathology, and fees to anesthetists. (an-ES-thuh-tists)

Numbers should be spelled out for easy reading. It is difficult to separate the billions and millions when reading before an audience. *Example:* One million, two hundred and eighty thousand parts have passed through this production line. (Some readers find it helpful to spell the number out and follow that with the figures enclosed in parentheses.)

Reading the manuscript

It is more difficult to communicate by oral reading than it is by extemporaneous speaking. The fact that the manuscript is before the speaker presents an obstacle to communication because the manuscript gets between the speaker and his audience. The speaker has a tendency to read, but not to read *to* anyone—to read words, not thoughts. Since the reader doesn't have to think of words, because the words are there before him, he may rattle them off in a dull, mechanical manner. Essentially, the key to good oral reading is learning to *think while you read.*

Rate of reading

Most inexperienced oral readers read too rapidly. The words flow so swiftly that the reader does not give them meaningful interpretation and the listener cannot comprehend the meaning. Fast reading may be caused by nervousness. If you practice reading aloud and become thoroughly familiar with the manuscript, you may reduce this nervousness and its accompanying tension.

The rapid rate may be due to self-isolation on the part of the reader. The reader is not reading to anybody but himself. He can go rapidly because *he* understands the material. A concern for the listener's comprehension may remind him to slow down so that the information can be absorbed. The use of the pause is a method of slowing down an overrapid rate of reading aloud. Try some of the following ideas:

1. Pause briefly before and after key words.
2. Pause between paragraphs.
3. Pause after a complex thought or sentence.
4. Pause before and after quoted material.
5. Pause between the main divisions of a report or paper.
6. Pause before any abrupt change in thought.

A few speakers read too slowly. A slow, dragging pace tires the listener. It makes the listener feel that the reader is either fatigued or lacks interest and enthusiasm for his material. Lack of familiarity with the manuscript may result in an overly slow pace. The reader has not taken time for practice. He is not sure of the sentence structure or the pronunciation of the words. He stumbles over phrases, pausing between subject and verb, verb and object, thereby breaking the logic of the thought. Practice in reading aloud is the remedy.

An overly slow pace may be the reflection of the natural speaking style of the reader. If pauses come in the wrong places, remedy this fault by a conscious effort to connect words for logic of thought, pausing only when necessary, being careful not to violate thought groups. If the speaker has this fault, he should force himself to read faster, trying to inject vigor and enthusiasm into his reading.

The interest of the audience is held by variety in pace. Variety cannot be achieved by a haphazard attempt to read rapidly at one place and slowly in another. The rate of reading is dictated by the meaning of the sentences. Observe the following general rules: (1) A slow rate can indicate finality, solemnity, dignity, emphasis significance, complexity, and calmness; (2) a fast rate is appropriate for excitement, enthusiasm, joy, fear, and nonessential phrases.

Variety of pitch, quality, and volume

Even though you are reading a paper, don't lose sight of the fact that a heightened conversational style is the ideal for communicating ideas to an audience. Variety will generally come naturally if you concentrate on meaning. To make the reading sound interesting and alive, you must make use of all the techniques of variation discussed in Chapter 3.

Pronunciation

Be sure you know the correct pronunciation of all words. Don't guess. (See the Appendix for material on pronunciation.) If you are not certain of pronunciation, consult a dictionary or an authority on the subject of your speech. Say aloud, repeatedly, all difficult words until your pronunciation is smooth and flawless.

The conclusion

Concentrate on the conclusion during the practice period. Many readers fail at this point simply because they are tired of practicing. The conclusion is very important because it contains the recapitulation of essential points, the repetition of the central theme, and the emphasis of vital solutions. You cannot afford to be weak at this point in your delivery. Pause when you reach the conclusion to renew your vocal energy and to glance ahead for a quick scanning to see the structure of the conclusion. Then proceed emphatically and definitely, planting each idea with firmness and conviction. If you practice in this manner, there is a good chance that you will read your conclusion with effectiveness during the presentation before the audience.

The illusion of the first time

Practice in reading aloud is essential for achieving familiarity with your material and an easy, flowing delivery. When you stand before your audience, however, read with enthusiasm, vigor, and interest as if you are seeing this material for the first time. This is called, "the illusion of the first time." Actors have a similar problem as they recite the lines they have taken tedious weeks to memorize. They may have said the lines of the play night after night for countless performances, but at each new performance they must deliver the dialogue as if it were for the first time.

Establishing contact with your audience

The oral reader must be concerned with audience's reception of the information. Can the listener hear? Does he understand? Is he accepting the ideas? These questions can only be answered by seeing the faces of the hearers. Try looking at the floor or out of the window when engaged in an animated, friendly conversation. It is difficult to do because it seems more natural to face the person being addressed. The same conversational approach should be brought to the public speaking situation whether you are addressing two people or fifty-two people. The listener likes to be looked at when someone is talking to him.

Resist the temptation to hide behind your manuscript. It is the personality, feeling, and purposefulness of the reader that communicates. No matter how well-written the manuscript may be, it is a dead thing until the reader brings it to life. The manuscript is an accessory device to assist the reader in ease and precision of communication. The manuscript cannot speak for itself. To see the reaction of the audience and to make the audience aware of your own personality, it is necessary to establish firm eye contact.

Become completely familiar with the manuscript. Read it over many times silently. Understand the organization so that the logic and sequence of the ideas are firmly in mind. Be at home with the form and layout of the sentences and paragraphs. Be so closely acquainted with the manuscript that a glance at an underlined caption or division heading will bring to mind most of the ideas in that part of the manuscript. Practice reading the manuscript aloud many times to avoid stumbling over words or halting over sentence structure. Be so accustomed to your paper that you can start reading at any given page and know exactly where you are in relation to the subject matter as a whole. Thorough knowledge of the manuscript will enable you to take your eyes from the page to look at the audience and return to your place on the page and to the train of thought. During the practice period, strive for eye contact. Appoint a lampshade, a picture of grandfather, or a chair to act as audience. Look at this object as much as possible while practicing the reading.

Listening to yourself

Utilize a tape recorder or a dictating machine. Listen to the recorded speech. Does the reading sound like natural talk? Listen for artificial or stilted expressions. Are there places where the voice sounds shaky or unsure? Reread these sentences to see how the interpretation can be improved. Perhaps these sentences should be rewritten or eliminated.

Check for lack of emphasis or misplaced emphasis. Perhaps the sentence is not well balanced. Rewrite it. Listen for hanging inflections, monotony, and fading out at the ends of sentences. Are there any mispronunciations, slurring of consonants, or distortion of vowels? Check the logic of the thought groups. Are any of them broken? Do the questions sound like questions? Are the affirmative assertions positive in expression? If any humor is included, is it read in a jocular manner or in a dull, matter-of-fact fashion?

Assignments and exercises

1. Choose a poem with short lines so that one entire line can be picked up easily by the eyes with a quick scan. Read the poem over silently for thorough knowledge of the theme and idea content. Practice aloud until you can scan each short line and read it while looking at your audience. Read the poem to the group.

2. Select a poem that is not too emotional in mood. Search out the central theme of the poem. Find the correct pronunciation and meaning of all words. After sufficient practice, read the poem aloud to the class, striving to communicate the meaning at all times.

3. Find an article in a professional journal in your field. Copy it, using the proper manuscript format for oral reading. After thorough preparation, read this article (or a portion of it) to the group.

4. Select an editorial or a news report of great interest to you. Rewrite the material to make it easier to read. Substitute some of your own words for those in the article, shorten and simplify the sentences for easy reading aloud. Read it to the group.

5. Write a report on some experimentation that you are undertaking. Take care that your sentences are not too complex. Use simple, direct language. Use the topic sentence form of paragraph writing. Avoid vague referents such as "this" and "it." Read the report to the group.

6. Write a speech on any subject which requires the use of the slide projector. Mark the manuscript for cueing in the slide projector and for assistance in reading aloud effectively. Deliver the paper before the group.

appendix **A**

Methods to locate optimum pitch

Hum the sound "ah" and then go down the scale, continuing a strong vibrant tone until you have reached the lowest pitch you can hum without "breaking" the tone. Find this particular pitch on a piano keyboard or an audio oscillator. Now hum loudly up the scale to the note *sol* or a fifth higher than your lowest full-sounding tone. Try talking in a monotone on that note. This particular pitch may be your optimum pitch.

Whisper a nursery rhyme or some piece of poetry or prose with which you are quite familiar, so that you can recite it readily from memory. Whisper it with as much force as you can muster so it carries to the far reaches of the room in which you are practicing. Start it again and have someone surprise you by pointing at you in the middle of this second whispered rendition. At that point, without stopping continue the recitation but change to a loud, strong voice. You may find this particular voice to be in a different tone from your habitual one. This pitch may be optimum for you.

Diacritical markings

CHART OF ENGLISH SOUNDS, AS REPRESENTED IN

NOTES

[The figures refer to *sections* in the GUIDE TO PRONUNCIATION, unless preceded by "p." (page).]

VOWEL SOUNDS.

Column I shows the *vowel symbols* used in the respelling for pronunciation in Webster's NEW INTERNATIONAL DICTIONARY, *Second Edition.*

Column II contains *words illustrative* of the symbols in column I.

Column III gives *equivalent symbols* which may be used in marking words without respelling.

Column IV contains *words illustrative* of the symbols in column III.

Column V shows various *other* spellings representing the same sound, with references to the GUIDE TO PRONUNCIATION, pp. xxii-lxxviii of the Dictionary, where the symbols are fully explained. See also KEY TO THE SYMBOLS, p. xxii.

VOWELS IN GENERAL are described in the GUIDE, §§ 27-39. For a description of each *vowel* sound in detail, see SOUNDS OF SPOKEN ENGLISH, Part III, §§ 76-268 of the GUIDE. For the function of *vowels* in syllable forming, see § 59.

ă, ĕ, ŏ, ŭ indicate sounds that vary considerably according to their position with reference to accent and to their neighboring sounds, and also according to the rate and style of speaking (§§ 8, 9). The symbols *ă, ĕ, ŏ, ŭ,* italic, used in unaccented syllables, indicate that, in ordinary speech, an obscure vowel is used, but that occasionally, in the most formal speech, the sounds indicated by the same symbols not italicized are used. For the symbol *ĭ,* italic, see §§ 73, 155.

For **diphthongs,** etc., see §§ 36-39.

For **accent,** etc., see §§ 60-75.

For the **apostrophe** as in *a'ble* (ā'b'l), *chasm* (kăz''m), *eat'en* (ēt''n), etc., see KEY TO THE SYMBOLS, p. xxii, and § 59.

For **ü** (French *u*) in words not yet naturalized, see § 247.

I	II	III	IV	V
ā	āle	e̦	they	pain, day, break, veil, o·bey', etc., § 77
ā̇	chā̇·ot'ic	e̦	me·lee'	ai·grette', § 88
â	câre	ê	thêre	pear, air, heir, prayer, e'er, §§ 78, 79
ă	ădd	. .	. . .	plaid, guar'an·tee', § 80
ȧ	*ȧc*·count'	. .	. . .	§ 91
ä	ärm	. .	. . .	calm, hearth, ser'geant, §§ 81, 82
a̤	a̤sk	. .	. . .	§ 83
à	so'fà	. .	. . .	§ 92
ē	ēve	ï	po·lïce'	feet, beam, de·ceive', key, field, etc., § 115
ē̦	hē̦re			deer, dear, weird, etc., § 116
ê	ê·vent'	ï	fï·as'co	heil'er, leop'ard, friend, feath'er, etc., § 117
ĕ	ĕnd	. .	. . .	§ 127
ė	si'*lė*nt			
ễ	mak'ễr	{ā,ī} li'ar, e·lix'ir {ō,ȳ} ac·tor, zeph'yr		§§ 121, 126
ī	īce	ȳ	mȳ	vie, height, aisle, rye, eye, sky, etc., § 152
ĭ	ĭll	ȳ·	pit'ȳ	for'eign, guin'ea, bis'cuit, sieve, etc., §§ 154, 155
ĭ	char'*ĭ*·ty	. .	. . .	§§ 73, 155
ō	ōld			oh, roam, toe, grow, sew, beau, etc., § 180
ȯ	ȯ·bey'	. .	. . .	§ 190
ô	ôrb	{a,au aw}	all, auk, law	ex·traor'di·nar'y, geor'gic, broad, etc., § 182
ŏ	ŏdd	a̤	what	knowl'edge, hough, etc., § 184
ô̇	sô̇ft	. .	. . .	§ 185
ŏ	*cŏ*n·nect'	. .	. . .	§ 191
oi	oil	oy	boy	§ 197
ōō	fōōd	ọ, u	dọ, rude	group, drew, fruit, ca·noe', rheum, etc., § 199
o͝o	fo͝ot	ọ, u	wolf, full	would, § 200
ou	out	ow	cow	§ 202
ū	cūbe	. .	. . .	beau'ty, feud, pew, lieu, view, cue, etc., §§ 240-242(5)
û	û·nite'	. .	. . .	§ 249
û	ûrn	{ē,ī} her, bird {ō,ȳ} work, myrrh		earn, guer'don, jour'nal, §§ 120, 245
ŭ	ŭp	ō	sŏn	does, blood, touch, etc., § 244
ŭ	cir'*cŭ*s			pi'ous, por'poise, at'om, na'tion, etc., § 250

☞ For accent, emphasis, and intonation, see GUIDE, §§ 60-75, and for "weak forms" of *an, and, her,* etc., see § 71 in WEBSTER'S NEW INTERNATIONAL DICTIONARY, *Second Edition.*

WEBSTER'S NEW INTERNATIONAL DICTIONARY, Second Edition

NOTES	VI	VII	? VIII	IX	X
CONSONANT SOUNDS.	b	ba'by, be	. .	. . . . . .	rob'ber, § 97
Column VI shows the consonant symbols used in the re-spelling for pronunciation in Webster's NEW	ch	chair, much	. .	. . . . . .	{ match, Chris'tian, right'eous, etc., § 104
	d	day, den	. .	. . . . . .	bdel'li·um, sad'dle, § 111
INTERNA-TIONAL DIC-TIONARY, Second Edition.	dū	ver'dure (-dūr)	. .	. . . . . .	gran'deur, §§ 111, 249
Column VII gives words il-	f	fill, feel	ph	phan'tom	laugh, etc., § 137
lustrative of the symbols in col-umn VI.	g	go, be·gin'	g̅	fog̅'gy	ghost, guard, plague, § 138
Column VIII contains equiv-alent symbols,	gz	ex·ist (ĕg·zĭst')	x̧	ex̧·ist'	§ 259
used to mark pronunciation without respell-ing.	h	hat, hen	. .	. . . . . .	who, § 149
Column IX includes words	hw	what (hwŏt)	wh	when, what	§ 258
illustrative of the symbols in column VIII.	j	joke, jol'ly	g̵,dg̵	g̵em, edg̵e	mag'ic, judge, etc., § 161
Column X shows various	k	keep, kick	₵,℮h	℮at,℮ho'rus	{ kick, bis'cuit, hough, sacque, etc., § 164
other spellings representing the same sound,	ks	tax (tăks)	x	vex	§ 259
with references to the GUIDE, where the sym-bols are fully	kw	queen (kwēn)	qu	queen	§ 210
explained.	l	late, leg	. .	. . . . . .	hol'low, § 166
For a general description of consonants, with	m	man, me	. .	. . . . . .	{ drachm, phlegm, thumb, ham'mer, etc., § 171
classification, see GUIDE, §§ 40-45. For conso-nants in combi-	n	no, none	. .	. . . . . .	{ sign, gnat, hand'some, knot, mne·mon'ics, pneu'ma, § 174
nation, see §§ 53-58. For the func-tion of conso-	ng	sing, long	. .	. . . . . .	tongue, ink, etc., § 177
nants in syllable forming, see § 59.	p	pa'pa, pin	. .	. . . . . .	hap'py, § 205
For a description of each consonant in detail, see	r	rap, red	. .	. . . . . .	{ mer'ry, rhi·noc'er·os, myrrh, mort'gage, §§ 211 ff.
SOUNDS OF SPO-KEN ENGLISH, Part III, §§ 76-	s	so, this	ç	çell, viçe	sci'ence, schism, hiss, psalm, lis'ten, sword, §§ 218, 225, 226
268 of the GUIDE.	sh	she, ship	çh	ma·çhine'	o'cean, schist, so'cial, con'scious, §§ 227 ff.
For x, as in German, see KEY TO THE SYMBOLS,	t	time, talk	. .	. . . . . .	{ baked, thyme, debt, in·dict', yacht, bought, phthis'ic,§§230, 236
page xxii, and GUIDE,§109.	th	thin, through	. .	. . . . . .	phthi'sis, etc., §§ 233, 236
For N, indi-cating nasals, as in French, see	t̶h	then (t̶hĕn)	. .	. . . . . .	§§ 233-235
KEY TO THE SYMBOLS, page xxii, and GUIDE,	tū	na'ture (-tūr)	. .	. . . . . .	§ 249
§ 95.	v	van, re·vive'	. .	. . . . . .	of, Ste'phen, §§ 137, 208, 254
	w	want, win	. .	. . . . . .	quit, sua'sion, etc., §§ 255, 256
	y	yet	. .	. . . . . .	on'ion, etc.; § 264
	z	zone, haze	s̱	is̱, lives̱	{ dis·cern', dis·solve', czar, rasp'-ber'ry, xe'bec,§§219, 221, 259, 265
	zh	az'ure (ăzh'ẽr)	. .	. . . . . .	{ rouge, pleas'ure, vi'sion, ab·scis'-sion, gla'zier, etc., § 266

Vocabulary test

1. An *inscrutable* face — 1. jovial 2. inexpressive 3. frightened 4. distinguished 5. emaciated ( )
2. *Bemused* by his message — 1. dazed 2. threatened 3. instructed 4. disturbed 5. reassured ( )
3. To *deride* a suggestion — 1. make 2. discuss 3. adopt 4. ridicule 5. disregard ( )
4. *Perjured* testimony — 1. judicial 2. forceful 3. objective 4. false 5. frightening ( )
5. A *diminution* of tensions — 1. decrease 2. stabilization 3. creation 4. increase 5. prevention ( )
6. *Turbid* water — 1. limpid 2. sterilized 3. cloudy 4. lukewarm 5. cold ( )
7. A *turgid* stream — 1. rippling 2. roaring 3. swirling 4. flowing 5. swollen ( )
8. *Mundane* affairs — 1. religious 2. illegal 3. business 4. recreational 5. worldly ( )
9. A *burgeoning* population — 1. growing 2. hungry 3. discontented 4. bilingual 5. creative ( )
10. Exposed to *calumny* — 1. disease 2. hardships 3. slander 4. treatment 5. travail ( )
11. *Somnolent* students — 1. intelligent 2. youthful 3. drowsy 4. forgetful 5. matriculated ( )
12. *Redoubtable* advisors — 1. respected 2. senile 3. weak 4. international 5. unconcerned ( )
13. A *maladroit* candidate — 1. astute 2. awkward 3. studious 4. experienced 5. egocentric ( )
14. A *sententious* oration — 1. clever 2. spellbinding 3. fascinating 4. hypocritical 5. pompous ( )
15. A *nocturnal* march — 1. military 2. tragic 3. stirring 4. night 5. funereal ( )
16. The *saturnine* doctor — 1. comforting 2. trustworthy 3. rambling 4. gloomy 5. skilled ( )
17. To view with *equanimity* — 1. alarm 2. approbation 3. misgiving 4. calmness 5. misunderstanding ( )
18. *Insouciance* of colleagues — 1. optimism 2. warning 3. indifference 4. attitudes 5. helpfulness ( )
19. *Myriad* uses of wood — 1. constructive 2. common 3. particular 4. questionable 5. numberless ( )
20. An *ineffable* quality — 1. indescribable 2. manly 3. measurable 4. transparent 5. desirable ( )
21. A *whimsical* taxi driver — 1. odd 2. reckless 3. talkative 4. stolid 5. experienced ( )

22. The science of *ornithology* — 1. trees 2. living 3. insects 4. flowers 5. birds ( )
23. *Fecund* plant life — 1. parasitic 2. prolific 3. decaying 4. aquatic 5. tropical ( )
24. An *invidious* comparison — 1. truthful 2. offensive 3. clever 4. silly 5. favorable ( )
25. Carefully *effaced* inscriptions — 1. copied 2. written 3. erased 4. preserved 5. transferred ( )
26. A *fortuitous* resemblance — 1. family 2. natural 3. faint 4. close 5. chance ( )
27. An *arch* foe — 1. foreign 2. cunning 3. arrogant 4. enervated 5. insignificant ( )
28. A *saline* solution — 1. logical 2. salty 3. satisfactory 4. medical 5. mathematical ( )
29. To participate in *chicanery* — 1. debate 2. frivolity 3. athletics 4. deception 5. ceremony ( )
30. An *evanescent* thought — 1. fleeting 2. pragmatic 3. farcical 4. reverent 5. philosophical ( )
31. A *droll* expression — 1. simple 2. trite 3. comforting 4. amusing 5. indignant ( )
32. Men given *kudos* — 1. scholarships 2. recognition 3. commissions 4. honors 5. sentences ( )
33. To establish *rapport* — 1. contact 2. policies 3. understanding 4. credit 5. bases ( )
34. To give *succor* — 1. relief 2. assurance 3. awards 4. satisfaction 5. suggestions ( )
35. An African *safari* — 1. emperor 2. expedition 3. aborigine 4. native 5. zebra ( )
36. *Furtive* glances — 1. bold 2. loving 3. respected 4. sly 5. habitual ( )
37. A *sardonic* look — 1. triumphant 2. wan 3. immaculate 4. weary 5. scornful ( )
38. He spoke *fatuously* — 1. tirelessly 2. impartially 3. sensibly 4. moodily 5. foolishly ( )
39. A *phlegmatic* disposition — 1. sanguine 2. dejected 3. calm 4. violent 5. troublesome ( )
40. *Dilatory* behavior — 1. dogmatic 2. puerile 3. wise 4. delaying 5. kindly ( )
41. *Exigent* problems — 1. omnipresent 2. critical 3. extra 4. domestic 5. confusing ( )
42. A *chimerical* undertaking — 1. expensive 2. complicated 3. unnecessary 4. dramatic 5. visionary ( )
43. A *paragon* of patience — 1. model 2. quality 3. lack 4. surfeit 5. reward ( )
44. Incredibly *gauche* — 1. impolite 2. powerful 3. awkward 4. intelligent 5. haughty ( )
45. To *avert* a strike — 1. arbitrate 2. end 3. prevent 4. foment 5. initiate ( )
46. A *rubicund* man — 1. ruddy 2. fat 3. gluttonous 4. elfish 5. rational ( )
47. To eye *truculently* — 1. slyly 2. endearingly 3. obtusely 4. fiercely 5. earnestly ( )
48. A *tacit* admission — 1. boastful 2. sworn 3. guarded 4. unspoken 5. foolish ( )
49. The *temerity* of youth — 1. skillfulness 2. pessimism 3. optimism 4. genius 5. rashness ( )
50. *Fulsome* praise — 1. unusual 2. fanatic 3. insincere 4. unexpected 5. endless ( )

NOTE: Answers to text on p. 237.

A list of some common prefixes

prefix	meaning	examples of use
1. a	not, less, without	amoral, amorphous
2. ab	away from	absent, abduct
3. ad	to	adjunct, address
4. ambi	both	ambidextrous, ambiguous
5. ante	before	antecedent, anteroom
6. anti	against	antipathy, antidote
7. bene	well, good	benefactor, benign
8. bi	two, twice	biweekly, bipartisan
9. circum	around	circumspect, circumference
10. com	together with	companion, combination
11. contra	against	contradict, contrary
12. de	down, from	descend, depart
13. dis	apart from	disengage, disgrace
14. epi	upon, over, on the outside	epilogue, epidermis
15. eu	well	eulogy, euphemism
16. ex	out, former	extract, ex-president
17. homo	same, man	homogeneous, homicide
18. hyper	over, above	hyperbole, hypersensitive
19. hypo	under	hypodermic, hypotenuse
20. in	in, into, not	infuse, invalidate
21. inter	between	interracial, interpolate
22. intra	within	intramural, intrastate
23. mal	bad, evil	maladjustment, malignant
24. mis	wrong	mistake, misapply
25. omni	all	omnipotent, omnivorous
26. para	beside	paragon, parallel

prefix	*meaning*	*examples of use*
27. per	through	pervade, permeate
28. poly	many	polygon, polygamy
29. post	after	postpone, postoperative
30. pre	before	precede, prepare
31. pro	forward, in favor of, in place of	proceed, proponent, pronoun
32. re	back, again	replace, restate
33. retro	backward	retrogress, retroactive
34. sub	under	subordinate, submarine
35. syn	together	synthesis, synchronize
36. trans	across	translate, transit
37. super	above	supersede, superficial
38. ultra	excessively	ultramodern, ultraviolet
39. un	not	unavoidable, unusual
40. with	away, against	withstand, withhold

Answers to Vocabulary Test, Appendix C:

1. (2); 2. (1); 3. (4); 4. (4); 5. (1); 6. (3); 7. (5); 8. (5); 9. (1); 10. (3); 11. (3); 12. (1); 13. (2); 14. (5); 15. (4); 16. (4); 17. (4); 18. (3); 19. (5); 20. (1); 21. (1); 22. (5); 23. (2); 24. (2); 25. (3); 26. (5); 27. (2); 28. (2); 29. (4); 30. (1); 31. (4); 32. (4); 33. (3); 34. (1); 35. (2); 36. (4); 37. (5); 38. (5); 39. (3); 40. (4); 41. (2); 42. (5); 43. (1); 44. (3); 45. (3); 46. (1); 47. (4); 48. (4); 49. (5); 50. (3).

A list of some common suffixes

suffix	meaning	examples of use
1. able, ible	capable of	tenable, discernible
2. ance, ence, ancy, ency	act of, state or condition of	surveillance, permanence, hesitance, clemency
3. dom	state or condition of	freedom, serfdom
4. er, or, err, ess, ist (feminine)	one who	owner, debtor, overseer, hostess, feminist
5. ful	full of	powerful, awful
6. hood	state of	priesthood, motherhood
7. ion, sion, tion	act of, state or condition of	rebellion, tension, termination
8. ish, y, ic, ac, al	like, pertaining to	womanish, pasty, choleric, elegiac, maniacal
9. ism	doctrine or practice of	paternalism, communism
10. less	without	childless, pitiless
11. ment	state, quality, or act of	punishment, astonishments aggrandizement
12. ness	state of	wilderness, happiness
13. ory	relating to	illusory, olfactory
14. ous	full of, like, having qualities of	cautious, ravenous, amphibious
15. ward	in the direction of	shyward, westward

Latin noun and adjective roots

root	meaning	common derivatives		
arm	arms	armor	armament	armature
art	make	artist	artisan	artificial
brev	short	brevity	abbreviate	brief
capit	head	capital	captain	decapitate
civ	citizen	civic	civility	civilize
clar	clear	clarify	declare	clarinet
commun	common	community	communicate	communion
cord	heart	cordial	accord	concord
corpor	body	corporation	corpse	incorporate
cur	care	curator	accurate	cure
domin	master	dominate	dominion	predominant
fid	faith	fidelity	confide	infidel
fin	end	final	finite	confine
firm	steadfast	affirm	confirm	firmament
flor	flower	florist	flourish	flour
fort	strong	fortify	fortitude	force
gen	race	gentlemen	gentile	generous
grat	pleasing	grateful	congratulate	gratitude
leg	law	legal	legislate	legitimate
liter	letter	literature	letter	obliterate
loc	place	location	local	allocate
magn	great	magnify	magnificent	magnitude
man	hand	manual	manufacture	manage
memor	memory	memorial	memorize	remember
mont	mountain	amount	surmount	dismount
natur	nature	natural	denatured	native
offici	duty	office	official	officious
ordn	order	subordinate	ordinary	ordain

root	meaning	common derivatives		
pac	peace	pacify	peaceful	appease
plan	level	plane	explanation	plain
plen	full	plenty	plentitude	complete
popul	people	popular	populous	population
prob	good	prove	probation	approve
propr	one's own	property	proprietor	proper
salv	safe, healthy	salvation	salvo	salvage
sen	old	senior	senile	senate
sol	alone	sole	solitude	solitary
solid	compact	consolidate	solidify	solder
ver	true	very	verify	veritable

Common Greek word elements*

root	meaning	common derivatives		
anthrop	man	anthropology	philanthropy	anthropoid
ast(e)r	star	astronomy	astrology	asterisk
aut	self	automobile	autonomy	automatic
bibli	book	bibliography	Bible	bibliophile
bi	life	biography	biology	biogenesis
chron	time	chronology	chronometer	chronicle
crat	ruler	democrat	autocracy	technocracy
dem	people	democracy	demagogue	epidemic
derm	skin	dermis	epidermis	hypodermic
dynam	power	dynamo	dynamite	dynasty
gam	marriage	bigamy	polygamy	monogamy
gen	birth	eugenics	genetics	genocide
ge	earth	geography	geometry	geology
graph	draw	graphic	topographical	photograph
heter	different	heterogeneous	heterosexual	heterodox
hom	same	homosexual	homogeneous	homonym
hydr	water	dehydrate	hydrophobia	hydrant
log	speech	monologue	prologue	epilogue
logy	study	sociology	geology	biology
megal	great	megalith	megaphone	megacephalic
metr	measure	diameter	perimeter	trigonometry
micr	small	microscope	microphone	micrographer
nom	law	astronomy	economy	autonomy
onym	name	anonymous	synonym	antonym
orth	straight	orthodox	orthography	orthopedic

* *The connecting vowel "o" often appears at the end of the first element in a compound word. It contributes nothing to the essential meaning, but it makes for ease and smoothness in pronouncing the words.*

root	meaning	common derivatives		
pan	all	Pan-American	panacea	panorama
path	feeling	apathy	sympathy	pathetic
phil	love	Philadelphia	bibliophile	philharmonic
phob	fear	hydrophobia	acrophobia	claustrophobia
phon	sound	telephone	phonetic	dictaphone
phot	light	photograph	photophobia	photosynthesis
pod	foot	tripod	antipodes	podium
poly	many	polygamy	polychrome	polygon
psych	mind	psychology	psychiatry	psychic
scop	see	telescope	horoscope	periscope
soph	wise, wisdom	philosophy	sophomore	sophisticated
tele	far	telephone	television	telepathy
the	god	atheist	pantheist	theology
tom	cut	atom	anatomy	appendectomy
zo	animal	zoology	zodiac	zoo

appendix **E**

Evaluation of a conference or discussion

Topic_____Group_____

Evaluator_____Date_____

Criteria	*Poor*	*Fair*	*Good*	*Excellent*

1. Was the conference well planned? Purposes, scope, and procedure clearly defined before coming together?

2. Did the discussion hold to its purpose and scope?

3. Were the right persons present? (Or did the presence or absence of certain persons handicap the discussion?)

4. How well was the group prepared for the discussion: either before coming together or through the use of adequate and appropriate reference materials?

5. Were the facilities for the meeting adequate? (Physical factors affecting comfort and efficiency.)

6. Did the discussion move ahead systematically?

7. Did everyone feel free to participate, bringing his real thoughts into the open?

8. Was participation well guided — "stay on the track"?

9. Was participation tactfully controlled, avoiding "personalisms" and useless conflicts?

243

Criteria	*Poor*	*Fair*	*Good*	*Excellent*

10. Was the discussion representative; not dominated by the leader or by certain members?

11. Was there effective use of notes or desk pads, blackboard, easel, charts, and graphs?

12. Were important comments spotlighted?

13. Were irrelevant comments postponed?

14. How well did the leader formulate and phrase his questions?

15. Was the leader prompt and accurate in summarizing the group's thoughts during the discussion?

16. Was there progressive summarization to make points clear and give the feeling of progress?

17. Did the group come to appropriate and logical conclusions?

18. Was the outcome worth the time and effort?

19. Were proper assignments made for carrying out the conclusions and for follow-up?

20. Any other comments?

Motions in order of precedence

	Precedence	Recognized by chair	Require a 2d	Debatable	Amendable	In order when another has floor	Vote	Reconsider	Renew
A. Privileged motions:									
Fix time of next meeting	A-1	Yes	Yes	No	Yes	No	Maj.	Yes	Yes*
Adjourn	A-2	Yes	Yes	No	No	No	Maj.	No	Yes*
Recess	A-3	Yes	Yes	No	Yes	No	Maj.	No	Yes*
Question of privilege	A-4	No	No	No	No	Yes	None	No	Yes*
Orders of the day	A-5	No	No	No	No	Yes	†	No	Yes
B. Incidental motions (no order of precedence):									
Point of order	B	No	No	No	No	Yes	None	No	No
Appeal from decision of chair	B	No	Yes	Yes	No	Yes	Maj.	Yes	No
Parliamentary inquiry	B	No	No	No	No	Yes	None	No	No
Withdraw a motion	B	Yes	No	No	No	No	Maj.	No	Yes*
Suspend the rules	B	Yes	Yes	No	No	No	⅔	No	No

Motion	Code							
Division of assembly	B	No	No	No	None‡	No	Yes	No
Division of question	B	Yes	No	Yes	Maj.	No	No	No
Request of information	B	No	No	No	None‡	No	Yes	No
Objection to consideration	B	No	No	No	⅔	No	Yes	No
C. Subsidiary motions:								
Lay on the table	C-1	Yes	No	No	Maj.	No	No	Yes*
Previous question (immediate vote)	C-2	Yes	No	No	⅔	Yes	No	Yes*
Limit debate	C-3	Yes	No	Yes	⅔	Yes	No	Yes*
Extend debate	C-4	Yes	No	Yes	⅔	Yes	No	Yes*
Postpone to certain time	C-5	Yes	Yes	Yes	Maj.	Yes	No	Yes
Refer to committee	C-6	Yes	Yes	Yes	Maj.	Yes§	No	Yes
Committee of the whole	C-7	Yes	Yes	Yes	Maj.	No	No	No
Amend	C-8	Yes	Yes	Yes	Maj.	Yes	No	No
Postpone indefinitely	C-9	Yes	Yes	No	Maj.	No	No	No
D. Main motions (no order of precedence):								
General main motion	D	Yes	Yes	Yes	Maj.	Yes	No	‖
Make special order of business	D	Yes	Yes	Yes	⅔	Yes	No	Yes
Take from the table	D	Yes	No	No	Maj.	No	No	Yes
Rescind	D	Yes	Yes	Yes	⅔	No	No	No
Reconsider	D	No	Yes	No	Maj.	No	Yes	No

* Motions marked "yes" may be renewed after change in parliamentary situation.

† ⅔ needed to change.

‡ Unless an appeal from the chair's rule is requested.

§ Unless the committee has begun its work.

‖ Not at the same session.

INDEX

INDEX

Description as support for points, 48
Diacritical markings, 232–233
Dickens, Milton, 166–167
Dictionary, use of, 63–64
Drucker, Peter F., 6

Emotional barriers in listening, 214–215
Emotions, memory of, imagination in, 100–101
and words, 65–69
Examples in support of points, 46
Eye contact with audience, 37

Fadiman, William, 69n.
Fairless, Benjamin, 201
Faulty extrapolation by listener, 213
Feelings and prejudices of audience, 17–19
Ferguson, Charles F., 66n.
Figures of speech, 47–48

Glennan, T. Keith, 205n.
Grammar, 64
Greek word elements, 63, 241–242

Haney, John B., 57n.
Harrington, C. Bennett, 2n.
Harris, George E., 170n.

Hearing aspects (*see* Auditory aids; Listening)
Horn, Francis, 1

Imagination, how to train, 103–106
need for, 95
to stimulate sensory memory, 197–199
to understand and appeal to audience, 95–96
in use, of experience of others, 101–103
of memory of emotion, 100–101
Interviews, 132–137
counseling, 134–136
conference profile, 135
preparing for, 136
job, 132–134
planning, 136–137
as research source, 110–111
sales, 169–170
Introducing the speaker, 173
Introductory part of a speech, 23

Jargon, 58
Job interview, 132–134

Knowland, Philip, 105n.

Language, 52–91
articulation, 52–54
dictionary, 63–64

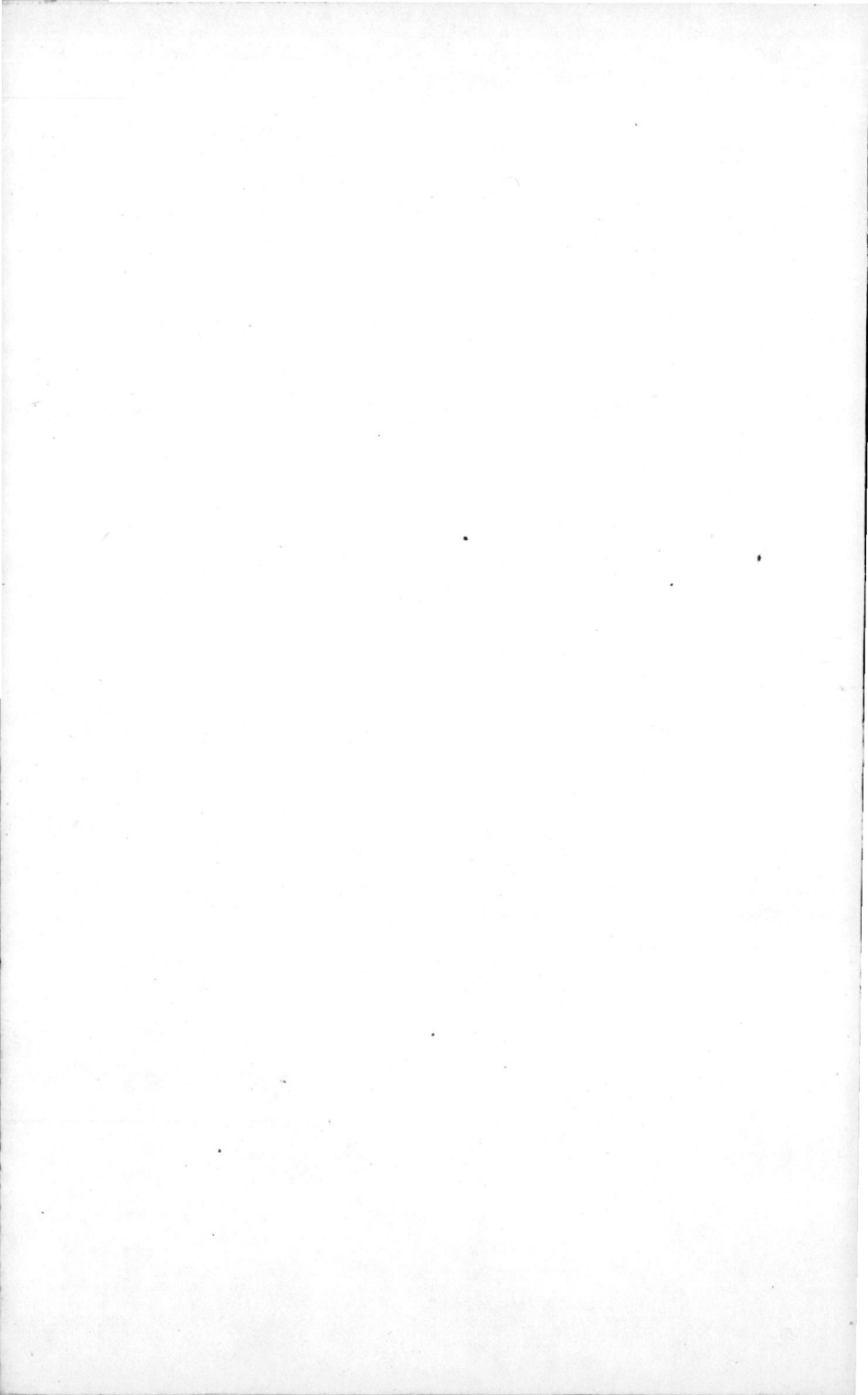